Risk
Balance
& Security

To Jim, Giorgia, Paige, Jesse, and grandparents
and
To Ilona, Alexis, Andrea, and grandparents

Risk
Balance
& Security

ERIN GIBBS VAN BRUNSCHOT

University of Calgary

LESLIE W. KENNEDY

Rutgers University

SAGE Publications

Los Angeles • London • New Delhi • Singapore

For information:

Sage Publications, Inc.
2455 Teller Road
Thousand Oaks,
   California 91320
E-mail: order@sagepub.com

Sage Publications India Pvt. Ltd.
B 1/I 1 Mohan Cooperative
   Industrial Area
Mathura Road, New Delhi 110 044
India

Sage Publications Ltd.
1 Oliver's Yard
55 City Road
London EC1Y 1SP
United Kingdom

Sage Publications Asia-Pacific Pte. Ltd.
33 Pekin Street #02-01
Far East Square
Singapore 048763

Printed in the United States of America

Library of Congress Cataloging-in-Publication Data

Van Brunschot, Erin Gibbs
Risk balance and security/Erin Gibbs Van Brunschot, Leslie W. Kennedy.
   p. cm.
Includes bibliographical references and index.
ISBN 978-1-4129-4069-6 (cloth)
ISBN 978-1-4129-4070-2 (pbk.)
   1. Emergency management—United States. 2. Crime prevention—
United States. 3. Terrorism—United States—Prevention.
4. Risk—Sociological aspects. I. Kennedy, Leslie W. II. Title.

HV551.3.V36 2008
363.10973—dc22   2007011267

This book is printed on acid-free paper.

07   08   09   10   11   10   9   8   7   6   5   4   3   2   1

Acquisitions Editor:	Jerry Westby
Editorial Assistant:	Melissa Spor
Project Editor:	Astrid Virding
Copy Editor:	Alison Hope
Typesetter:	C&M Digitals (P) Ltd.
Proofreader:	Joyce Li
Indexer:	Juniee Oneida
Cover Designer:	Janet Foulger
Marketing Manager:	Jennifer Reed

Contents

Preface

This book was originally conceived at the time that risk was becoming of central interest in criminology. Increasingly, scholars recognized that individual decisions by offenders and victims involved a risk calculation. At the same time, law enforcement was increasing its focus on technological solutions to enhance risk management. With the catastrophic events of September 11, 2001, and the rapid surge of concern about terrorism, law enforcement was quickly caught up in a new enterprise, responding to national threats while continuing to operate at local levels. Interestingly, the shift that had taken place toward risk management provided an awareness of the value of information, intelligence, interdepartmental cooperation, and strategic awareness, themes with which policing agencies had become familiar, along with the increasing demands for police accountability and community engagement. The law enforcement community became a central point around which risk management and preparedness developed, ranging from emergency management in natural disasters, to public health threats, to challenges that face the economy. In addition, the public was mobilized to prepare and to remain vigilant in the face of threats, and people were challenged to form their own assessments of personal risk, including evaluations about threats in their surroundings and their environment.

In preparing this book, we established that individuals and agencies cannot simply respond with endless resources to mitigate the damage that hazards create: they have to find a balance in managing risk. Our focuses are the processes and structures in the establishing of this balance in crime, terrorism, disasters, and threats to a nation's health. We believe that we have taken some important steps in improving our understanding of how risk runs through all decisions that are made about threats and hazards. With a new understanding of how risk balance works, and how it has been applied in our preparedness, prevention, and response strategies, we will be able to better conceptualize our task of enhancing future security.

As we followed the risk thread, we found that it wound its way through many different topics and many different disciplines. A product of our interest in security is the realization that the study of it is profoundly interdisciplinary. While we would argue that our primary target audience for this book is criminal justice students interested in new topics in public security, we realize that there are many other groups (for instance, those in public health, disaster research, and security studies) who will come away from this book with a better understanding of how their interests fit into a larger risk perspective. We have tried to do justice to these many sources of information and points of view, but we realize that there is still much work to do in explaining these ideas to a broader audience. We believe that the research needed in this area must start now, beginning with a detailed assessment of the ideas promulgated by agencies developing programs and spending large amounts of money in ways that have not been held up to careful scrutiny. This evaluation does not presume that other approaches to security are poorly conceived or malintentioned: only that these should be reviewed for their effectiveness, using the standards of risk assessment laid out in this book.

Acknowledgments

The authors would like to thank Jerry Westby and his staff at Sage Publications for providing encouragement and support throughout this project. They would also like to thank the Social Sciences and Humanities Research Council of Canada for their initial support of the "Contexts of Risk" project.

Erin would like to thank Les for his unfailing enthusiasm and steady stream of great ideas. Leslie-Anne Keown, Jay Laurendeau, Gillian Ranson, Gus Brannigan, and Daniel Béland deserve special mention for their good humor, advice and friendship. She thanks Jim, who has balanced exceptionally well the demands of three kids and the demands of a book-writing partner. Giorgia, Paige, and Jesse have been extremely patient with their mother and provide daily reminders of who and what really counts.

Les starts with his admiration for Erin for her patience, resolve, and, of course, real scholarly talent. He would like to thank the staff, students, and faculty at Rutgers School of Criminal Justice for their support. In particular, he thanks Norm Samuels for his moral and intellectual guidance; Steve Diner for his support for the Center for Public Security and other initiatives at SCJ; Louise Stanton for her fine work for the Center; and Bil, Thomas, Edith, Deborah, Cheryl, LaWanda, Teresa, Sandra, and Irene, who tolerated his occasional absences to let him get this work done. His friend Mark Anarumo deserves special mention as someone who has taught him a lot about security and golf. Of course, Ilona, Alexis, and Andrea get special thanks: he learns something new from each of them every day. Finally, a special bow to his Dad for soldiering on so well, his brother Trev for helping him so much, and to his late Mom for providing such a great model to live by.

Finally, the authors are most grateful for the reviewers who spent considerable time providing quality feedback and expertise during the development phase: Dave Andersen, Minnesota State Community and Technical College; Tom Birkland, University at Albany, State University of New York; Chris Demchak, University of Arizona; Ralph Garris; University of South Carolina, Lancaster; Pam Griset, University of Central Florida; James L.

Jengeleski, Shippensburg University; Matthew Lippman; University of Illinois at Chicago; Gus Martin, California State University, Dominguez Hills; Peter J. May, University of Washington; David A. McEntire University of North Texas; Jeryl Mumpower, University at Albany, State University of New York; Tom O'Connor, Austin Peay State University at Fort Campbell; Terrence O'Sullivan, Homeland Security Center for Risk and Economic Analysis of Terrorism Events (CREATE), University of Southern California; Gary R. Perlstein, Portland State University; and William L. Waugh, Jr., Georgia State University.

1

The Centrality of Security

In April of 1999, the event now known simply as Columbine occurred. This shooting spree masterminded by two teenagers against their peers at Columbine High School in Colorado received copious media coverage. While this event was the most devastating school shooting in U.S. history—there had been other such events—the shooting also highlighted how dangerous everyday life can be, depending on who you are and where you happen to be. A normal, even mundane aspect of life—going to school—was drastically transformed from routine to deadly. The images associated with Columbine were numerous: from the expressions of pain on the faces of those on the ground hearing the gunfire, smelling the smoke, and experiencing the wounds, to graphics found on the Internet providing school blueprints detailing where students and faculty had been hiding and where bodies had subsequently fallen. In fact, Columbine has become part of the social commentary and imagery of the uncertainty and insecurity imbedded in everyday American life. The event underscored how threats of extreme violence from alienated youth emerged from a society characterized by strong political support for freedom to own firearms which is justified, ironically, as a defense against the unbridled violence directed against homeowners and others. Columbine illustrates, on the one hand, the complexity of the various threats to safety and security and, on the other hand, the legitimate steps that we need to take to ensure that we are free from violence.

Two years after Columbine, in the fall of 2001, media images of another sort of violence prevailed. In surreal, nearly Hollywood-inspired footage, images of the planes crashing into the World Trade Center towers dominated the news media for months, in an event, 9/11, which has come to signify in highly provocative terms insecurity at a national level. While worldwide audiences may not relate to living and working in New York City, or even being American, observers can relate to flying in airplanes and being at work. Benign, everyday occurrences—the routine use of airplanes and going to work—were suddenly transformed, intersecting with death and destruction on a massive scale. The experience of this terrorist event, if only vicariously, deftly lodged itself into the psyche of citizens around the world. Again the transformation of routine events, coupled with the monumental symbolism of the World Trade Center as the heart of American economic power, threw into sharp relief questions of safety and security and their restoration at an international level. Immediate responses consisted of bolstering security efforts in locations identified as central to the terrorist effort, particularly in terms of airport and border controls.

Although airports and borders were the immediate focus, this event highlighted vulnerability and insecurity in ways that had not previously been apparent. Furthermore, the methods that had formerly been used to address security were seen as insufficient. International condemnation of terrorist action does little to protect the water supply, for example. Still, the anthrax-laced letters sent to U.S. politicians helped to put bioterrorist security on the map in a way previously ignored, and more recent threats of avian flu have, again, catapulted health security to the forefront. The vulnerabilities of geographical areas that house key infrastructure—such as electricity, water, and sewerage—have come into focus, as have the threats to other distribution systems such as public transportation and harbors.

The events that rocked our sensibilities and brought issues of security to the fore were not limited to North America. In the fall of 2004, viewers around the world were shocked by the violent events transpiring in Beslan, in the former Soviet Union. Having hidden an arsenal of explosives over the summer school break, rebels from the Republic of Chechnya waited for the September return of school children before detonating a number of explosives in a school gymnasium and elsewhere. More than 300 perished, most of them children. Those who were not killed by the explosions were witness to a bloody standoff between the police and the rebels holed up inside the school. Viewers who were transported to the scene by instant media coverage could not help but be engaged—and horrified—as they were again witness to an event with which much of the world has routinely dealt: the beginning of a new year and the return of children to school.

In July 2005, terrorists detonated bombs simultaneously on three subway cars in London, and forty-five minutes later on a double-decker bus. Reminiscent of an incident in Madrid two years earlier, and of the 9/11 attacks, this bombing provided stark reminders of the vulnerability of a routine activity, such as traveling to work. Furthermore, this vulnerability occurred in London, despite its extensive experience with bombings by the IRA over the past two decades, which many had believed was better prepared than many cities to divert this type of attack. Two weeks later, terrorists launched a similar attack against the London transit system, but this time the attackers' bombs failed to go off.

Safety and security concerns are not limited to terrorist acts. The most devastating tsunami on record took place on Boxing Day (December 26), 2004, with South Asian countries such as Sri Lanka, Thailand, India, and Indonesia particularly hard hit. Both professional and home video cameras portrayed images of rushing water and frightened people clinging to trees and buildings or being swept away by the rising tide. In hindsight, it appears that a simple communications system warning people to move to higher ground could probably have saved thousands of lives, yet the costs of the communications system, and the low probability of a tsunami of this magnitude ever occurring, meant that no such warning system had been put in place. Particularly striking about this event, as well as some of the other examples mentioned earlier, is that it was preceded by a failure to anticipate what could scarcely be imagined, leaving us to ask, "How can we prepare for the unimaginable?" and similarly, "How should we prepare for the unlikely?"

September 2005 will be remembered as belonging to Katrina—the hurricane that devastated the U.S. Gulf Coast. Its brutal winds and tide action submerged much of the coastline and brought the city of New Orleans, Louisiana, to its knees. Although well forecasted as a likely event, choices made in the years and months prior to Hurricane Katrina left the Gulf Coast without any feasible emergency plan, all the while ringed by levies that many experts had predicted would fail in the face of a hurricane of this magnitude. Immediately following the hurricane, the devastation ushered in questions about responsibility and blame. Who was to pay for the event's mismanagement, from the failed evacuations prior to the hurricane to the delayed rescue response? Despite the recognition that an event like this could happen, and was even likely to happen, neither the onset nor the evolution of this disaster was adequately prepared for.

In October 2005, an earthquake devastated Pakistan, leaving more than 73,000 dead. Registering 7.5 on the Richter scale, the earthquake struck about 100 km north of Islamabad, the capital of Pakistan. Reporter Robert Tanner describes the scene: "They can smell the bodies. They haven't found them yet, but they're digging, heaving one rock at a time from a home that's now a grave " (Tanner, 2005). The devastation accompanying this disaster was exacerbated by poor building construction.

These examples of disaster illuminate human vulnerabilities and hint that serious misfortune is sometimes never all that far away. Although many of these major disasters have a direct impact on relatively few victims, they contribute to a perceived lack of security for many, combining with and reinforcing the day-to-day anxiety that many people experience. For some, disaster appears to be imminent. While in so many ways our routine lives provide us with reassurance and comfort, routines may also expose us to unanticipated dangers over which we have little control. At the same time, disasters of the magnitude of the examples mentioned here are exceedingly rare events—but it is not only extreme events that remind us of and expose our vulnerabilities.

Each and every day we encounter routine situations that threaten our security, whether we remain within the confines of our homes or venture into the outdoors. Within our homes, for example, we may be exposed to household chemicals or harm from other family members. Outside the home, we may be exposed to airborne toxins, or find ourselves riding in an elevator with a psychopath. Many of the hazards that we face are not even known or recognized as dangerous—we are not able to detect if acid rain is falling on our heads, or if the preservatives in the food we eat contain carcinogens. Furthermore, some of what we do to enhance security may have the opposite effect by either reminding us of our vulnerabilities, therefore undermining our perceived security, or by creating vulnerabilities in other areas. For example, purchasing home security devices over the Internet or phone may result in our credit card numbers being publicized and used in ways that threaten our financial security. Most of us learn ways to cope with or accommodate the harms that impinge on our everyday circumstances, often through modes of protection or avoidance, or we rely on others to provide accurate information.

Individuals, government agencies and private institutions face a wide variety of dangers that may undermine security. As Beck (1992, 2003) and others explain, we live in a historical period where anxiety prevails: we do not necessarily know what might harm us. If and when we do identify particular hazards and threats, we may not necessarily know how to protect ourselves, or have the resources to protect ourselves against them. As the number of self-help and "success" manuals indicates, even taking advantage of opportunities to enhance security may be as problematic as avoiding hazards. At least some of the problems that we face are unavoidable: for these, we must gear ourselves to minimizing the harm that may result. Still other hazards are identifiable and may be avoided or eliminated altogether, while other hazards occur without notice. Our ability to eliminate, diminish, avoid, and control hazards and threats is limited by the resources that we have at our disposal, and by the choices that are, very often, constrained. Priorities and agendas may also vary with respect to spatial and temporal perspectives—threats identified as immediate or imminent will be viewed differently from those seen as less likely or temporally (and spatially) further removed.

To summarize, we define *hazards* as sources of danger or harm. We define *threats*, on the other hand, as warnings that something unpleasant such as danger or harm may occur. What distinguishes the two concepts is the time frame to which each applies. Hazards are associated with the present, possibly producing harm or danger right now. In contrast, threats signal or foreshadow future harm or danger, or the intention to cause harm or danger: harm has not yet been actualized and is merely a possibility. In either case, measures may be taken to minimize or preempt the harm or possibility of harm. Furthermore, hazards may also be threats. For example, we may define *smoke* as a hazard, or a source of harm or danger (i.e., fire is present). We may also define smoke as a threat—signaling or foreshadowing future harm because of its association with fire.

Some of us are more likely to know of and be informed of the hazards that we face through varying levels of awareness and knowledge, as well as access to expert advice. Access to advice and information increases the likelihood that we may take various precautions to protect ourselves. While knowledge of danger is critical to enhancing security, some of us are better positioned to protect ourselves from the harms that we encounter, through either personal resources or professional support. Differential access to resources, including access to expertise, wealth, and knowledge, results in varying levels of security between individuals, and among institutions and states. At the same time, certain disasters may strike and deliver harm regardless of the extent to which efforts are made to mitigate that harm. Yet even in the aftermath of harm, those with resources are better positioned to return to normal than are those without resources.

Security Matters

Our discussion to this point highlights a number of factors that affect security. First, if we cannot imagine certain negative events, then we can hardly put protection in place in order to prevent or mitigate their impact. We must be able to perceive and recognize threats and hazards—to imagine them—before we can undertake any attempts to address them. Security may be general or specific, but security requires the identification of "something" as threatening: a referent object. (We consider this more fully in Chapter 2, this volume.) Furthermore, what is defined as threatening or hazardous is a result of the interplay between particular social and cultural forces, therefore perspectives vary with respect to what is identified as hazardous or benign.

Second, the identification and recognition of particular types of harm are tied to the perceived nature of their consequences. Nevertheless, how we perceive or anticipate our ability to deal with consequences of harms is centrally linked to the resources that we have at hand to cope with consequences and to anticipate possible future events. Resources include economic, social, and cultural capital (Bourdieu, 1983). Differential access to resources influences our ability to cope with consequences and simultaneously influences the extent to which we can prepare for and are able to respond to particular events. For example, we may recognize that certain areas of a city are "dangerous," but we may consider ourselves to be capable of defending ourselves (of course, we may be wrong). Alternatively, we might expect that responsibility for our safety is the purview of the police, who have access to information and resources to address crime in ways not accessible to individual citizens. Differential access to resources, including information, both at the individual and institutional levels, affects the a priori identification of hazards and threats.

Even if we can perceive and recognize dangers, we may not be able to achieve security. The urgency with which we address these harms will be influenced not only by the presumed probability associated with them, but also by a willingness and ability to apply resources in particular ways. For instance, while the governments of the South Asian countries affected by the 2004 tsunami may have recognized that the possibility of a tsunami existed, the pressures to address more likely, although arguably less devastating, events competed with preparations for unlikely events of tsunami proportions. If an event is unlikely and resources are limited, how much sense does it make to use limited resources to prepare for unlikely events? The ability to address a variety of harms in meaningful ways often has to be balanced against the reality of scarce or limited resources, and against competing and often diametric priorities. In a different example (discussed in greater detail in Chapter 3, this volume), the Toronto Police Service failed to issue public warnings regarding a known rapist for fear that public warnings would drive the rapist out of the city to another jurisdiction. By choosing to prioritize and, hence, secure their own investigations, the police acted in a manner that was detrimental to those who the rapist subsequently attacked. The policing agency prioritized "closing the case" (preserving the security of the case), which was counterintuitive to individuals who sought to prioritize information that could be used for self-protection, and the security of their own personhood. In situations where resources are limited and priorities diverge, individuals, institutions, and states make choices that may simultaneously enhance security at one level or for a particular party, while undermining security at another level or for another party.

Finally, security is dynamic and is continually created and recreated in different ways. Ten years ago, for example, the threat of international terrorism on domestic soil was not on the radar of the U.S. government, let alone on the radar of the average North American citizen. Furthermore, not only does security vary over time, but it also varies both within and across particular domains: a state of security may be elusive in certain domains or spheres, yet be far more attainable in other domains or spheres. For example, we may be able to protect our houses from certain types of crime through home security systems, but we may be far less able to protect ourselves against bioterrorist threats. Similarly, while border security may be tightened to ensure that terrorists from other countries are not allowed into a particular state, border security does not protect a nation against homegrown terrorist groups. The nature of the particular threats and harms that we face makes simultaneously achieving security across a variety of realms seem elusive.

A final point related to the dynamic aspect of security has to do with respective positioning relative to the identified hazard. Whether at the individual or institutional level, we may perceive danger or potential harm as ranging from very likely to very unlikely. For example, we may recognize that school shootings are a possibility, now that we have collectively witnessed such events, but we may still understand the likelihood of such events as remote. Similarly, while we understand that tsunamis are possible, we might also know—often by relying on expert opinion, because few of us have direct experience with many identified threats—that tsunamis are extremely rare events. Perceiving a particular threat as either remote or likely, as well as being able to imagine the extent of the harm that can be done, will influence the level of preparedness undertaken in advance of such an event. For example, once Hurricane Katrina moved from being highly likely to inevitable, security also changed (in this case, for many, the change was to a diminished state). Furthermore, the security at the pre-event stage of Katrina was different from the security experienced while the event was ongoing, just as security in the aftermath of the hurricane was not the same as when the event was occurring. Perceived likelihood of harm therefore varies depending both on one's temporal and spatial proximity to the hazard itself.

Risk Positions

Certain individual and institutional characteristics may be associated with increased sensitivity to particular cues in the environment, which may in turn be associated with particular (perceived and real) vulnerabilities.[1] If individuals and institutions are differentially attuned to cues in the environment, then vulnerabilities will also vary, presumably influencing the likelihood of harm. Women, for example, may view themselves as more likely to be criminally victimized than men, and may interpret particular environmental cues in light of this perception. Similarly, organizations that provide emergency health services, for example, interpret certain elements of the environment differently from, say, agencies geared toward the provision of financial services. The differing perceptions as to what is threatening and what is beneficial are exactly why we see that security (as well as endangerment) is relative to and is influenced by both environmental and contextual factors and perspectives described here as risk positions.

If individuals and institutions are differentially attuned to cues in the environment, then vulnerabilities will also vary, which presumably influences the likelihood of harm. One avenue through which criminology has taken up the investigation of vulnerabilities is a consideration of repeat victimization. Essentially, the task has been to determine how particular characteristics make certain individuals more or less vulnerable to victimization, as well as how experiences figure into vulnerability. The insights from the repeat victimization literature facilitate our consideration of baseline differences among individuals and institutions, and how it is that these differences may influence detection of and responses to harm.

In the repeat victimization literature, the concepts of risk heterogeneity and of (event) dependence figure prominently and relate specifically to risk positions (see, for example, Tseloni & Pease, 2003; Farrell, Phillips, & Pease, 1995). The term *risk heterogeneity* suggests that individuals are more or less vulnerable to criminal victimization due to specific, unchanging characteristics. For example, young males are more susceptible to victimization than are older females: youthfulness is characteristic of vulnerability, as is being male. Other, more macro characteristics also come into play—household or neighborhood characteristics, for example, make targets more or less attractive to offenders. As Tseloni and Pease state, "Some targets are repeatedly victimized because they have always been more attractive to offenders compared to other potential targets" (p. 197). Simply put, there may be unchanging characteristics of individuals and contexts that elevate the likelihood of victimization.

Dependence refers to characteristics of individuals that may have changed due to a victimization experience. "Dependence" focuses attention on whether, for example, the experience of criminal victimization changes an individual in some particular way, making him or her more vulnerable (or, in other cases, less vulnerable) to future victimization. In this view, vulnerability depends on experience. As Tseloni and Pease (2003) note, "The successful completion of a first crime renders the target more vulnerable and/or attractive. In principle, the longer the victimization history, the closer to certainty is the probability of suffering a subsequent crime" (p. 196). By extension, experience with other types of noncriminal hazard such as poor health or disaster is important when considering the subsequent identification of hazard and threat, perceived vulnerabilities, and the types of behaviors individuals engage in after such experiences.

Tseloni and Pease (2003) have focused on how it is that a victimization experience increases vulnerability and hence the likelihood of a subsequent victimization. For our purposes, their ideas help us to recognize and account for differences in the identification of hazards among parties, and how perspectives on what might cause harm are a reflection of particular characteristics, as well as past experience summed up in risk positions. With regard to individuals, particular characteristics such as sex and income may make females and individuals with low income, for example, consider their environment in ways that differ substantially from those who are male and have high incomes. Furthermore, the identification of hazard will vary by geographical characteristics. Rural residents who live next to gas plants, for example, may consider flared emissions as more hazardous than do urban residents. Similarly, organizations such as the police define hazards in ways that reflect their particular characteristics and experiences as law enforcement agencies. As Anarumo (2005) notes, policing agencies across the United States perceive a greater threat emanating from domestic terrorist groups than from international groups. For the majority of these agencies, the likelihood of having had experience with domestic terrorist groups is far greater than is the likelihood of having had experience with international terrorism. Experience, in other words, focuses attention on harms that are familiar; this is discussed in terms of the availability heuristic in Chapter 2, this volume.

Security is the outcome of managing risk in the face of a variety of harms, assigning differential and often limited resources to sometimes incompatible priorities; and identifying respective location relative to harm. What we can begin to appreciate is that security is, in large part, a relative term. *Security* is often defined as absence (Freedman, 1992), rather than as a type of attainment. For our purposes, we can broadly define security as freedom from danger, fear, or anxiety. Exactly how freedom is defined and may appear between individuals or among states, and the shape it may take, can vary widely. Furthermore, the sources of security and insecurity are always changing: what may instill feelings of safety and well-being today may be sources of insecurities tomorrow.

Approaching Security

While some individuals may take calculated risks, suggesting a rational approach to balancing behavior against possible harm, others may engage in certain behaviors without being aware of the dangers they face. This implies that ignorance may also contribute to assessments (or lack thereof) of potential harm. Rather than being simply an individual-level phenomenon, however, Giddens (1990) suggests that patterns of risk may be institutionalized within certain trust settings, such as investing in the stock market or participating in sports. When an individual chooses to play hockey, for example, she assumes that every person playing is conforming to the structure known as "the hockey game," and that everyone is playing by the same rules. Similarly, in the context of investing in the stock market, individuals purchase stocks with the full knowledge that losses may occur. Success is not a given, but the expectation of fair play among those purchasing and selling stock is assumed—the investor trusts that the market is not being unduly influenced by anything other than expected market factors.

In recognizing risk, we must accept not only the possibility that things might go wrong, but also the fact of that possibility. Stated another way, Clarke and Short (1993) point out that regardless of whether the probability of technical failure has increased over the past years, the social conflict over the probability of certain outcomes has intensified. In essence, Clarke and Short indicate that risk is a concept used to mean different things: risk may imply a future outcome, either negative or positive (in classical probability theory, 1 [future event] = P [event] + Q [nonevent]), or it may mean the probability of a certain outcome (again, in classical probability terms, P [event] = 1 [future event] − Q [nonevent]). Giddens (1990) suggests that where risk is known to be risk (where we know, for example, that negative outcomes are a possibility), harm is experienced differently from where notions of fortuna (fate) prevail (p. 111). Fate suggests that we are powerless; recognizing and anticipating risk implies a degree of empowerment.

While the academic literature and general usage define risk as the possibility of a negative outcome, risk may include the probability of either a positive or negative outcome. The tendency of most actors is to maximize the probability of a positive outcome (benefit), while minimizing the likelihood of a negative outcome (harm). We seek to minimize negative outcomes and take action to reduce harm to what we might consider acceptable levels. What is important for our investigation is that measures taken in the name of security not only apply to managing the present, but may also be designed to establish a particular future.

Measures taken in the name of security then are often designed specifically with the future in mind. An easy example is the person who limits his alcohol intake one particular evening in anticipation of driving home later that night. Drinking less alcohol now is a matter of securing the future—one would not be charged with driving under the influence and would not cause harm to self or others if limits are placed on alcohol consumption now—at least the probability of such negative outcomes is presumably reduced. Likewise, the U.S. government's color-coded system for terror alerts suggests that individuals must be vigilant; individuals now undertake vigilance with the expectation that future harm will be averted because of current efforts. These examples suggest that security is a process involving the future, but security also involves interpretations of the past.

Although risk is central, especially with respect to anticipating the future, understanding security is also an exercise in looking backward. While history may not exactly repeat itself, an understanding of what has come before is critical to understanding the present and anticipating the future. In particular, problem solving is a large part of security and involves the idea of looking back. Once we have identified a problem, we need to consider what preceded it to determine the ingredients of that problem. The concepts of risk and problem solving reinforce our position that security is an ever changing process, moving through time and space.

Modeling Security

Guiding our discussion in this book is the central premise that to begin to achieve security we must understand how individuals and institutions balance risk. As a framework for our discussion, we offer a "risk balance perspective." The balance derives from the elements that we identified above: (1) the values that we retain that shape our views of the dangers and threats that we face; (2) the choices that are made when calculating risks based on information that is available; and (3) decisions regarding allocating resources to mitigate or alleviate harm. This balance will be constantly adjusted over time as threats and hazards evolve; and will change, as we will see, depending on what types of security challenges emerge and recede, for example, crime, terrorism or natural disasters. Addressing security from the point of view of risk balance conforms to the ways in which we talk about confronting dangers; it is increasingly common for agencies to discuss their responses to dangers in terms of risk balance. Risk management programs, insurance and crime prevention program, for example, all contain elements of balancing our resources against potential hazards.

As stated, risk is a calculation, based on values, choices, information, and perspectives of the likelihood of harm or benefit. This calculation of harm or benefit takes into consideration the types of hazards faced, along with the resources available to address (diminish) the likelihood of harm that hazards pose. At the same time, the calculations of harms and benefits depend on the temporal stage of the hazardous event. Security therefore requires balancing between the hazards themselves, the means available to address various hazards, and the stage of the hazardous event. Security may result when hazards are balanced with resources, yet the balance changes depending on the temporal phase of (exposure to) the hazard.

According to this model, there are numerous and dynamic *security states*—defined as the intersection of hazards (or threats), resources, and temporal phase (exposure). Each of these security states involves an effort to balance harm (or the possibility of harm) with the application of assets (such as knowledge and money) according to the exposure stage of the event. Importantly, not all hazards weigh in evenly to particular security debates. For example, in the recent past the threat of terrorism has outweighed other hazards that also potentially undermine security. Similarly, the application of resources at each of the individual, institutional, and state levels differs over time according to the nature of the hazards under consideration, influencing the overall risk balance. Importantly, however, we need to think of each of these security stages as snapshots of security—as parts of a security dynamic. Over time, at different stages of the event, the balance can change, either because of prevention measures taken prior to an incident, reduced exposure during an incident, or prevention measures that are developed in learning from previous incidents. Across hazards, these balance calculations can vary greatly, with different interventions developed according to the type of hazard, but also according to the stage of the event. The implication of this model is that some or all of these hazards may combine to affect overall exposure to harm and influence the risk balance calculation that may characterize any particular and all realms. This is not unlike the idea behind an "all-hazards approach."

In the end, this model represents a security dynamic consisting of evolving and changing security states that is influenced by the interaction of hazards, which generate a level of risk, over time. These risk levels can potentially be brought into balance according to the amount of effort expended. Strategically, this risk balance can then be influenced by the stage of the event. As an example, good preparation, including identification of a particular threat, can mitigate exposure to a threat, which in turn can reduce the amount of resources needed to create security in the face of responding to the event itself. In addition to reducing exposure to negative outcomes, risk balance can also incorporate opportunities that lead to positive security outcomes. This approach deals directly with our view that risk is relative and can be both a positive or negative influence in bringing about security states.

Our model of risk balance centers on balancing hazards with resources and temporal and spatial positioning to enhance the ability to achieve a degree of security. Because we recognize security as fluid and dependent on context—as well as dependent on perspective—we begin to move toward a more process-based conceptualization of security. In traditional criminology, the primary view has been one that eschews security as a state of being. This view is not dissimilar to one that views crime as acts. Our approach adds to a growing literature (Miethe & Meier, 1994; Sacco & Kennedy, 2002) that views security not as the product of willing offenders or vulnerable victims, but rather as the convergence of a variety of factors stemming from individual and institutional sources. We can see security in terms of an event.

The event perspective is a tool or framework that highlights spatial and temporal factors. The spatial aspect of the event perspective draws attention to the various stakeholders and how it is that stakeholders contribute to and become involved in particular events. For example, stakeholders in a criminal event include witnesses, bystanders, offenders, victims, the police, the courts, and so on. Each of these stakeholders views the event differently because each occupies a different structural position and is more or less attuned to particular aspects of the crime or situation over other aspects. In their explication of the temporal component of the criminal event perspective, Sacco and Kennedy (2002) draw attention to the precursors to crime, the criminal transaction, and the aftermath of the transaction. In other words, understanding events must include a consideration of what happens before an event (the past), what happens during an event (the present), and what happens after an event (the aftermath). Despite seeming rather linear, in fact, this framework allows for a spiraling process, whereby the aftermath of each event becomes the precursor stage of the next event. The event perspective draws attention to the spatial and temporal aspects of particular processes by suggesting that different elements come into play at different times in the event.

The notion of an event draws on the familiarity that most of us have with narratives (Agnew, 2006). As is common with narratives and stories, an event has a beginning (pre-event), a plot (transaction), and an ending (aftermath). For our purposes in addressing risk balance, how individuals and institutions are positioned within these narrative structures has much to do with the ways in which hazards are identified and defined, and also depends on available assets. Security narratives—including the identification of harms and responses to them—vary depending on the spatial and temporal elements that are brought together in each story. As we will see in Chapter 2, this volume, when we discuss the social construction of security, certain security narratives dominate others, particularly when specific parties have greater access to resources and therefore have the power to write security narratives as they see fit. This approach allows us to make use of the idea presented above as parts of a risk calibration to which individuals, experts, and institutions have contributed.

The concept of event draws our attention to how it is that various pieces of the security puzzle converge during the transaction—or plot—of the security narrative. What is interesting about the event concept is that the pre-event and post-event stages could be considered open ended, due to the potentially extended period both before and after the harm. Furthermore, some threats do not emerge as a discrete type of event and instead remain chronic or continuous. For certain parts of the population, for example, residential radon does not go away, and is therefore prevalent. Such a problem must be taken into account not as variable, but rather as a constant, along with other types of more or less discrete or continuous hazards, that must be continually addressed.

Furthermore, pre- and post-event periods may be difficult to circumscribe by particular spatial or temporal parameters. For example, take the case of the 2004 tsunami. Geologists may have recognized that the potential existed for a tsunami of these proportions to occur, but it was impossible for them to pinpoint the actual date or place that it would occur. The time lag between knowing that harm could occur and actual harm occurring may be, for certain forms of harm, large—and, often, largely theoretical, especially when dealing with unique events. Tsunamis occur with some degree of regularity, but tsunamis of this magnitude are rare. The theoretical possibility, therefore, constitutes the pre-event stage; however, fixing on particular spatial and temporal coordinates was impossible far in advance. As noted in the case of Hurricane Katrina, even with spatial coordinates locked in—at least in terms of being able to specifically identify which levies would fail—without a specific associated time frame, preparations for this failure did not occur. The pre-event stage was indeterminate in terms of timing until the hurricane changed from possible to inevitable.

The post-event stage is, in many ways, similarly open ended. In the aftermath of harmful events, at the same time that various recovery responses are put into effect, plans are often made to reduce the probability of devastation or harm should another similar event occur. This seems like a straightforward response to the experience of trauma or harm. In certain instances, we can learn much from past events in terms of coordination of services and response procedures. The aftermath of particular events, however, may be plagued by a similar open-endedness in terms of how to address recovery, enhance protection, and anticipate future harm. For instance, with respect to the 9/11 terrorist attacks, airport security has been greatly enhanced. In the aftermath of 9/11's devastation, it is easy to imagine that airplanes could again be used as weapons in future terrorist attacks, even though prior to this event we had not imagined such use. (We discuss the representativeness heuristic in Chapter 2, this volume). Terrorist events, however, are social events, making these events less predictable than certain natural events—less predictable both in terms of timing and character. There are no tectonic plates that can be monitored for movement, nor are there water and air temperatures to be recorded as in the case of hurricanes.

Responding effectively to harmful events after they occur means anticipating the variety of ways that future events might unfold. The criticism in the aftermath of 9/11 is that although the government has tightened airport security, it has paid less attention to securing ports and harbors which are other potentially vulnerable venues. Preparation in the aftermath of a harmful event must include thinking outside the box. Perhaps more damaging criticism was evidenced in the response to and aftermath of Hurricane Katrina, with the suggestion that efforts to anticipate future terrorist attacks had moved resources away from other realms of potential security threats such as hurricanes.[2]

On the one hand, thinking outside the box means anticipating types of harm that have yet to occur—but can be imagined. Anticipating bioterror incidents, for example, or preparing for tsunamis, are examples of thinking outside the box. On the other hand, a potential peril associated with thinking outside the box is the possibility of reductive thinking and immobilization. In terms of technological innovation, for example, attempts are made to detail the consequences of applying particular solutions. Often, there is an effort to address consequences in terms of a hypothetical future and its associated spatial and temporal parameters. Given the unknowns associated with the future, there may be less willingness to apply certain technologies today. An example is that of genetically modified crops. There has been some hesitation to embrace this technology because the consequences of using such foods have not been fully determined as either harmful or positive.

Some would argue that the best way to deal with the uncertainty of potential negative outcomes is to take no chances at all. Often referred to as the precautionary principle, this view means that in public and private policies, we do not allow for even the possibility of any harmful effect. We do not allow certain types of activity unless research has proved that it does not have harmful effects. According to the Wingspread conference in Racine, Wisconsin, in 1998, the precautionary principle suggests that "when an activity raises threats of harm to human health or the environment, precautionary measures should be taken even if some cause and effect relationships are not fully established scientifically" (quoted in Appell, 2001, p. 1). The precautionary principle therefore does not rely on conclusive evidence, but rather is motivated by particular values over and above conclusive (or nonexistent) evidence. Appell explains, "In other words, actions taken to protect the environment and human health take precedence. Therefore, some advocates say, governments should immediately ban the planting of genetically modified crops, even though science cannot yet say definitively whether they are a danger to the environment or to consumers" (p. 1).

The precautionary principle can also promote the view, in the non-scientific realm, that we should take all measures possible to reduce or avoid harm, even if there is little evidence to show that these harms are likely to occur under any circumstances. Hence, we could argue that it is a good idea to provide security funding against terrorism to all constituencies in a country, even though certain areas have a remote likelihood of being attacked. The underlying assumption is that the lack of evidence of these areas being targets does not mitigate the damage that would be done if they were targets. Even though this distribution of funds might have the consequence of increasing the threat to high-risk targets that are unable to defend themselves fully, the argument persists (Sunstein, 2001).

Can we anticipate all negative consequences of our actions? The answer, obviously, is no. But this realization is at odds with our frequently expressed belief to the contrary: that we should be able to manage risks with certainty as a result of greater knowledge and technology that is more effective. This optimism is supported by the great successes in medicine and in wealth building that has come through global economies. But the complete reduction of risk at the hands of determined criminals, the attacks from terrorists, or the forces of nature is out of our reach. The insecurity that results from this reality makes us try harder to manage these risks and to hold those who fail us in this effort accountable for the devastating consequences of these failures; this response is exemplified in the condemnation of authorities after the Katrina disaster discussed earlier.

Before we conclude that we are better safe than sorry, however, we must confront the reality that we cannot always be perfectly safe, although we can understand more about what contributes to security through preparedness, prevention, and response that comes from a balance in the management of risk that we face in our lives.

Studying Security From Many Perspectives

Studying security is a multidisciplinary project. It is not possible to think about security without recognizing that boundaries between realms such as health, crime, and the environment, for example, are often blurred, both in theory and in practice. This means that we must draw on a number of different fields of study to make sense of how balancing risk leads to security (or insecurity). While the primary target of much of the work on security has been criminal justice agencies, particularly law enforcement, the issues raised in addressing hazards from health and natural disasters include public health officials, engineers, scientists, and others. While the specific responses and the information used to craft these responses may differ across disciplines, the model of balance is the same for all. The importance of understanding balance in terms of what we value, the choices we make, and the resources available for response is central to all realms.

The recent crisis on the Gulf Coast caused by Hurricane Katrina shows a need to understand the interconnectedness of security issues, but also exemplifies the evolution of security and the degree to which threats to security can vary between members of the same population. As with other disasters, the immediate response during Katrina was to save lives and move people out of harm's way, and to provide shelter and food to those in need. The crisis affected various groups within the population in a variety of ways with income figuring prominently in the abilities of hurricane victims to cope with the aftereffects of the disaster, as well as to protect themselves from further harm. Contaminated water, power outages, and failed facilities took their toll differentially even among the poor: those poor who were in bad health, as well as the young and the aged, were particularly vulnerable.

Although we bring to this project our backgrounds in sociology and criminology, we maintain that security is a subject that has yet to be adequately covered by any specific discipline or in a satisfactory interdisciplinary fashion. Furthermore, concerns over security are never far from issues that pervade the public and private domains. While public health officials might concern themselves with flu epidemics and other transmissible diseases, for example, the goal of keeping populations healthy is ultimately a national and, increasingly, a global security issue. While providing free flu shots to the elderly ensures freedom from illness for a vulnerable segment of the population, it also secures the public health system by alleviating it from having to deal with the expenditures incurred if such epidemics were to occur.

Conclusion

Since all categories grow from the same ambient experience of generalized insecurity of no visible internal structure, their boundaries are blurred: their semantic fields, at least in part, overlap. Their separation, always an artifice of classifying efforts, tends to exaggerate the differences at the expense of the affinities. (Bauman, 2002, p. 65)

Security may be a contested zone, involving many contradictions between and among individuals, institutions, and states. We suggested earlier that security varies widely by perspective—what security is, what threatens security, and what needs to be done to attain or improve security depends on the perspective from which it is viewed. Security is not the exclusive purview of state, or of institutional or individual actors, but rather depends on the intersection of these levels. These intersections are not necessarily hierarchical—individuals may undermine institutional security, just as institutions may undermine individual security. As Bauman (2002) suggests, security blurs and overlaps semantic fields: security in one realm seeps into and influences security in other realms. The social and physical elements that we perceive as threatening or hazardous pervade the fabric of our lives—at work, at play, and at home. Our risk positions (in terms of, for example, age, gender, and income) may preclude exposure to certain hazards, at the same time that social location may increase the probability of exposure to other hazards (e.g., Cohen & Felson, 1979).

Our theoretical framework outlining risk balance is detailed in Chapter 2. In that chapter, we provide an overview of risk society and the implications of our current historical context for the developing (and increasing) emphasis on security. Some theorists, for example, claim that risk society is characterized by heightened individualism and general unease. This unease has been exacerbated by recent events, not least of which are the events of September 11, other recent and continuing terrorist events, as well as the host of disasters witnessed over the past few years. We consider whether these sorts of events have served to crystallize, as well as provide objective evidence of the nature of the threats that abound in this historical period. In particular, we draw on Beck's (1992) and others' explication of the risk society and explore the applicability of risk society to the burgeoning interest in security. We then draw on literature by Amos Tversky, Daniel Kahneman, and Paul Slovic on how individuals assess hazards and threats and the resources they need to respond to them.

An examination of this sociohistorical period and the relationship between individuals, institutions, and states provides a context for our discussion of the social construction of security. While the sociohistorical context contributes to and fosters the identification of particular harms, a consideration of the social construction of security does not necessitate taking the objective reality of this context or the particulars of certain events to task. As Spector and Kitsuse (2001) point out, the focus for the sociologist is to consider the process set in motion with the identification of some problem, at the same time that she does not need to determine the objective reality of the problem's identification. We do not need to establish the reality of terrorist threat that the United States faces, for example, any more than the objective threat of war was determined in other historical periods. Instead, our focus is on the processes that unfold with respect to an identified hazard or threat—a process that involves a particular dialogue among individuals, institutions, and the state.

After establishing the historical and sociocultural context, we draw on a variety of potential hazards in the realms of crime, terrorism, health, and the environment. We consider these arenas as part of the security landscape. The second part of our book therefore considers particular hazards and threats more specifically and considers how the elements of our model serve to highlight and begin to reveal the complexity of achieving security in various threat contexts. Chapter 3 focuses on crime and how the contexts of crime affect security. In Chapter 4, we consider terrorism as a matter of security that, although it has tended to operate at the national level, has been recreated as an issue germane to individual security. In Chapter 5, we consider health and the environment as security issues; each of these realms has much to teach us with respect to prevention, warning, and response systems. We highlight the commonalities found between realms that are as seemingly divergent as health and terrorism.

The final chapters draw together common threads relevant to risk balance, and consider more specifically the ways in which responses to risk balance unfold. Here, we consider the means of addressing hazard in the pre-event stage, focusing in particular on means of preparing for hazards that may occur but have not done so. We then consider various responses to hazards as seen from the incident phase of the event: what sorts of responses are associated with hazards as they occur? Finally, we consider responses to risk balance in the aftermath of incidents and focus our discussion particularly on the notion of prevention. The aftermath of hazard often allows for reflection on how hazards might have been avoided, and what might have been done to reduce harms incurred.

Notes to Chapter 1

1. We use the term *environment* in a broad sense, and define it as including the social, spatial, and political environment.

2. In the aftermath of Hurricane Katrina, there was much criticism that the infrastructure to deal with security issues other than terrorism had been greatly compromised. This criticism was acknowledged by the Department of Homeland Security when, in the late fall of 2005, it issued a document calling for an approach to security that was inclusive of a variety of threats and potential harms—from terrorism to natural and man-made disasters.

2

Values and Choices
in Constructing Security

The Values of Security

Cultures provide a menu of choices with respect to what is considered hazardous and what is considered safe (Purcell, Clarke, & Renzulli, 2000). As Purcell and colleagues indicate, cultural mediation highlights certain behaviors and objects as dangerous and others as safe, while still others are simply left unaddressed. Culture serves as a lens through which the environment is interpreted, with perspectives on hazards and threats often as varied and numerous as there are cultures themselves. Sunstein (2005) argues, furthermore, that considerations of hazards and threats are contingent on cultural or social determinants. In Europe, for example, there is a great deal of anxiety about the dangers posed by genetically altered food, a threat of much less concern to North Americans who are far more concerned with biohazards entering the food chain. North Americans also tend to view the running of the bulls in Spain as clearly dangerous behavior, but tend to view bungee jumping, skydiving, and mountain climbing as relatively benign. In order to study security and think about harm, we need to know the contexts in which hazards are identified—the social, spatial, and political environments—and how it is that culture serves to mediate these environments.

The identification of hazards from an institutional perspective has implications for the identification of hazards at the individual level, and vice versa. Furthermore, the actions taken at one level to enhance security may work at cross-purposes to actions taken at another level. The menus of choice may look quite different from an institutional than from an individual perspective due to the cultures that surround each respective level. Clearly, part of the reason for the distinction between these levels has to do with orientation to the environment. Individuals, for example, operate within their environments on a level that tends to be defined primarily by more proximate and embodied concerns. It is difficult, for example, to identify or respond to a threat that may be interpreted as particularly distant or improbable; we refer to heuristic devices in more detail later in this chapter. Global warming may be one example: although some experts have identified this threat, the immediate implications of this phenomenon are not apparent to most individuals, effectively serving to remove this concern from their personal radar. At the institutional level, the orientation can better be described as more abstract and removed from the embodied concerns of individuals. Agencies and institutions often have to think in terms that are larger than any one particular individual, and that are more (or less) inclusive of groups and individuals. The goals of particular health agencies, for example, are to maximize the health of a number of people, rather than to focus on any particular individual. The specifics of individual cases may therefore be left unaddressed by such agencies and their respective policies. Policing agencies might view failing to close a case as similarly hazardous to individuals who may be concerned that particular offenders are arrested. Potential and actual victims, on the other hand, care little about closing a case and are more concerned with personal safety and protection against offenders. What registers on individual or collective radars as hazardous and threatening varies, and may result in each of these levels unknowingly undermining efforts to protect against harm at other levels.

A further example of the differing menus and how these result in varying responses to possible harm are the recent security measures undertaken by the U.S. government in response to the terrorist attacks in 2001. On the one hand, we note the proliferation of antiterrorist devices (most significantly at airports), as well as the creation of a color-coded terrorist advisory system. Such measures are perceived to increase security from an institutional point of view, as airline travel, which was highly implicated in the mass destruction associated with 9/11, falls within the purview of government vigilance. In terms of the warning system, the government seeks to keep the public apprised of recent developments through its identification of various color-coded threat levels. For individuals who travel by air, however, enhanced security may not be the result of such measures. Airline passengers may experience greater annoyance, versus actual or perceived security, because they are delayed by measures that restrict the comparative freedom they enjoyed pre-9/11.

Cultures provide us with the means of ready identification of certain elements in our environment as safe or harmful. For those elements that do not appear on the menu, we often rely on others to help us identify and interpret our environments. As Purcell and colleagues (2000) note, how culture is mediated has important implications for the exercise of power—who has it and who does not—as well as for legitimacy. Some individuals and agencies are in positions of power that maximize the likelihood that their identification of hazard and threat will be acknowledged.

Security is influenced by the ways in which society refers to these dangers and the appropriate accommodations that can be made in response to them. The social construction of security involves accounting for the values of society. Values are reflected in the ways in which we describe what we fear, in the messages that we impart to our families about the dangers they face, and the ways in which we legitimize certain actions that we take to create security. The issues that gain salience depend on a complex set of relationships between politicians, the media, educators, and others. What we know is that the social construction of security and the management of risk have changed dramatically over the past century as a result of large-scale shifts in our views of nature and science. We increasingly believe that we can beat the odds if we only can anticipate the threats. The notion that we must accept our fate has been replaced by the expectation that intervention is possible.

The Invention of Risk Society

Ulrich Beck is the writer who has had the greatest impact on our thinking about how changes in societies have affected how we view risk and security. He suggests that a central tenet of this change is the shift from an emphasis on the distribution of material wealth to the distribution of risk. He states, "we are therefore concerned no longer exclusively with making nature useful, or with releasing mankind from traditional constraints, but also and essentially with problems resulting from techno-economic development itself" (1992, p. 19). Beck suggests that this transition has occurred primarily in the Western world where needs for food and shelter are, or can easily be, satisfied. Historically, science and technology provided the answers to questions of consumption and livelihood, but today technology and science are problematic in our search for security. This shift in emphasis comes with a change in the ways in which we communicate about what is dangerous and what is not, and is instrumental in how we respond to these hazards. Beck summarizes the product of these changes as risk society, offering a new way of considering risk as primary, and hence risk balance as central, rather than as secondary aspects of modern life.

Within the risk society model, the concept of risk plays into everyday experiences. We expect the future to unfold in predictable ways and we act according to the future we presume. This is especially true with respect to how and what we have defined as harmful or as potentially harmful. As we will discuss, Slovic and others (2002) have argued that our security depends on how well we have made these decisions. These individual choices are influenced by larger factors working in society, though, which make the outcomes of these decisions uncertain. One of the most fundamental choices is the use of scientific intervention itself. For example, if the overproduction of cropland has depleted naturally occurring nutrients and minerals, is it legitimate to address this problem with the application of synthetic fertilizers? If science and technology created the condition of overproduction, does it make sense to use science and technology, in the form of synthetic nutrients, if overproduction was itself a product of science? Beck poses the interesting dilemma that security is both ensured by—and challenged by—our use of technology. We must weigh the decisions that we make based on probabilistic choice against the uncertainty that we face because of incomplete knowledge and unproven interventions.

In Beck's view, the predictability of life is undermined because we have entered a period characterized by pervasive doubt; uncertainty has replaced certainty in science. What we thought was known, as well as what we thought experts knew, is no longer a source of security but is increasingly seen as a source of potential endangerment. This view projects deeply into our understanding of how societal values and norms affect the ways in which we manage risk. These issues transcend individual and institutional choices and become an integral part of the political and cultural discussions and debates that swirl around security.

Beck (1992) explains that we are "eyewitnesses—as subjects and objects—of a break with modernity . . . [where classical industrial society is] forging a new form—the (industrial) 'risk society' " (1992, p. 9). In the 19th century, modernity emerged against a background of opposites: tradition, in terms of rank and religion, and scientific challenges to the forces of nature. Science has identified, exposed, and challenged the flaws found in other ways of knowing the world (i.e., tradition and religion), but is now entering a period where the challenges to know and control the world stem from the advances of science itself.

The problems created by technology are widely recognized, such as the pollution associated with manufacturing various goods. With this knowledge, we are able to monitor our choices and choose particular paths into the future. Through what Lash and Wynne (1992) call a "reflexive process," there is the possibility of a change in the relationship between social structure and social agents (p. 2). Rather than being predetermined, outcomes can be influenced by individuals and institutions. Destiny, at least to a large extent, may be modified. Reflexivity, therefore, opens up the door to greater possibilities, but it also holds liable those who fail to adequately anticipate the future. Essentially, controlling the future rests on a variety of conditions, including a willingness to restrict our behavior or the behavior of those around us. Moreover, it suggests the aggressive use of scientific intervention in controlling the negative aspects of technology. While this type of risk management can be shown to be stunningly successful in areas such as the management of air traffic, it seems less likely to succeed in areas such as crime control.

It can backfire on us, as well. We now know, for example, that exposure to particular chemicals can have long-term negative consequences. Asbestos, a common product used in building materials and household products, has been hailed as one of the best heat resistors available. However, the long period between exposure to asbestos and subsequent ill effects has resulted in continued use of asbestos far beyond what might have occurred if these ill effects emerged temporally closer to exposure. The result of being unable to immediately associate exposure with harm has resulted in a large proportion of the global population unwittingly exposed to this carcinogen. Large asbestos industries worldwide are expected to result in the deaths of many around the globe (see, for example, Barbalace, 2004). The realization that this wonder product has and will continue to cause this sort of suffering suggests that we may be exposing ourselves to other sources of harm that appear benign now, but whose deleterious effects might be registered only at some time in the future.

The Context of Risk Society

Summarizing the challenges we face, Beck (1992) characterizes five central theses of risk society. First, risks induce systematic and irreversible harm that may be invisible. Beck suggests that the threats we face today are distinctive from threats in previous eras. Historically, the threats faced were personal; now they are global. He argues that in an earlier period, risk implied a note of "bravery and adventure, not the threat of self-destruction of all life on

Earth" (p. 21). Today, consequences of particular actions are widespread, moving well beyond geographic boundaries. We have tended to focus our preventative actions on the realms of behavior that are proximate and personal over those that are public. For example, in terms of the harms associated with criminal behavior and the generalized insecurity this produces, the focus of criminological concern has been at the local level and has not tended to focus on the more global crime hazards that are characterized by temporally and spatially extenuated criminality. In other words, we focus attention on preventing crimes against persons, in our homes, and in our neighborhoods, not on preventing crimes such as price-fixing and embezzlement, whose effects are less immediately tangible.

Furthermore, endangerment in the risk society differs from earlier eras in that we are unable to *directly* detect that which may harm us or threaten us. After providing an example of the stench of medieval cities, Beck (1992) notes,

> it is nevertheless striking that hazards in those days assaulted the nose or the eyes and were thus perceptible to the senses, while the risks of civilization today typically *escape perception* and are localized in the sphere of *physical and chemical formulas* [italics in original]. (p. 21)

The expectation that grave hazards may be imperceptible to the senses is illustrated with respect to the war in Iraq and the emphasis on weapons of mass destruction, as well as the U.S. focus on hypervigilance, which amounts to an attempt to make the imperceptible perceptible. As technology has advanced, threat can no longer be assessed on that which is obvious: endangerment has gone underground.

Beck indicates that the hazards faced in the past were due to an undersupply of technology, while today the hazards are due to an oversupply; in other words, technological advancement has taken over. Once perceived as the answer to our problems ranging from food shortages, disease, and shelter, technology in the risk society is increasingly seen as the source of problems. The hazards we face are due to industrial overproduction, yet overproduction is far from evenly distributed, with the benefits of globalization having different effects in different regions of the world.

Beck's second thesis is that while social position, what we call risk position, matters in terms of exposure to hazards, risk distribution has what Beck (1992) refers to as a boomerang effect. The boomerang effect is that the "risks of modernization sooner or later also strike those who produce or profit from them . . . which breaks up the pattern of class and national society" (p. 23). Those who profit from environmentally damaging manufacturing processes are also subject to the harms that manufacturing causes. Furthermore, the risk society is a world, or global, risk society because those who live in certain regions are subject to the harms produced by other regions. Just as the benefits of globalization have no boundaries, the hazards associated with globalization also respect no boundaries: actions are no longer unilateral. For example, the depletion of the cod stocks in the Northern Atlantic Ocean is not simply a problem for the cod-fish industry. Rather, as part of a larger ecosystem, the depletion or destruction of part of the entire system will affect other types of fisheries as well as consumption patterns the world over. In the transition from industrial to risk society, a change occurs in communality: communities based on shared values are traded for communities based on shared threats. Beck observes, "the place of the value system of the 'unequal' society is taken by the value system of the 'unsafe' society" (p. 207). The risk society is based on a communality of fear and insecurity.

Third, risk is self-referential: risks create more risks. Beck (1992) states that while economic needs can be satisfied, "*civilization* risks are a *bottom-less barrel of demands* [italics in original]" (p. 23). With economic exploitation of the hazards that industrial society itself has created, the will to reduce what has become economically viable will be diminished. Risk management—the quest to reduce fear and establish security—has become a big business unto itself (a point to which we return in Chapter 6, this volume). For example, it remains to be seen whether the strategic focus on new surveillance technologies will benefit society in the same way the advances in wartime aviation technology led to major innovations in the contemporary airline manufacturing process. Examples of dual benefits have already appeared, however. Protecting the goods in container ships keeps them safe from terrorists but also reduces the likelihood of theft and pilferage, reducing loss in the overall costing of goods. So, while there may be a dead hand of security that adds costs to business, this may be offset by the benefits (e.g., the reduction of loss) that accrue in other ways.

Fourth, Beck (1992) argues that risks are "*ascribed* by civilization" (p. 23). Traditional structures of ascribing one's place, such as class and income, have been replaced with new structures that rest on proximity to hazards, with the revamping of the old class structure along the dimension of endangerment. Through knowledge one can avoid dangers, although perhaps only in the short term. At the same time, however, knowledge of risks is a commodity that only some possess. As Beck (1989) states, "one comes across the hard law earlier rather than later, that as long as risks are not scientifically recognized they do not exist, at least not legally, medically, technologically, or socially" (p. 100).

Fifth, Beck highlights the relationship between the public and private realms in the risk society. When public harm is created within private operations of business, for example, those operations become open to public scrutiny. Privacy no longer exists in the risk society. Furthermore, Beck (1992) indicates that what "emerges in risk society is the *political potential of catastrophes*" (p. 24). Simply put, the threat of catastrophe, the possibility of hazard unleashed, can be used as a political tool (p. 78). Societies are subject to terrorism and its associated harms, yet the threat of terrorism is as powerful as its reality. The identification of the slightest hint of possible harm, let alone catastrophe, opens the doors to levels of surveillance not experienced in earlier eras. This is illustrated in the aftermath of the London bombings, in 2005, where the success in tracking the bombers after the fact has been attributed to the extensive surveillance network that was already established throughout Britain—not only in transit stations, but also throughout the city of London, which houses many closed-circuit television monitors in a variety of public venues. The public versus private aspect of risk society relates to the often-competing perspectives involved in establishing security states through risk balance.

The distinction between private and public security is becoming increasingly blurred. As an example, prior to 9/11 the management of global supply chains of manufactured goods was left, for the most part, to the scrutiny of corporate security, with the provision that material entering the country would be subject to inspection by customs officials. The loss of goods or the assurance that the suppliers were trusted was primarily left to the companies themselves. This has changed with the strong initiatives implemented by the federal government through customs and border control to ensure that the material coming into the United States does not threaten security. Companies must adhere to security protocols and meet strict importation guidelines; even though this is presented as a voluntary program, nonparticipation almost guarantees that companies will come under much greater and slower (hence more costly) scrutiny by customs. What was primarily a private enterprise in managing supply chains has now become the purview of the public sector, all in the name of reducing the possibility of harm.

Applying Risk Society to Risk Balance

Although Beck refers to the boomerang effect with respect to never truly being able to escape the potential damages that may result from particular choices, the likelihood of being able to establish negative outcomes as attributable to any one particular cause may be minimal. Theoretically, and in the abstract, the notion of a boomerang effect makes sense. As we noted earlier, however, what characterizes at least some of the hazards inherent in risk society is the elongated time frame between exposure and outcome. It will be difficult to establish, for example, that particular actions at one time result in particular outcomes at another time. If it was possible to control for other factors, much as what is done in experimental models, we might then be able to establish that a particular factor or factors causes a particular outcome. While holding various factors constant works in experimental models, in real life we are unable to hold all potential influences constant, therefore we are unable to establish with any degree of certainty that outcomes are due to particular causes. While this should not prevent us from taking relevant and smart actions that might contribute to various positive outcomes, it remains difficult to establish causality, hence the challenges with the precautionary principle noted earlier.

Beck's analysis of the merging of the public and private realms is somewhat paralleled in our risk balance model by our emphasis on levels of analysis. We suggest that individual efforts to protect and guard against hazards must be considered within the larger social and institutional contexts in which they occur. Furthermore, efforts to establish security at one level might undermine security efforts at other levels. For example, individuals may feel that carrying firearms enhances their personal security, but clearly the security of other individuals may be jeopardized by these individual security efforts. The Department of Homeland Security suggests that behaviors that might have formerly been considered private, or at least inconsequential, must be re-evaluated in light of possible threats to national security, hence the emphasis on vigilance. The boundaries that characterized the private versus public spheres are blurred in risk society because of directives from institutional and state levels that often emphasize personal responsibility. Reichmann (1986) suggests that, in private arenas, rules of behavior are more obvious and transgressions of these behaviors more visible. In other words, should we take offense in a private arena, there is someone to whom that response can be directed. The offense that we might feel in a public place, by the very nature of the location in which it is occurring, reduces our ability to pinpoint, and essentially lay blame, for the offending action. Part of the reasons for threats to security being more interpretable in private contexts is because we have a clearer sense of what is going on around us; that is, we have better knowledge of our surroundings in a closed area. In the public context, the same behaviors and cues may be more open to interpretation: the motivations of persons and characteristics of public situations make interpretation as to intent and motivation less clear-cut, and hence, security more problematic.

Public spaces become an even greater source of insecurity in a risk society. As Beck points out, much danger is hidden, in any case. We can never know everything about every person and every situation in the public context, but our knowledge presumably increases as the boundaries close in on increasingly private venues.[1] The merging of the personal and public realms, especially as undertaken in the name of security, suggests that higher levels of political participation should mark risk society: as risk society becomes increasingly pervasive, an accompanying tendency to create, recreate and question boundaries should also prevail. That is, politicization may result if agents do not become immobilized by the heightened responsibility they have for their own security. We return to the political implications of security momentarily.

Finally, hazards are "particularly open to social definition and construction" especially by professionals in charge of defining risks. Decisions produced within the context of the risk society are not simply about information (i.e., an objective calculation), they are also, at the same time, decisions made with respect to the extent that people will be affected and consequences will emerge (Beck, 1992). This calculation influences how individuals or institutions ready themselves against threats and seek resources to balance against high levels of hazard. Furthermore, as explained by the event-based nature of our risk balance model, this calculation can be influenced by the time relative to the actual event that creates harm, allowing for the occurrence of prevention, readiness, or recovery.

Culture and Messages About Security

If we take into account Beck's views about the changing nature of society, we see that risk has become a central focus for communities and individuals to manage security. The emphasis that is placed on risk, however, is set in the context of the general value system of society. Douglas (1992), for example, contends that the risks that are paid the most attention are those connected to legitimating moral principles: if there is no moral value attached, there is little reason to talk about any associated risk. We strive to find a reason for why things happen. One has only to consider the explosion in lawsuits and the phenomenon of suing individuals in attempts to place blame and to receive material compensation or to legitimate particular points of view. Douglas maintains that the late 20th and early 21st centuries are characterized by heightened sensitivity to issues of danger, due primarily to the politicization of what is named as dangerous. This is a theme that is reinforced in by Mueller (2006), who makes a strong case for the overblown nature of the current threats from terrorism, arising from the claims made by politicians and the so-called terrorism industry.

In *The Culture of Fear*, Glassner (1999) explains that the means by which individuals begin to fear particular events and phenomenon over others is due, at least in part, to what has been referred to as the Cuisinart Effect (Schwartz, 1995) promoted and used by the media. This refers to the "mashing together of images and story lines from fiction and reality" (Glassner, p. xxiv). The public is prone to pulling fragments of knowledge together from a variety of sources, both from experts and experience, but Glassner provides examples of the media doing the same thing. In a story by NBC's *Dateline*, Glassner describes how clips of *Outbreak,* a movie about a lethal virus, were woven throughout a story about deaths in Zaire. The Cuisinart Effect produces a type of hybrid risk knowledge, with disparate information pulled together with the effect of creating a social problem, or security issue, where none previously existed.

Wildavsky (1995) suggests that security may be bolstered if the biases created by media coverage of scientific issues were better controlled. In his book, *But Is It True?*, Wildavsky suggests that bad media reporting inadvertently leads to the creation of a false public consciousness about where risks might actually lie. The bad media practices that Wildavsky refers to include taking findings out of context, as well as failing to consider issues beyond the results of any particular study, which can vary widely. The media do not contribute exclusively to the creation of bias. Newspaper readers, for example, often do not read beyond headlines or the initial paragraphs of reports. Wildavsky suggests that citizens could far more effectively assess what they are reading, and he offers rules for evaluating scientific evidence about risks. As Wildavsky notes, the democratizing effect of threats in risk society is only democratizing to the extent that the population is scientifically literate. The CNN effect, for example, refers to the impact that "continuous and instantaneous television may have on foreign policy, in the making of foreign policy and the conduct of war" (Brookings, 2002, p. 1). Instead of engaging with issues directly, the volume of television coverage may sway citizens and politicians alike to perceive particular issues as more important or relevant than they might actually be. Rather than becoming more critical of what is seen and heard about hazards, citizens may continue to rely not only on the media to evaluate findings for them, but also on experts whom they trust, despite the variation that often characterizes both media and expert opinion.

(We return to the role of the media in risk and security communication in Chapter 6, this volume.)

Moore and Valverde (2000) highlight how it is that hybrid risk knowledge relies on a highly mixed knowledge format. Rather than relying on one source or type of information, knowledge fragments from a variety of sources are combined. In the date-rape threat, information contributing to this risk came from "medical information, Victorian melodrama, . . . War-On-Drugs, 'scared straight' discourses, . . . graphs providing quantitative information, and community-police-type lists of 'safety tips'" (Moore & Valverde, p. 521), the effect of which is that all women acknowledge some snippet of information and may subsequently realize that they, too, are in danger. The larger the number of fragments of knowledge, and the larger the variety of sources from which these fragments emerge, the greater the likelihood of identifying a problem than any one of the fragments could have otherwise created.

How does all of this apply to security as a social issue? The concept of security houses a number of fragments, like tiles in a mosaic, with particular fragments resonating for particular individuals, institutions, and states. The concept of security is so broad and involves so many aspects that it would be difficult not to have at least some fragment resonate with most parties, increasing the likelihood of and ease with which security has become a social issue. Given a social milieu characterized by generalized anxiety, information that may be interpreted as having anything to do with safety and security due to heightened sensitivity toward such matters will be that much more likely to resonate. Living in a risk society increases the likelihood of being particularly attuned to information that may serve the purpose of either establishing where our vulnerabilities lie, or establishing what we might be able to do about these vulnerabilities in order to enhance security and our perceptions of it.

Judging Hazards, Threats, and Risks

Our culture has changed in the ways in which we view science and technology and in our control of our own destinies. Nevertheless, we still make choices about risk as individuals, institutions, communities, and governments. These choices are influenced not only by values, but also by perceptions of successful strategies and views of appropriate and attainable outcomes. Offsetting uncertainty, the means by which hazards and threats are identified have much to do with the assessment of probabilities.

Figure 2.1   Perceptions of Security

SOURCE: www.CartoonStock.com.

On what basis do individuals arrive at estimates of future events? How do individuals assess the probability of harm? Few have devoted as much time to answering these questions as Daniel Kahneman and Amos Tversky using prospect theory. Beginning in the 1970s (for example, Tversky & Kahneman, 1974), these authors conducted studies that considered, among other issues, the methods that people use to judge the probabilities of various events under conditions of uncertainty. While individuals might be able to predict with 100 percent accuracy the likelihood of the sun rising each day, clearly other events are far less predictable. It is difficult to predict the outcome of elections, for example, or the likelihood that an offender will reoffend, or the possibility that a person will come down with the flu. Much of what we do to protect ourselves, we do under conditions of uncertainty—never really knowing the chances that we will face particular harms, or knowing if the protections that we put into place are effective. If we happen not to catch the flu, for example, was it because we had a flu shot and took a precaution we believed necessary based on our belief that this would help, or because we were never exposed to that particular strain of flu virus in the first place?

The means by which events are judged as likely or unlikely, as well as identified as hazardous or benign, are the result of relying on a limited number of clues and biases (Tversky & Kahneman, 1986). Tversky and Kahneman suggest there are three heuristic devices, or mental shortcuts, that are commonly used in identifying harm and estimating the likelihood of its occurrence: representativeness, availability, and adjustment and anchoring.

The representativeness heuristic enables individuals to judge hazards and threats based on how close or far away that particular event might be from that which is known or has been experienced before. In other words, individuals determine how close B is to A. If B is close to (representative of) A, then the two are judged to be of the same kind and therefore are determined as having similar probabilities of occurring.

Despite using what we know, representativeness may lead to misjudgments due to a number of factors. For example, associations are often made through the use of inaccurate stereotypes. Personality traits such as aggression and egoism may be more likely associated with lawyers than with librarians. We may also fail to account for the prior probability of particular outcomes. For example, even though B may seem like A, if A is rare, then the probability of B being representative of A is less likely. In other words, knowing that B is of type A does not make the probability of B more likely. Similarly, representativeness may lead to the illusion of validity. The illusion of validity occurs when input information leads to false predictions. As Tversky and Kahneman (1986) explain, a positive description of a student, for example, is often associated with a positive prediction as to his or her future grade-point average. The student who is described as an A-student, for example, is predicted to fare better on examinations than is a student who earns As and Cs. Marketing companies and politicians play on this bias and describe a product or a candidate, or a political response, in positive terms which may work to construct the illusion of validity; if events or phenomena are described in positive terms, then positive predictions are more likely associated with these descriptions.

A further bias associated with representativeness has to do with regression toward the mean. Consider, for example, performance on a test. An excellent performance on a test is likely to be followed by a poorer performance, independent of what occurs after the first performance, whether the initial performance was rewarded or punished. Similarly, a poor performance is likely to improve on a second testing. What this means is that responses or reactions to certain types of phenomenon may play into their subsequent occurrence far less significantly than might be expected. Regardless of whether a poor test mark is punished or a good test mark is rewarded, marks and other such phenomena tend to average out over the long term.

Tversky and Kahneman (1986) refer to the second shortcut as the availability heuristic. As they note, this is characterized by "people assess[ing] the frequency or the probability of an event by the ease with which instances or occurrences can be brought to mind" (p. 46). For example, observers might readily diagnose the chest pains of a 65-year-old man as evidence of a heart attack, given that many have heard of older males having heart attacks. Furthermore, instances of classes of more frequent occurrences are easier to remember than are those of less frequent (smaller) classes, so observers might name certain afflictions as part of the larger and more well-known class (for example, cancer) than the less frequent and less well-known class (Parkinson disease). As with representativeness, the availability heuristic enables judgments about events or probabilities of events using information about what is known to judge against what is unknown. Use of the availability heuristic again, however, leads to particular biases and inaccuracies.

A difficulty with the availability heuristic has to do with familiarity. While events and instances might be more readily named as being of a certain class, we may misjudge a particular event or instance because we tend to categorize according to the familiar, or according to the largest class. This point has to do with salience: we can more readily name instances as being of a certain class, as well as predict probabilities of a certain class, depending on how salient the event or class is to us. For example, having just witnessed a fire or terrorist event, we may judge the likelihood of such an event as being far greater than it actually is given our recent experience with it. As Tversky and Kahneman (1986) further note, salience is also influenced by direct versus indirect experience. Those who have experienced a terrorist event will be more likely to judge the future occurrence of such an event as greater than those who have simply read reports of a terrorist event in the newspaper, or have otherwise only heard of such an event.

Another important bias stemming from the availability heuristic identified by Tversky and Kahneman (1986) is the effectiveness of a search set. We have learned to organize our thoughts and categorize events according to specific criteria. In terms of the identification of hazards and threats, we may conduct our search sets in ways that fail to identify threats that are equally probable. In the days following September 11, 2001, for example, the directive to remain vigilant to suspicious activity may have been erroneously biased by the means citizens were directed to employ and, in fact, did employ. The identification of suspicious activity appeared to be based on a limited search set involving overt interest in public places, photo-graphing buildings, and racial identification. This restricted focus worked to the detriment of many citizens of Arabic descent in the period immediately following 9/11. Rather than using a search set that was wider, more inclusive, and less prone to the biases generated from one specific event or from a limited set of events, the search set consisted of a relatively narrow range of behaviors and identities with resulting large inaccuracies.

Crucially, the availability heuristic is also biased by the limits of imagination. As we observed earlier, the difficulties we have in imagining certain events affect the perceived probability of those events. The harder an event is to imagine, the less likely we judge its probability (Tversky & Kahneman, 1986, p. 47). The opposite is also true. The ease with which we imagine a certain event does not make that event any more likely than the unimaginable. One example (Young, 1996) works both ways: In the 1980s, a four-year-old boy, James Bulger, had been out shopping with his mother. When his mother turned her back, two young boys led James from her. Their images were captured on videotape as they were leaving the shopping center holding James by the hand. James's bludgeoned body was later found and the two boys were charged with murder. In the first instance, it was unimaginable that two young boys would commit murder, but having seen just such a case, a concerned public felt that this type of murder was indeed more likely than ever to occur again, despite the actual probability being very low.

Tversky and Kahneman (1986) explain that "the risk involved in an undertaking may be grossly underestimated if some possible dangers are either difficult to conceive of, or simply do not come to mind" (p. 48). Similarly, probabilities may be overestimated if we are better able to imagine possible dangers. The limits to imagination are evident again with respect to 9/11. The "9/11 Commission Report" (National Commission, 2004) indicates that early cues as to what was occurring were not interpreted correctly for good reason: no one had conceived that terrorists would use a domestic aircraft to commit a terrorist event, other than hijacking. Until seconds before impact, people did not believe that the pilots were actually aiming directly for specific buildings.

An additional bias created by the availability heuristic is referred to as "illusory correlation" (Tversky & Kahneman, 1986, p. 49). This occurs when certain characteristics are believed correlated, however falsely. For example, in recent years, certain policing agencies have been highly criticized for targeting particular groups over others. African Americans, for example, figure disproportionately in crime statistics. What appears unclear to the police and, often, to the public is that overrepresentation in crime statistics does not mean that particular minority groups actually commit more crime than others but rather that certain groups are more likely to attract police attention because of stereotypes. As a result, crime rates cannot be readily correlated with the criminogenesis of particular groups. The same problem with profiling is emerging in the treatment of Muslim Americans when they cross borders and travel by plane. Although it is illegal to profile according to religion or race, the heavier scrutiny that Muslims receive reinforces their view that they are being selected for special attention solely because of their ethnicity.

Tversky and Kahneman (1986) identify a third mental shortcut as adjustment and anchoring (p. 49). As they explain, estimating probabilities is often the result of using a particular anchor from which adjustments are made: probabilities are anchored to particular levels, and adjustments are made from that anchor point. The difficulty with this strategy is that the anchor point may be wrong, and therefore the adjustments tend to be inaccurate given the starting place. For example, when asked to estimate the product of a series of numbers—$8 \times 7 \times 6 \times 5 \times 4 \times 3 \times 2 \times 1$ compared with $1 \times 2 \times 3 \times 4 \times 5 \times 6 \times 7 \times 8$—people estimated the products were greater in the former than in the latter presentation, although the answer is the same. A further bias results when considering disjunctive and conjunctive events. Conjunctive events are a series of events with each subsequent step depending on an earlier step, while disjunctive events do not rely on the success of previous steps for success or failure. In complex systems, when there are many steps, the likelihood of the system failing is high, even though the probability of success at each particular step may be relatively high. Tversky and Kahneman provide the example of the human body: even though each component is likely to succeed, if one component should fail, the entire system fails. Similarly, in any complex system or plan, many things have to go right for the plan to succeed. How does this apply to hazards and threats? We may anchor the probability of crime, for example, to wrong events. Given that the media tend to focus on crimes that are more sensational (despite their rarity), we might estimate that crime consists primarily of serious crimes; we have anchored to the sensational and thereby potentially reflect on changes in levels of crime against the wrong anchor. On the other hand, if we anchor to the less severe crimes, we might estimate the overall crime problem as being far different from those who anchor to sensational crimes. Posner (2004), though, warns us that we should not avoid considering low probability (sensational) events as creating threats when they can have a devastating effect should they occur. Balancing the true threat with the need to allocate resources creates a real dilemma in how we develop security responses at national and local levels.

Tversky and Kahneman's (1986) work provides us with a great deal of insight into the identification of hazards and threats and how these might begin to affect security. Although these authors focused much of their research on judgments of probability, for our purposes their insights help to illuminate how it is that particular events or items come to be identified as hazardous or benign in the first place. The perceptual shortcuts highlighted here—representativeness, availability, and adjustment and anchoring—provide a framework of the processes by which hazards and threats are identified and named. The identification of hazards and threats is facilitated by the same processes as judgments of probability, as well as the associated biases that influence estimates of their probabilities. Judging hazards and threats and their associated probabilities must relate to what we know, or what we think we know. The use of heuristics does exactly that: it makes use of information that is at hand. The knowledge that we have about other, related events provides the baseline against which we are able to assess what we face and the likelihood of harm and how this plays into security overall.

Heuristic devices, as Tversky and Kahneman (1986) acknowledge, are used and misused by both laypeople and professionals; even experts are subject to the biases these shortcuts entail. By extension, we argue that heuristic devices are not entirely the domain of individuals alone. Heuristics also underlie the ways in which organizations and governments orient to hazards and threats and their associated probabilities. Although organizations and states operate at a different level of abstraction than do individuals, "institutional think"—drawing on frames of reference relevant to particular organizations—guides the means by which institutions and organizations respond to their environments, both internally and externally. A research method known as institutional ethnography, for example, highlights the means by which institutions and individuals working within them recreate particular institutional understandings and interpretations through the application and reapplication of specific procedures and processes.

Experts

In related work, Paul Slovic (1993) has focused more specifically on the ways in which individuals' judgments may be seen as distinct from experts'

"They're fake. Part of the new false
sense of security system."

Figure 2.2   The Security Era

SOURCE: www.CartoonStock.com

judgments of risk. There are two ways in which to characterize the split
between experts' and individuals' understandings of risks. Technocrats
maintain that the public is ill-informed regarding risks and that the regulation of risk needs to follow science and facts rather than public opinion
(Sunstein, 2001, p. 2). On the other hand, the populist perspective, and one
that would conform to the skeptical views of science embodied in Beck's risk
society model, is characterized by distrust in experts, abiding by the notion
that government should follow what the citizenry is telling it rather than
government being guided by technocratic elite (Sunstein, p. 2). Slovic has
dedicated much study to understanding the division between individuals
and experts when it comes to risk and risk perception. Rather than seeing
either side's view as correct, Slovic, according to Sunstein, suggests that citizens simply are working with an alternate or rival rationality, a rationality
that is informed by different elements than the rationality used by experts.

Slovic and his colleagues (2002) point out that highly publicized events are more likely to produce fear, despite statistically low probabilities of their occurrence or reoccurrence. Similarly, other affective influences come into play, including the incorporation of values into our judgments of risk. Rather than confining analyses to the examination of numbers and statistics, which can only take into consideration that which is countable, such as number of deaths attributed to certain phenomenon, Slovic and his colleagues argue that the lay public takes more qualitative elements into consideration, such as the notion of dread, and voluntary versus involuntary exposure. However, in his examination of Slovic's work and the implications of his work for public policy, Sunstein (2001) suggests that ordinary people may not necessarily use qualitative elements to judge hazards. Rather, based on the criticism of the psychometric paradigm by Margolis (1996), Sunstein observes, "when ordinary people diverge from experts, it is because ordinary people see the risks but not the benefits, whereas experts see both" (p. 20). Furthermore, experts may simply have more information at hand with which to make their judgments.

Slovic and colleagues (2002) have also carefully considered the role that *affect* (or emotion), plays in laypersons' judgments of risk. They suggest that affect plays a major role in how risks are judged. In fact, affect comes prior to assessment, therefore guiding or directing judgments. The emotional response therefore "operates as a heuristic, much affecting people's judgments about both benefits and dangers" (Sunstein, 2001, p. 25). The suggestion that affect influences judgements about risk makes intuitive sense: the horrors associated with certain kinds of hazards often crowd out estimates of probability. Consider, for example, flight insurance for "losses associated with terrorism," versus flight insurance for "losses" (Sunstein, p. 27). The graphic images we have of terrorism may make us more willing to pay for terrorism insurance than other forms of insurance, despite the low probability of terrorist losses.

Sunstein (2001), however, provides some criticism of the centrality of affect by observing that it is difficult to separate affect from cognition; we feel certain emotions because of our ability to cognitively assess various hazards. At the same time, from a policy perspective, appealing to the emotions of the public is a sound strategy and is one that has been increasingly taken up; consider, for example, state-produced television commercials regarding drunk driving or smoking. The idea of appealing to emotion has more recently been put into effect in areas such as Florida, which is particularly prone to hurricanes. In an effort to counteract the complacency that has tended to characterize hurricane preparedness,

Florida's emergency management director, Craig Fugate, is quoted in the *New York Times* as saying, "We're going to use a sledgehammer" to drive home the message of preparedness (Goodnough, 2006, p. 1). Part of this sledgehammer approach includes the radio replay of emergency calls from the previous year's hurricane season, in an attempt to appeal to the emotions of listeners who hear the panicked voices of victims who learn that emergency services are often out of reach.

In his overview of Slovic's work, Sunstein (2001) addresses another major component of risk judgment—the notion of trust. Trust is central to how hazards and threats are identified in the first place. Slovic suggests that much controversy surrounding the management of hazardous technologies is due to the lack of the public's trust of experts. Furthermore, as we note below, Slovic emphasizes the fragility of trust as something that can be more easily destroyed than created (Sunstein, p. 30). If the public were more trusting of experts, the gulf that now exists between the public and experts in their judgments of risk would be attenuated. However, as Sunstein observes, the manner in which trust might be created and strengthened poses its own special problems. Unlike Slovic, Sunstein suggests that engaging public participation in decision making may not always prove effective. While public participation might enable power sharing to some degree, it may also foster distrust. (We return to the topic of public participation in Chapter 6, this volume.)

Giddens (1990) suggests that there are specific relationships between trust, confidence, and risk that contribute to security. Giddens maintains that trust integrally connects space and time, transcending the boundaries of particular situations. Trust relates specifically to a lack of transparency; trust would not be necessary if the actions and intentions of others were continually visible. Rather, trust assumes a lack of information and assumes some degree of uncertainty. In other words, our concern with trust operates in the connection between the uncertainty about risk as detailed by Beck and the need for information in making choices about security as outlined by Tversky and Kahneman.

What about the uncertainty associated with the use of technology to address risk? Individuals and experts can agree that certain scientific solutions are appropriate to responding to certain hazards. Science is not the creator of harm, but inappropriate scientific applications can be harmful. Yet the extent to which interventions are effective needs to be the subject of scrutiny. For example, in a study that considered more than 20,000 articles related to terrorism, Lum, Kennedy, and Sherley (2006) find only a fraction (about 200) that includes any form of empirical data in making the case about the origins and responses to terrorist actions. Of these, only seven evaluated systematically the actual effects of counterterrorist interventions, which included studies of metal detectors at airports. The paucity of research on the large-scale responses to terrorism that have cost billions of dollars reinforces the view that experts have little more reliable information to understand what works than the well-educated citizen. Science could help us address these uncertainties, but the commitment to collect and analyze information about program effectiveness is not currently in place.

This vacuum leads to concerns about the authority with which experts can truly be trusted to manage risks and ensure our security. Giddens (1990) suggests that "trust carries the connotation of reliability in the face of contingent outcomes" (p. 33). We trust because of what we do not know, not because of what we know. Trust may be defined as "confidence in the reliability of a person or system, regarding a given set of outcomes or events" (Giddens, p. 34). It is important to remember that how we identify hazards and threats, and our calculations of potential harm depend on the reliability and accuracy of the information provided to us. If out-of-date or incorrect information is provided by those in positions of trust, such as government agents, security may be undermined. Also, if there is a general distrust of the information or of those who provide it, such as experts or front-line workers, we may opt to search for other ways to inform ourselves and make decisions about security. This can wreak havoc in emergencies where people actively resist government information and refuse to comply with its orders, putting themselves and others in danger (a situation clearly illustrated in the aftermath of Hurricane Katrina in 2005).

Routines, Experts, and Trust

This leads us back to our discussion of routines presented in Chapter 1, this volume. Our routines are specifically based on the notion of trust: we trust that what we have done in the past will work for us in the situations that we face today. For example, we do not know if we are dealing with a psychopath or an average individual when we bump shoulders in a crowded elevator. We do know that when we have bumped shoulders in the past, saying sorry and looking up at the floor indicator or down at our feet has proven successful so that we do not offend the other individual. We trust that our previously established routines will work in the absence of new information. We trust the past to predict the present, as well as short-term, if not long-term, future. Similarly, we follow certain structured routines that are less individualized, but that provide a sense of security nonetheless.

We get up at specific times, arrive at work, stay a designated number of hours, and return home. All of these routine behaviors are based on trust: we trust that our alarm clocks will go off, we board public transportation, assuming that we will get to work on time; and so on. Even in situations where routine behaviors may be characterized by misfortune, great efforts are made to return to normal and get back to the ordinary. Essentially, the desire is to re-establish the perceived security that is implicit in much routine behavior.

The significance of trust in the identification of and responses to hazard and threat cannot be understated. Much of what we believe in and maintain to be true is not the product of direct experience, but is rather the result of information gleaned from and provided by experts and expert systems. We expect experts and their systems, such as policing agencies, to accurately identify hazards for us and to facilitate our responding accordingly. We expect experts to map out the landscape for us in order that we may reach some degree of heightened security provided through routines or the re-establishment of routines.

Because we cannot manage all the details of modern life that could potentially affect us, we rely on experts to manage this information for us, as well as to alert us both to dangers (such as the police warning us of neighborhood threats) and opportunities (such as financial advisers who suggest that we buy certain stocks, and so on). Risk assessments differ depending on the degree to which we trust those who provide us with information: "perceptions of risk, including judgments as to the acceptability of particular risks, are a function of the degree to which the institutions which are responsible for the assessment and management of risks are trusted" (Short, 1984, p. 714). We trust that those in the know will provide us with what it is that we need to know, which has the effect of reducing the complexity of the world that we encounter on a daily basis (Luhmann, 1988). Those who trust institutions assess security and estimate probabilities (of harm or benefit) differently than do those who do not trust institutions. Furthermore, trust is basic to security; it transgresses the boundaries of the present and affects the future. In addition, it influences our assessments of the past. Giddens (1990) establishes trust as an individual-level condition and product of individual experience, whereas Beck (1992) suggests that trust (or lack of trust) inhabits the societal-level and is a characteristic of society regardless of individual experiences.

In his analysis of the relationships between lay people and experts, Wynne (1996) considers the importance of trust to these relationships and the responses of English hill-farmers to the contradictory instructions that they had received from experts regarding the safety of the fields where they grazed their animals after the nuclear reactor accident at Chernobyl. Out of an increasing sense of frustration, at first over delays in which they were banned from selling their sheep on the market, the farmers increasingly began to doubt not only the contradictory advice that had been provided to them by experts, but also that the experts themselves held knowledge that was any more useful to them than were their own experiences as farmers. Frustration eventually turned to disbelief as the farmers' assessments came to be completely at odds with expert opinion regarding where contamination was greatest. Similarly, in a study by Ali (1997) examining the process by which a landfill location was determined, the dominant discourse between the public and the risk management experts revolved around inherent uncertainties. The resulting communications between the public and experts became more about the relationship between these two parties than it was about the knowledge that these experts presumably possessed.

Wynne's (1996) study of lay–expert relations emphasizes the contextual aspects of risk and how it is that the relationships between experts and the lay public become propelled away from the opinion or information transmitted by experts, and move instead toward issues of trust (p. 57). There is a realization that the science that experts convey is problematic due to uncertainty and contingency, which is characteristic of all prediction but is especially significant when uncertainty accompanies what is thought to be expert knowledge. As well, the competing claims of experts reduce the trust that the public may have in the claimed expertise. Bradley and Morss (2002) further suggest that the natural knowledge that farmers possess, for example, often derived from established routines, may be at odds with the knowledge conveyed by experts. Experts may fail to take this natural knowledge into consideration, and transmit their expert interpretation of events tabula rasa. Finally, they note that natural knowledge may remain invisible to experts precisely because of their roles as experts, and the assumptions of laypeople who may first hesitate to voice their opinions "out of habitual trust for or deference to the experts" (Bradley & Morss, p. 524).

These images illustrate the tension between forms and sources of knowledge and how it is that information, data, and experiences may play a role with certain issues coming to the foreground of specific security landscapes while others fall away. As some have noted (see, for example, Plummer, 2003), what counts as knowledge evolves over time, such that "pluralization, individualization and multiplying choices mak[e] social lives very different from any previous era" (p. 520). Plummer's insights apply to security, which does not "harbor . . . an essential unitary core locatable within a clear framework . . . [there is no] essential truth waiting to be discovered: there are only fragments" (p. 520). Fragments of knowledge become the basis on which security issues are illuminated within the context of risk society, with the specific fragments under consideration often differing among the individual, institutional, and state levels.

The difficulties faced by experts in understanding risk and in convincing the public of their abilities to guarantee security have led to a trend toward the individualization of security. Beck explains that every actor, whether individual or institutional, assumes responsibility for his, her, or its own safety. Similarly, O'Malley (2004) describes *prudentialism*, whereby actors are motivated (if not actually coerced) to secure themselves through various means, such as insurance policies. Actors are often expected to take responsibility to ensure their fit with particular standards—standards that have been defined, often, by expert others. As Alexander (1997) further explains, individualization may also involve "people making up answers to questions that are often very complex in the absence of believable answers provided external to the person" (p. 30). Contradictory or fragmentary advice from experts as well as from the media and other sources paves the way for the self-reliance characteristic of this era. For Kelly (2001), the point of convergence with respect to self-government (governmentality) and risk society lies in what is referred to as conditions of possibility: harm need not be proven. It is enough that particular conditions are able to germinate the possibility of harm.

This individualization may not be a bad thing: we find lots of evidence that the most effective responses to hazards are those that are based on individual initiative. Taking precautions in one's home, buying insurance, and working out plans to contact relatives in an emergency all suggest individual risk management. Observers at the aftermath of disasters talk about the importance of individual initiative in providing spontaneous support to first responders, either through assistance in evacuation or by providing basic medical assistance (Clarke, 2006). The challenge in this arena is encouraging and enabling individuals and experts to collaborate in prevention, response, and recovery; this collaboration is often undermined by a lack of trust.

In the new security era, individual action or inaction weaves in various ways with institutional and state-level efforts to bolster or undermine security. Security gaps illuminate sources of vulnerability, with vulnerability readily transferring from one realm to another, and across levels. Furthermore, while security has become more entwined and enmeshed among the individual, institutional, and state levels, security has also become increasingly disengaged; individuals are becoming ever more responsible for security, as are institutions for their own security. Security today may therefore suggest a compression of responsibility with individual and institutional actors taking on more independent security efforts than in the past. While previously the role of the state was to provide security, there is now an increasing emphasis on the responsibilities that individual actors must take for their own safety. Reliance on the state simultaneously increases (the state often identifies what is threatening) and decreases (by off-loading responsibility for security to individuals and institutions).

In the above discussion, we highlight the distinctions that may arise from the perspectives of individual actors, and how those perspectives may differ from the institutional or state perspective, especially with respect to wide-ranging harms. Nevertheless, separation between these levels can often only be made in theory. In practice, it is difficult to suggest that any particular perspective—individual, institutional, or state—can be understood without reference to each of the other respective positions. By considering risk balance as the application of differing weights to different factors depending on perspective, we get a better sense of how it is that elements emerge and recede in efforts to enhance security.

Types of Resources

As we have already stressed, it is difficult to separate the identification of hazards and threats from access to resources. The identification of hazards and threats is clearly linked to the types of resources that we have at hand, and resources may come in a variety of packages. It is difficult to imagine being able to identify particular harms without access to knowledge— whether that knowledge comes by way of others, or by one's own experience. For example, riptides are clearly a hazard at certain beaches. Knowledge of this hazard may be gleaned from a variety of sources: a familiarity with how currents work, word of mouth from other beachgoers, or personal experience. Those who do not have access to any of these forms of knowledge may be more likely to be harmed than those who are equipped with this information, assuming that it will be used to effectively deal with the possible harm that riptides pose.

Another obvious resource is money: those who have more of it will be better equipped to deal with the consequences of various hazards and threats, as well as better equipped to avoid harm in the first place. Consider the devastation caused by Hurricane Katrina. Those who suffered the most were those who had the least economic resources. Poor residents are struggling to rebuild since the hurricane, while those with higher incomes have greater monetary resources to draw from in order to rebuild. In terms of avoiding the hurricane, those with access to their own transportation (that is, economic capital) were able to remove themselves from the path of the hurricane before it hit.

While the examples above focus on economic resources, theorists such as Bourdieu (1983) and Coleman (1993) have elaborated on the notions of cultural and social capital. According to Bourdieu, *economic capital* may be defined as that which can be "directly converted into money and may be institutionalized in the form of property rights" (p. 243). On the other hand, *cultural capital* may be converted to economic capital, but it cannot be passed on in the same way that economic capital may be. Cultural capital requires an investment of time by the holder of such capital. For example, cultural capital is the result of efforts made and time spent on acquiring specific skills or knowledge through an extended training period. While there is a certain acquisition of cultural capital that occurs by osmosis—such as the development of an accent that earmarks for listeners exactly where one is from—Bourdieu notes that "[cultural capital] cannot be accumulated beyond the appropriating capacities of an individual agent; it declines and dies with its bearer" (p. 245). Having said that, while an art collection (that is, economic capital) may be passed from mother to daughter, for example, what is not readily passed from mother to daughter is the taste that was involved in the acquisition of the paintings, as well as the taste required to appreciate the paintings. It could be argued that economic capital without cultural capital is somewhat like power without legitimacy. In many ways, cultural capital may be seen as the grease that turns the wheels of economic capital.

Cultural capital is a resource that enables its holders to see the environment in particular ways. As we noted with respect to the riptide example, knowledge of tides and currents may be the result of formal schooling or it may be the result of direct experience. Whatever its source, knowledge of riptides is a form of cultural capital; it is a product of investing time and exposure.

A final form of capital is *social capital*. Over the past 30 years, the importance of social capital has been widely debated, primarily in terms of facilitating its acquisition for those who may not otherwise have access to this resource. Social capital is essentially about belonging, or about having social ties and social networks that matter. Membership in particular groups is akin to a credential—you either have it or you do not—and this credential provides its bearer with credit. For example, there are different chapters of the Hells Angels scattered throughout the world. Membership in this association affords out-of-town members a form of credit at local clubhouses. Membership is a credential that enables access to clubhouses across locations. In many circumstances, the greater the number of memberships and networks to which one belongs, the greater one's social capital. Membership in certain networks, however, prohibits the possibility of membership in others; an example is gang membership. Further, social capital is not a resource that is specific only to individuals, it may also be characteristic of agencies or institutions. Agencies that are tied to other agencies have more social capital on which to draw than agencies that exist independently. For example, insurance agencies that have some degree of credibility with local police forces will be facilitated in their efforts to check claims against police records. In contrast, the social capital that exists between federal and local policing agencies may be minimal if there is competition between agencies, as has been the case in the past. Tensions between police at the federal level and police at the local level are often a result of the perception that resources, primarily economic resources, are limited.

The ability of actors to mobilize resources in terms of economic, social, and cultural capital in response to security issues, including the ability to correctly judge the threat of injury or loss, is *efficacy*. Not surprisingly, individual efficacy can be diminished if there is an effort to remove from individual actors the power to make decisions to protect themselves. Efficacy at the individual level may either coincide or be at odds with institutional efficacy; the latter is particularly true if the models of institutional responses are assumed to be expert and not accessible to the average individual. Efficacy also relates to the competency of organizations in assessing harms and understanding the resources needed to deal with these.

Institutional and individual efficacies may also come into direct conflict. There are many examples, but illustrative of this conflict is the comment made by a public health expert. He said that, although he understood clearly that the best strategy to achieve overall security in New York City in the face of a widespread attack would be to evacuate, he knows that he and many others would not leave Manhattan until they were assured of the safety of their loved ones [personal communication]. Similar choices were made in the face of Hurricane Katrina: officials first requested evacuation on a voluntary basis, but were subsequently forced to remove residents who refused to leave. This choice to stay is not rational but makes sense to individuals who are confronted with this situation. Many individuals would seriously resist acting, or leaving a situation, before assurances of their loved ones' safety had been given. This is a form of personal efficacy that runs counter to the expert view that evacuation is the most prudent strategy overall. (We consider strategies for dealing with hazards in Chapters 6 and 7, this volume.)

The pathways toward as well as away from security are fraught with contingency. Balancing risk may be more or less successful depending on the type of hazard focused on. The social context in which we exist directs our attention to particular elements and away from others, suggesting that security is, in large part, a social construction. For the remainder of the chapter, we consider how it is that general references to security do little to enlighten; security requires a referent object and a referent subject. Without establishing object and subject, we cannot fully take into consideration how wide-ranging and, at other times, excessively narrow security interests can be, and how security interests may come into conflict.

Security From What?

Security must involve a referent object—something physical, mental, or symbolic that is being secured. Although references are made to, for example, national security, adjectives accompanying security do not necessarily make the referent object clear. National security does not establish whether the nation is symbolic or geographic, nor does it establish which aspect of national security is the focus. In order to speak meaningfully of security, the referent object must be clearly specified. Furthermore, if we consider security as freedom from danger, fear, or anxiety, the nature of the endangerment (hazard or threat) must be determined before freedom from it can be established. Endangerments (to individuals, institutions, or even states) include physical endangerment, economic endangerment, endangering of rights, and endangering status or position (Buzan, 1983, p. 20). Buzan observes that once the referent object of security is established, the conditions of establishing security, from a particular perspective, can follow. The effectiveness of efforts, for example to bolster security, depends on identifying what exactly is endangered.

Paradoxically, recognizing and confronting various security issues may also undermine one's sense of security. In other words, recognizing vulnerability or insecurity may debilitate and bring to the fore, and keep in the foreground, perceived vulnerability. Efforts to quell insecurity or increase security could, however, backfire, creating responses ranging from anxiety to terror. A further difficulty in establishing security is that certain aspects of security may, in fact, be contradictory, at least in the short term. Health security, for example, may mean exposure to vaccinations that bring about the symptoms of the illness against which the vaccination is said to guard. Similarly, security within one particular realm may be threatened by security in another realm. Income security may be undermined by health security, or vice versa. We have all heard of workaholics who jeopardize their own health and the health of their relationships by overworking. Other individuals may find themselves having to work less in order to maintain their health yet their financial security may suffer. Although prioritizing certain types of security is inevitable, security in one particular realm may undermine security in another.

For individuals, the choices made with respect to security priorities have much to do with personal beliefs and values, past experiences, and risk positions. Clearly, some individuals are more at risk or endangered than others due to demographic characteristics such as age, sex, and residence (urban versus rural residents, for example). Risk positions may also be influenced by family history (for example, genetic links to cancer), work history (exposure to various hazards, for example), or beliefs and attitudes. Certain individuals can protect themselves from what they have determined is a source of danger or potential danger, while others may be exposed to endangerments but have fewer resources with which to protect themselves. For corporate actors, choices with respect to security must also be made, although the bottom line no doubt figures prominently in the determination of corporate security priorities. While a corporation may indeed value the security of health that producing environmentally friendly products might generate in terms of healthy workers, healthy consumers, and positive public impressions of the corporation, the very existence of a corporation depends on achieving a level of financial security that may be at odds with environmental security.

The budgetary considerations of nation-states also focus on a bottom line of sorts. States are charged with providing citizens with a particular level of security, although the level and means by which states provide security and the individuals or institutions to which these efforts are directed varies widely. Certainly there is variation among nations by level of development, political orientation, political leadership, demographic composition, international relations, world events, and so on. Furthermore, the realms of security emphasized at the state level depend on the nation under examination. Social security, which is primarily internally focused, may be a priority in some states, while other states may prioritize military security, which is primarily externally focused.

Security for Whom?

Just as there is a distinction between individual and expert views of security, there is a central contradiction between individual and state security: the state can really only protect or provide security through the imposition of sanctions against individuals, such as the use of legal sanctions. Further threats to security stemming from the state can be largely grouped into four categories (Buzan, 1983, pp. 25–26), including, first, "threats arising from domestic law-making and enforcement," or failure to make law. Until recently, for example, it was considered impossible for rape to occur within a marriage. Law did not recognize or validate the potential vulnerability of women within marital contexts. Second, threats to individual security stem "from direct political action by the state against individuals or groups." An example is the October Crisis in 1970 in Canada. Then–Prime Minister Pierre Trudeau invoked the War Measures Act in response to the FLQ (Front de Libération du Québec) terrorist threat. The Act effectively suspended the protections afforded citizens in the face of state power, at the same time hugely expanding the powers of police and government (Bélanger, 2000). Buzan observes that the state can impose drastic measures against various groups, if these measures are cloaked in the garb of addressing national security threats. Third, endangerment stemming from struggles over state machinery may occur among states characterized by political struggle and threats to overthrow the government. These struggles provoke insecurity in the general population, and not simply among those directly involved in the struggle. Finally, there may be threats arising from the state's external security policies or foreign policies. Clearly, foreign policy may work to the disadvantage of individuals by making them targets outside of their home countries. One has only to consider the relative danger that certain travelers experience in various parts of the world. Overall, state security may work against individual security and state interests may override individual security.[2] While individual security interests may be usurped by state interests, the actions of both individuals and the state act as a feedback loop: individual action has implications for state-level security, and state-level security has implications for individual security.

Beyond the central contradictions of individual and state-level security, security is often characterized as a zero-sum game—security at one level or for one party may be seen as undermining security or creating insecurity at another level or for another party. Furthermore, the action that is undertaken at one level or by one party to enhance security may be interpreted as a source of endangerment from other perspectives. In an increasingly global world, it is more difficult to defend actions as unilateral, or as contained by and within borders. Not only do claims to independence become less legitimate in a global world, but also the very legitimacy of the borders themselves is clearly in question. Terrorist networks such as Al-Qaeda, for example, do not recognize political borders. They are not associated with particular geographic states or regions, but rather their connections are supra state, working outside the boundaries of traditional state borders. Threats to national security, therefore, no longer come explicitly from other nations; rather, threat has networked and gone global. Interdependencies created by a global economy ensure that actions taken in the name of security at the nation or state level are likely to create insecurities elsewhere. Globalization will be discussed more thoroughly in Chapter 5, this volume, when we consider security as it applies to terrorism.

While reference may be made to security at the individual and institutional levels, in reality these levels cannot effectively be separated. Clarke and Short (1993, p. 385) remind us that the individual and institutional levels are not distinct: "individuals and their decision procedures are placed within institutional contexts," and focusing on individuals might easily neglect how organizations and institutional contexts shape perception. Starr (1969) makes a similar point: "decision-making is separated from the affected individual, society has generally clothed many of its controlling groups in an almost impenetrable mantle of authority and of imputed wisdom" (p. 1234). Individuals cannot be secure independent of the state, because the state may work either to undermine or enhance personal security through its internal workings or through its foreign policies and relationships with other states. Similarly, states are not secure in contexts where civil uprisings and revolts are under way or may threaten, or where incursions from other states have occurred or appear likely.

Conclusion

The characteristics of risk today—its global nature, imperceptibility, and ties to technological advancement—make identification and calculation of future harm difficult, if not impossible. All of these factors make risk balance complicated and inexact. It is not just the uncertainty of harm but also the lack of information relating to certain sources of harm that may confound individuals and institutions in the pursuit of security. Attempts to balance risk become more difficult and less certain in their results.

The context of risk society suggests that the means by which we identify harms and threats may be largely influenced by doubt, information gaps, and lack of trust. While the emphasis on experts and expertise grew over the course of modernity, expertise today is increasingly viewed with suspicion. Furthermore, competing claims of experts contribute to security as a social construction. Weaving together various fragments of expert and other knowledge creates many security landscapes which may hinder "seeing the forest for the trees."

The risk balance perspective differs from other examinations of security in three important ways: first, in terms of highlighting the disparate images of security and recognizing the variability in how security is constituted; second, by building on an intuitive notion of risk; and, third, by recognizing the dynamic nature of security. As we have been suggesting, security and insecurity are relative. What constitutes security depends on perspective, with various elements emerging as threatening or nonthreatening depending on the point of view taken. Security from one perspective may undermine security from another perspective. Furthermore, particular individuals may define security much differently from the institutions to which they belong. As we know, the resources that we have at hand are limited. Our goal over the next few chapters is to highlight the common and divergent themes that underlie these differing images in order to better understand and ultimately enhance overall security.

Freedom is incorporated in our definition of security, with security as freedom from danger (harm), fear, or anxiety. Endangerment, fearfulness, and anxiety are the products of both hazards and threats. Hazards are sources of danger, while threat reflects an intention to inflict harm or damage. Hazards suggest a present orientation, while threats are oriented toward the future. Establishing freedom from either requires clear identification of what exactly poses a danger. A foundation of security is knowledge—both in terms of identifying harm, but also through recognizing that knowledge alone may be insufficient. The identification of a source of (possible) harm cannot alone achieve security, as effectively responding (exerting control) is required to achieve security. Control, in its most general sense, is the ability to effect change, but there is little control without power.[3] Power enables one to define, reveal, and see situations and circumstances as one sees fit. Control is a corollary of power, in that control allows for action and change, or at least their possibility. Most importantly, power enables but is also a product of access to resources. Those with greater power will define security in ways that differ significantly from those who lack power. Together, knowledge and power underlie security, with both control and vision the outcomes of these two factors.

Knowledge and power play into security in a variety of ways. Security requires navigating what is known with what is unknown. Without knowledge or awareness of harms, achieving security is impossible; although hazards and threats must be named as such and security can only be achieved with respect to what has been identified as endangering.[4] Security requires information: individual and institutional actors cannot be secure if they do not have the knowledge to process whether harms indeed exist (whether hazards are really hazards or something else), what to do with respect to identified threats (how to control threats), and the ability to carry out specific action to deal with threats. Knowledge plays into security by allowing for assessment, choice, and consideration. Conversely, ignorance means there can be little assessment and due consideration of that which threatens. Knowledge may also, of course, be compromised by less access to power.

If we were to look at the relationship between knowledge and power in real terms, we see the difficulties that emerge with the ways in which information about terrorist threats are handled. It has been the case that law enforcement agencies, when dealing with these threats, have kept information under wraps, arguing that releasing this information would compromise their investigations. This has resulted in a restricted view on the public's part concerning the role that it can play in deterring terrorism. The public is told to be vigilant and to report suspicious behavior but the public is also rarely included in discussions about effective strategies for preventing terror groups from operating in its midst. As a result, the public lacks knowledge and lacks power to make a difference in addressing this threat. This does not mean, however, that the public is complacent about the problem. In fact, there is clear indication that the public has strong feelings about threats of all sorts and make judgments about these, with or without comprehensive information. While characterized by little direct power to influence responses to these harms, the public's interpretations and reactions become an important part of the equation that needs to be addressed in understanding security.

As was mentioned earlier, Sunstein (2001) talks about the clear distinctions between the public and the experts in the ways in which they interpret and respond to identified harms. While the publics' views may not look rational, their assessments are deeply imbedded in personal experiences, in contrast to the ways in which experts may make judgments based on scientific evidence. What is important is not whether judgments are accurate but rather the actions and reactions that these judgments precipitate.

Notes to Chapter 2

1. Despite knowing the people and situations better within private contexts, endangerment is not necessarily reduced in the private realm. We know, for example, that threat and opportunity are evaluated much differently in the context of intimate relationships than with stranger relationships. Research on domestic violence suggests that intimacy plays a key role in how one calculates the threats posed by significant others.

2. We will more fully consider this phenomenon in Chapter 5, this volume, when we consider terrorism and security.

3. Buzan (1983) notes the conflation of the concept of power with the concept of security, particularly as occurring within the context of the Cold War. He suggests that in this context,

> security necessarily shrank conceptually to being a way of saying either how well any particular state or allied group of states was doing in the struggle for power, or how stable the balance of power overall appeared to be. Reduced to little more than a synonym for power, security could have little independent relevance. (p. 7)

4. While this seems to be suggesting that what we do not know will not hurt us ("ignorance is bliss"), there is more to security than simply the subjective identification of endangerment: there may be objective hazards that one can safeguard against. We refer in Chapter 3, this volume, to the case of Jane Doe—a woman who sued the Metropolitan Toronto Police Force for negligence for failing to warn the public of a rapist active in a particular neighborhood. Jane Doe won her case, claiming that had she known of this hazard, she would have taken appropriate steps to secure herself against such harm.

3

Crime and Security

In the spring of 2005, Canadians were bombarded once again with news about one of Canada's most notorious convicted killers, Karla Homolka.[1] After she had served her 12-year sentence and on the eve of her mandatory release, attention turned to the conditions of her release, as well as her future plans including, especially, the question of where she would live. The presiding judge weighed a number of factors, including her behavior in prison, circumstances surrounding her original crime, and the sentence she had served. In the eyes of the public, the Crown, and the Judge, however, the most significant factor was whether Homolka still posed a threat to the Canadian public. By all accounts, Homolka was a model prisoner, yet doubt remained as to whether a person involved in such heinous crimes could ever be trusted not to "return to the dark side." Section 810 of the Canadian Criminal Code allows for the courts to impose various behavioral restrictions on a released convict if there are reasonable grounds to believe a person may commit a criminal offense again.

Judge Allan Beaulieu appears to have agreed that there were, in fact, reasonable grounds to believe she would commit another offense, and ruled that Section 810 would be imposed in Homolka's case, despite objections from her defense attorney (ctv.ca, 2005). This ruling paved the way for the Crown to require Homolka to inform the police of her whereabouts; supply the police with her address, occupation, and contact information for any roommates; report to police on a monthly basis; inform police if she leaves her home for more than 48 hours; have no association with individuals who have a criminal record; maintain no contact with Bernardo (her former husband and co-offender), his family, or the families of their victims; take no drugs other than those prescribed to her; use none of the intoxicants applied in the murders; undergo therapy for one year; provide a DNA sample to authorities; and assume no position of authority with young people under the age of 16. Although criticized as toothless, these conditions were meant to reduce the likelihood that Homolka would reoffend, as well as to quell public fears about her return to society.

The curiosity with Homolka's case has been accentuated by the role of the police in the early stages of the criminal event. The approach taken by the criminal justice system also elicited further public scrutiny with respect to how this case was handled by the courts. Tales of botched police investigations and courtroom plea bargains ("deals with the devil") highlight the importance of the police and courts in determinations of public and individual security, as well as the importance of transparency, accountability, and responsibility. The approach to this event by both the police and the Crown also serves to demarcate the distinctions between public perceptions of security against crime, which focus primarily, although not exclusively, on personal safety; and institutional considerations, which focus more on case management and on closing or clearing cases. The Homolka case also illustrates the importance of data and the means by which perceptions of security or insecurity might be manipulated by the provision of, or lack of, certain information. Once a list of conditions was attached to Homolka's release, did knowing this make the average citizen more or less secure? Did it enhance security to know where she resides or when she reports to police? We must consider both the meaning and relevance of various types of information in the quest to establish security. In Homolka's case, not only was the substance of particular types of information crucial, but, more specifically, the timing of particular pieces of evidence was central to the outcome of her case.[2]

This chapter begins to untangle some of the issues that arise with respect to establishing security in the realm of crime. We consider the role of the police and other agencies in protecting the public against crime. We then examine the distinctions between individual and institutional definitions of security with respect to crime and how this relates to the types of information that counts for individual versus institutional assessments of security. To illustrate some of these distinctions, we draw on the notions of profiling offenders and profiling victims.

How Much Crime and How Can It Be Addressed?

Crime is a political hotbed, with most politicians studiously avoiding the appearance of being soft on crime. But has the nature and rate of crime actually changed over the past few decades? Because policing statistics are a product of mandates and orientations, as well as the practicalities of numbers of police on the street and recording practices, the use of statistics provides only partial insights into the true story of crime. Official data are further called into question by victimization studies suggesting that the so-called dark figure of crime looms far larger than revealed by official statistics. Because of the official crime picture provided by policing and criminal justice statistics, or the dark figure of crime revealed by victimization data, crime remains a concern. As Reiner, Livingstone, and Allen (2001) note, "the conventional popular and political understanding . . . is that we have—for disputed reasons—become beset by ever more numerous and ever more serious crimes" (p. 175).

Part of the perception of rising numbers of crimes and criminals may be due to the increasingly blurred boundaries between criminal and untoward behavior. As Bauman (2002) notes, the actions that were once "placidly and meekly suffered without resistance are being recast as illegitimate," and are increasingly seen as needing to be dealt with. While the relationship between media reports and fear of crime also remains unclear, there is little disputing the increasing frequency with which violence and crime are presented by the media. Furthermore, perceptions of increasing frequency and severity of crime may also be simply the result of heightened insecurities that individuals feel more generally: "anxiety generated in ever larger quantities by existential insecurity and fears of an uncertain future seeks more tangible, close-to-hand estuaries" (Bauman, p. 54). Becoming wary of and vigilant against crime may be one such estuary: it is one possible way of reducing anxiety through the implementation of protective measures.

The blurred boundaries between criminal and noncriminal behavior, and right and wrong, are characteristic of the risk society. While clearly not all actors feel a sense of foreboding about environmental damage, for example, a large proportion of the population has tangible worries about crime. Although police are officially mandated to address crime and criminal behavior, the emphasis on community involvement and its attendant message that crime is everyone's business may be reflected in the trend toward private policing and the hiring of security professionals. Embedded in the notion of responsibility for crime is the more obscure emphasis on blameworthiness. Those who take responsibility may begin to feel that others, who either undermine their own security or who have failed to take responsibility for security, are blameworthy. In other words, there may be a sense of entitlement among law-abiding citizens and those who take measures to protect themselves against crime: certain people deserve protection, while others do not. Zero tolerance, involving strict interpretations of behavior and an unwillingness to allow for the benefit of doubt, may be a manifestation of these notions of entitlement and blameworthiness.

Policing and Crime Risk

In a recent keynote address, David Bayley (2005) describes the pressures that face public policing in the 21st century. He explains how public policing has morphed into an institution markedly different from the 20th century images of the uniformed officer in a patrol car. Policing, Bayley suggests, now faces demands from above, from the side, and from below. For example, he notes that public police now face demands from national (and international) organizations and government sectors keen to access local data, hence the pressure from above. In terms of pressure from the side, municipal police forces and private police or security institutions compete for contracts that were once the purview of the public police alone. Private policing has now usurped many public policing functions. At the same time, private companies often hire off-duty police officers. Finally, in terms of pressures from below, citizens have come to expect far more of public police than simply catching criminals, and now expect that police will prevent the occurrence of crime in the first place.

As first responders to many criminal events, all of these pressures play into perceptions of security and the role that police and others play in insulating society from crime. These obligations are not necessarily new to public police forces, but have acquired new intensity over the past decade. In terms of pressures from above, the events of September 11, 2001, for example, have transformed the need for information, or intelligence, at an international level. Although the collection of this information is often motivated by national and international requests for and considerations of security, local policing agents are often presumed best able to provide this information. Because members of Al-Qaeda presumably lived everyday lives in the United States for some years prior to committing any terrorist activity, security against terrorism is argued to best start at the local level. At the same time, these terrorists did not commit local crimes and therefore were not on the radar of local police forces. Despite the increasing interest in the idea that terrorists can be detected at the local level, it seems increasingly likely that terrorists would take great pains to avoid bringing themselves to the attention of local authorities. Furthermore, local police forces often suggest that they have few resources to police the local level, let alone become watchdogs for national and international security threats. Not only do we begin to identify a change in the expectations of police—with an increasing emphasis on prevention—but we also see a focus on control via suspicion of wrongdoing, and the increasing permeability of the boundaries between state, institutional, and individual expectations of social control.

Protecting the Public: Community Policing and Intelligence-Led Policing

In policing today, much has been made of appeals to community, partnership, and intelligence as key metaphors for service delivery. The prevailing idea is that the service the police are able to deliver hinges increasingly on the involvement of the community (for example, Karp, Bazemore, & Chesire, 2004), despite the difficulties in defining exactly who or what that community consists of, or what the expectations are with respect to community participation. Ericson (1994) suggests that rather than attempting to maintain responsibility for crime and its occurrence, police are better off embracing the community policing philosophy, whereby problems of crime and disorder become joint property. In this scenario, responsibility for criminal activity shifts from the police to other institutions. In essence, the boundaries are blurred, and we all become responsible for crime. Police must admit the impossible mandate—that they can actually provide complete protection from crime (Manning, 1977, in Ericson)—and allow other institutions and individuals to become more responsible for their own security. Under a community-policing regime, police shift their attention to the provision of information and away from the provision of security.

The motivation for the police to become knowledge brokers is in part the recognition that relevant information with regard to reducing crime comes from a number of sources, including the community. In their efforts to *rationalize* (enhance the cost-effectiveness of) the information they collect, police organizations "should be structured to collect, analyze and interpret information from a *range of sources* [italics added], construct it as intelligence and use this to inform how, when, why and against whom they take action" (Innes, Fielding, & Cope, 2005, p. 42). The idea behind intelligence-led policing and the increasing rationality of the investigative process is that, rather than policing being an ad hoc and intuitive enterprise, it is an enterprise that requires greater objectivity and rationality to counter these difficulties.

One of the means by which these goals have been tackled is through the program COMPSTAT (COMPuterized STATistics), which is a computerized mapping system coupled with state-of-the-art management principles (Willis, Mastrofski, & Weisburd, 2004). COMPSTAT has enabled police executives' easy access to crime data, at the same time ensuring accountability at a more local level. Studies of the COMPSTAT approach indicate that key elements of the program, however, may not be evenly applied across policing departments, with the result that some applications of this approach have actually "reinforced the traditional control elements of the military model of police organizations" (Willis et al., p. 467).

Despite the difficulties regarding its implementation, COMPSTAT retains at least the possibility of public accountability and community participation. The emphasis on transparency, for example, involves the community being informed of policing activity and the police providing information to the public and press about how crime problems are being addressed (Willis et al., 2004, p. 467). The other component of transparency consists of mechanisms to ensure that the public has a means of providing its input on policing issues. As Willis and colleagues (p. 488) explain, however, this is one of the more difficult elements of the COMPSTAT program, as well as in community policing programs generally: policing agencies are often loath to share information with the public. Some police officers maintain that the knowledge they have is a product of experience and expertise and are hesitant to reveal what they know. In other words, knowledge is a form of power (Willis et al., p. 487).

As Innes and colleagues (2005) explain, there is a dual emphasis within policing, one of which is low policing issues and the other high policing issues; this echoes Bayley's observations presented above (see also Brodeur, 1983). Low policing issues revolve around the recognition that there are particular groups who commit a disproportionate amount of crime, with policing efforts therefore most efficiently directed toward these groups. If police direct their investigations toward these groups, they increase the efficiency of their efforts at controlling crime. High policing, on the other hand, refers to the increasing pressures on the police to participate in national and international security efforts such as those directed toward reducing threats posed by terrorists, drug cartels, and organized crime networks. Both community policing and intelligence-led policing fit in different ways to these low and high policing orientations.

Community policing and intelligence-led policing work hand in hand. Those who become involved in community policing are held accountable for their decisions, and professional standards are encouraged. Furthermore, community policing facilitates a change in focus from offenders to victims: many victims have complained that their perspective on their victimization is simply not acknowledged in more traditional approaches to policing. The focus of policing changes from a concern over crime rates to problem solving. Innes and colleagues (2005) define intelligence as a mode of information that "has been interpreted and analyzed in order to inform future actions of social control against an identified target" (p. 42). With various sources involved in the identification of crime, and the exchange of some information regarding crime, we next consider how these parties and associated philosophies may or may not work together to enhance security.

As we pointed out earlier, risk society theorizing recognizes that there is an array of potential hazards in the environment, including crime hazards. These hazards require sorting and different priority levels. In response, we see the application of actuarial thinking, whereby threats are determined in part by their allocation into specific groups or groupings. For example, individuals become more or less threatening depending on the characteristics associated with the groups to which they belong. Law-abiding young minority males, for example, may find themselves unfairly lumped together with other young minority males who have been identified as criminogenic, thereby increasing the likelihood of their being found guilty by association, or guilty by virtue of shared characteristics. *Actuarial placement* (placement into various groupings based on shared characteristics) governs the amount and type of policing to which one may be subject, just as actuarial placement governs insurance rates depending on the risk group into which one has been placed. (We consider insurance in detail in Chapter 6, this volume.)

Technological sophistication associated with the information era allows for the previously impossible development of models of crime, and predictors of crime. While actuarial placement reinforces categorical inclusions and exclusions, globalization reinforces the permeability of national boundaries and pushes police to begin to think about how their efforts to address local crime may have an impact at the national or international level. Local police agents are being asked to consider crime on a scale that was once considered well out of their jurisdiction; at the same time, citizens are being forced into providing their own security.

Who Polices Whom?

This July, when the squad cars, the foot patrols and German shepherds rolled in, vandals and thieves seemed to disappear. But this was no victory of cops over robbers. In fact, it didn't involve any police at all. Instead, the nearly 200 residents had begun pitching in $45 apiece each month to hire guards. ("The rise of the rent-a-cop," 2004)

Murphy (1998) suggests that a central accomplishment of the modern state in the United States is the "appropriation and monopolization of the policing function from citizens, communities and private industry" (p. 14). Yet, traditional policing has been criticized for being inefficient and expensive, and for failing to prevent crime. The challenge for the state, Murphy suggests, is to rethink how costs can be reduced, and simultaneously to avoid diminishing the overall security of the state. Another challenge has been to reconceptualize expectations of public police and shift responsibility away from government with a view to redefining security as a marketable commodity (Murphy, p. 14).

Perhaps what must first be considered is the extent to which the government has off-loaded some of its policing responsibilities to private agencies. Private security measures have advanced well beyond locks on doors and bars on windows, to the more recent wave of hiring private security guards. Data from the 2001 Canadian Census (Taylor-Butts, 2004) indicate that the appeal of private security companies is not a minor phenomenon: security guards outnumber police officers by about 10,000 (approximately 73,000 to 63,000), with other estimates suggesting that the number of private security guards may actually be double that of police officers. As Rigakos (2002) points out, early attempts to distinguish between private and public policing functions were dichotomized along the lines of corporate versus state security, as private security emerged along with the "mass private property" of corporate holdings (p. 15). Associated with this dichotomy was the suggestion that private police were concerned more with property issues, while public police concerned themselves with controlling crime and personal harm. The attempt to differentiate between the functions of private and public police, however, affirms the blurry line between what it is that each actually does. While the power of private police to arrest is limited, other differences between private and public police are often less discernible. Concerns with the division of duties, however, may obscure a more important question such as "What functions should the public police service provide?" Clearly, the neighborhood that is able to pay $45 per month per person for heightened security places the issue of equitable distribution of security on the table. Is the power to pay a legitimate basis for differences in security within a society? Are potentially large differences in personal security simply a by-product of the manifestation of individualism, which is typically encouraged?

In addition to the off-loading of various services to private policing agencies, the move to reduce the responsibilities of public police is facilitated by emphasizing community involvement in security issues. Murphy (1998) notes, the "new community policing rhetoric admonishes the community for its reliance on the police and declares the need for communities and individuals to accept their responsibilities and actively participate in policing their own communities" (p. 16). Communities are expected to shoulder increasingly greater responsibility for their own security needs than ever before, but all of this depends on being able to legitimate the commodification of security in the public perception. Rather than being viewed by the public as within the realm of public service and a right of citizenship, security against crime tends to be sold as a commodity on the market. Once sold as a commodity, marketplace principles apply, whether security is provided by private or public police. Murphy suggests that community policing and crime prevention rhetoric have reduced public expectations of policing to the point where the community is directed toward policing alternatives, or a do-it-yourself kind of policing. O'Malley (1992) argues that "privatization of security practices and costs—to be seen in the trend toward private security agencies, security devices, domestic security practices, neighborhood watch schemes (with attendant insurance underwriting)—generate the rudiments of a user pays system of policing security" (p. 266). Variation in income means that some are obviously more secure (that is, better able to pay) than others.

At the same time that the line between public and private policing is increasingly blurred, the line between public and private affairs is also increasingly blurred. What was previously considered private behavior has now become fodder for suspicion and investigation in a post–9/11 world. The USA PATRIOT Act (Uniting and Strengthening America by Providing Appropriate Tools Required to Intercept and Obstruct Terrorism Act of 2001), instituted 45 days after September 11, 2001, expanded the definition of terrorism to include domestic terrorism, which opened the doors to the surveillance of behavior once considered private. For example, the PATRIOT Act allows law enforcement to conduct secret investigations, including phone and Internet surveillance, and also gives the state access to personal records such as medical and employment records, documentation previously considered private. Furthermore, the PATRIOT Act allows police to conduct investigations in the absence of evidence of crime, in the name of intelligence gathering. Noncitizens fare much worse: the Act allows for them to be detained indefinitely on suspicion of wrongdoing alone, without benefit of judicial review for 6 months.

The concern over the intelligence-gathering associated with the PATRIOT Act has registered beyond U.S. borders. Rather than allowing U.S. authorities to be able to scrutinize the topics of interest to Canadian academics, a number of Canadian universities have recently chosen to remove their on-line accounts with a popular U.S.-based Internet research tool. The fear is that research conducted by Canadian professors and students will be subject to the same scrutiny as their American peers (Alphonso, 2006).

The PATRIOT Act could be viewed as a means of ensuring that the signs of disorder and crime itself are not left unchecked, with the expectation that the use of this Act will maximize security and safety. The PATRIOT Act redefines the signs of crime, such that certain characteristics and behaviors once considered benign are now seen as indicative of involvement in terrorism. The fear is that failing to deal with disorder and various transgressions increases the likelihood that communities will become disenchanted with both their neighborhoods and the police, and will let disorder slide unchecked. In the case of the PATRIOT Act, police and other social control agents are seen to be doing something about terrorism, even though the method is not of citizens' choosing.

The view that these are times of danger substantially affects policing, both how it is done and exactly what and who are policed. Lianos and Douglas (2000) discuss the process of dangerization, and how it is that security seeking has placed the possibility of victimization at the center of what we do and how we understand and evaluate what is done to others. While Lianos and Douglas do not directly refer to zero tolerance, the kinds of policies that they discuss help to sharpen public perception of danger. They note, "instead of helping us to overcome primitive fears of otherness, contemporary trends encourage us to redefine and dread the 'Other'" (p. 262). Policies such as zero tolerance and the PATRIOT Act imply that danger and disorder are all around us, encompassing a greater range of behaviors than in the past. In such a context, opportunities for crime and suspicion expand as the range of questionable behavior increases: everything counts as potentially threatening. Rather than having the effect of making danger normal and therefore less threatening, fear and anxiety are heightened with the continuous search for threats resulting in ever-greater demands for control and compliance (Mueller, 2006).

Lianos and Douglas (2000) argue that security has become synonymous with access, and that access to controlled spaces is a predominant marker of acceptance and acceptability or, in the case of failed access, a marker of danger. Institutionally managed spaces stratify access, allowing certain people in while keeping others out. Spaces that appear unmanaged—characterized by open access—are viewed as potentially threatening. Institutional processes work to exclude or include, and "the more actors are subjected to institutional processes of 'clearance,' the more such processes become identified as the new coordinates of social belonging and, by the same token, social stratification" (Lianos & Douglas, p. 272).[3] The presence of items such as candy wrappers and broken bottles in abandoned lots no longer "signify the lack of education and the weakening of local community bonds: they indicate non-managed—therefore dangerous and lawless—territories" (Lianos & Douglas, p. 273). It is not behavior as such that is of interest in conditions of danger, but the "connotations assigned to behavior in terms of social belonging" (Lianos & Douglas, p. 273). How behavior is labeled determines whether one belongs or not.

Securing Against Crime

In the sections that follow, we examine security threats as these apply to crime, particularly with respect to possible offending or possible victimization. We begin by briefly examining individuals as security threats and consider attempts to profile potential offenders. From the perspective of those targeting criminals, the idea behind profiling is to thwart crime before it occurs and to increase security for others. These measures, of course, are seen quite differently from the perspective of those being targeted, who would view profiling as threatening their own personal security. We then closely examine the story of Jane Doe, a woman who was raped and subsequently filed suit against a police agency for failing to provide her with information that could have been used in her assessment of her personal risk of victimization. The Jane Doe story is significant for a number of reasons, but clearly indicates the difficulties that can result due to differences in the ways in which harms are defined between individuals and institutions. Finally, we turn to the notion of profiling places, and look at the ways physical and social geographies are studied as a means to reduce harm and bolster security.

Profiling Offenders

It is common in criminological literature to see references to risk factors, as well as to levels of risk (i.e., high risk or low risk), but the fact that risk is about possibility, and not certainty, often appears to be forgotten. (This usage differs from risk position or vulnerability, as we explain in Chapter 2, this volume.) Risk factors identify what experts believe to be indicators of likely behavior, predictors that attract attention and action. Various state police, for example, have in the past based their policing of drivers according to the risk that particular demographic groups have been presumed to pose in terms of traffic enforcement and participation in other types of crime. Minorities have been overrepresented in official (policing) crime statistics, with targeting (or harassment) based on assumptions about the increased likelihood that these members of society might offend. Race is often used, wrongly, as an indicator of a possible future event. Reichmann (1986) explains this shift:

> When regulation shifts from individual offenders to the probability that some offence might occur, traditional presumptions of innocence are transformed into assumptions of guilt. When guilt is inferred from how closely your behavior matches some profile of likely offences—a form of "statistical justice"—constitutional premises based on reasonable doubt may be undermined. (p. 165)

As Levidow (1994) further indicates, the tendency within criminology and policing has been to reify risk—to treat possibilities as though they have meaning today beyond a theoretical future (p. 440).

Bradley and Morss (2002) comment on the notion of "statistical justice" and how it is that a "risk factor becomes synonymous with 'independent variable' or causal variable in such a way that the vocabulary of risk simply re-glosses a long-standing . . . approach to research on vulnerable populations" (p. 520). Risk factors as synonymous to causal variables are problematic for a number of reasons. First, this would suggest that the determination of cause can be improved with the inclusion or substitution of independent variables. In prediction (regression) analysis, attempts are sometimes made to improve models' predictions (increase variance explained) by adding more explanatory variables to models, with the expectation that more variables will get us that much closer to explaining particular phenomena. Adding more variables, however, does not necessarily improve the explanatory power of a model. Second, these procedures cannot be used for the purposes of forecasting; the identification of risk factors is typically post hoc or after the fact, at best. In other words, regression models only apply to what has taken place—they cannot be used to predict what could happen. Furthermore, Shannon (1985) reminds us that we cannot claim to be able to predict the future behavior of particular individuals based on aggregate probability analysis. We cannot tell what any specific individual will do simply by considering the characteristics of the group to which he or she belongs. Finally, these procedures often compare the risks of one particular vulnerable group to a less-vulnerable group, or the rest of the population. In risk society, and as actuarial practices underscore, there is no group that can be a comparison in the traditional sense of being vulnerable or dangerous (Bradley & Morss, pp. 522–23). The problems with these forms of prediction have not deterred the Transportation Security Administration, which provides airport security in the United States, from developing a terrorist prediction model that attaches a score to each traveler based on, among other things, past travel patterns, seat selection, and food choices.

Profiling can also be understood as a form of statistical justice. A number of previous events are considered in order to ascertain common characteristics of offenders, or of crime victims or situations. These characteristics are then used to identify those individuals who are predicted to be most likely to commit future actions. These characteristics are then used to mark or identify a theoretical future with the expectation that there is an identifiable relationship between the past and the future. In other words, characteristics associated with past behaviors positively predict future behaviors. Those who happen to have similar characteristics as past offenders are deemed more likely to commit future offenses and may be targeted regardless of any past wrongdoing on the basis of shared characteristics with those who have committed particular actions.

Profiling typically operates by using characteristics of one group to identify characteristics of future groups. Studies that have considered reoffending run into similar problems, given the relationship between past and future. It is predicted that those who have offended in the past are those most likely to offend in the future. Such predictions, however, are not necessarily accurate, and may generate both false positives and false negatives along with correct future predictions (Figure 3.1). It is entirely possible that a previous offender, for example, will again offend in the future (Cell A, a positive prediction in which an offender subsequently reoffends). Similarly, it may be the case that previous nonoffenders do not offend in the future (Cell D). But predictions can be wrong: it is also entirely possible that a previous offender will not offend in the future (Cell B). This is referred to as a false positive: on the basis of previous activity, it is wrongly expected that this individual would commit future offenses. Equally troubling is Cell C, which occurs when those who have not committed crimes are expected not to offend in the future, but actually do commit future crime.

Past activity	Future activity	
	Offends	Does not offend
Offends	**A – Correct prediction** **(Positive)**	**B – Incorrect prediction** **(False positive)**
Does not offend	**C – Incorrect prediction** **(False negative)**	**D – Correct prediction** **(Negative)**

Figure 3.1   Profiling Future Offending

Profiling provides a false sense of security, as do predictive models of offending that rely on indicators of past activity as a means of determining future behavior. The murky waters of prediction are complicated by the sometimes-tenuous and perhaps nonlinear connections between the past, present, and future, and the role that contingencies (such as opportunity, or lack thereof) may play in informed predictions.

Profiling Victims

Social environments are rife with elements that might be identified as hazardous, neutral, or beneficial. We have also suggested that security may be viewed in a variety of ways depending on the perspectives taken. Individuals vary in terms of what they might identify as dangerous due to their risk positions and previous experiences. Organizations also view the landscape differently depending on their institutional goals and purposes. The case of Jane Doe provides a revealing example of the distinctions between individuals and institutions regarding the security landscape and the implications of these differences.

In the 1980s, Jane Doe was a single, White female living alone in a downtown community in Toronto, Canada. Jane Doe was raped at knife-point by Paul Douglas Callow, and later learned that the Toronto Police Service had had information about the rapist that they had failed to divulge to the community. Doe subsequently sued the police for breech of duty. Doe claimed that had police warned her that a rapist had targeted not only her neighborhood, but also women who looked like her, she would have taken specific measures to provide for and ensure her safety and, ultimately, to prevent her rape. In other words, information that could have been provided by police would have allowed Doe to make a choice with respect to how to behave. Doe indicated that she would have perceived the presence of the rapist as a threat. Doe was not informed of this danger, and had no way of knowing that her safety was potentially compromised, therefore she did not (and did not realize that she should) take action in response to this threat. Doe governed her behavior unaware of the hazard in her neighborhood and was therefore oblivious to the possible harm associated with this particular threat (Callow). Because Doe was not informed and therefore could not choose how to act in the face of this threat, she could not realize that the actions she was taking or failing to take may have increased the probability of a future negative outcome, which in this case was being raped.

Before the courts, the police framed their argument in terms of a general threat, whereas Doe framed her argument in terms of a specific threat. The extension of the argument offered by police is that the police cannot be seen as liable to any particular individual when the police are charged with responsibility for and to numerous individuals.[4] Doe charged that the police were statutorily obligated to protect citizens, and that by failing to define and communicate to the public the presence of a threat (the rapist), the police were negligent in their duties. Ultimately, Doe successfully argued that the police must take some responsibility for the rape because of their failure to inform the public. The police were found liable because they withheld knowledge that would have, theoretically, prevented a future negative occurrence. The warning that was never issued represented a failed opportunity for Doe and others like her to choose to protect herself from a danger that was otherwise not identified.

In her assessment of the case (Ontario Court of Justice: *Jane Doe v. Board of Commissioners of Police for the Municipality of Metropolitan Toronto*, 1998), Justice J. MacFarland indicates that "it is accepted that one of the consequences of the pervasiveness of male sexual violence in our society is that most women fear sexual assault and in many ways govern their conduct because of that fear." In their defense against Doe's claims, the police, in fact, used this exact argument. Specifically, the police argued that if fear of rape is ever present, then issuing a warning with respect to this threat (the rapist) should not have altered the conduct of women who already operate in a state of heightened alert, anticipating the presence of a rapist. The threat, they argued, is pervasive. In other words, women, by virtue of being women, already perceive, and have been socialized to perceive, a general threat, regardless and independent of police warnings that would have made little difference to women who were already cautious. Police argued that they should not be held responsible for future negative events because of failing to warn women who are already, in effect, warned by their status as women. Again, by viewing women in categorical terms as those who are generally threatened, the threat posed by Callow to specific women (those with dark hair living in second-floor balcony apartments) was not recognized by police. Ultimately, the categorical (actuarial) thinking characteristic of the institutional level undermined security at the individual level.

Assessing Crime Information

The identification of particular elements of the social and physical environment as hazardous or beneficial has implications for behavior within that environment. Response to hazards, for example, is typically geared toward reducing the harm that a hazard presents, whereas reacting to opportunities may be geared toward maximizing the benefits an opportunity presents. It comes as little surprise that, given our earlier discussion of risk positions, the identification of hazards and opportunities varies not only among individuals, but also between organizations and individuals. Among individuals, for example, the elderly might consider certain elements in the environment as hazardous that young people would not identify as such. Similarly, the police might view particular regions of a city as opportune in terms of catching and locating offenders, while city residents might see these regions as hazardous. The differences in the ways in which hazards and opportunities are viewed will affect the ways in which information about these elements is communicated and received.

If individuals and policing organizations view hazards and opportunities differently, what are the implications of these differences for personal safety, as well as for obtaining institutional goals, such as crime management? Different perspectives as to what constitute a hazard and how hazards are interpreted suggest that appropriate and relevant information may not be delivered to respective parties. The recipients of information regarding crime may interpret information in ways that are more or less attuned to particular formats. Providing information to organizations, for example, may be more straightforward than delivering knowledge to individuals. Information offered by police to organizations is often general information and more appropriate to an actuarial model of crime prevention that identifies particular risk categories or groups. The distribution of such knowledge would likely involve the police identifying groups of people who represent more or less danger—and, hence, more or less harm—to particular organizations and their respective goals. For example, the police might warn businesses of scam artists who use fax machines to set up appointments to defraud unsuspecting businesses. Information packaged in this general format, however, tends to be unsatisfactory when dealing with individuals and does little to enable individuals to calculate their personal risk of harm. Specifically, individuals may or may not recognize themselves as being members of the group to which general information applies.

In the case of Jane Doe, policing experts from across North America insisted that although it was important to release information about crimes through the media when appropriate, the contents of the warning must be carefully weighed. On the one hand, a warning that was too general would be ineffective, but on the other hand, one that was too specific may provide a false sense of security. Given the information at their disposal, investigators chose not to issue any warning at all. This was another of the bases of the police argument against Doe's lawsuit—that police did not have enough information at their disposal to provide a warning with any substantive meaning.

What is critical, however, is that the individual (Jane Doe) and the organization (the police) constructed differently the meaning attached to the rapist. In fact, the police probably did have enough information to satisfy the public's desire to have threats communicated. The differing definitions of threat for institutions versus individuals, however, were revealed. Definitional differences as to what constitutes a threat had obvious ramifications for behavior at both the individual and organizational levels, as well as for expectations about what acting or failing to act would mean for the future. This case illustrates how divergent definitions of threats may have laid the groundwork for both a future occurrence and for divergent assessments of liability and responsibility for the respective outcome.

The way in which Doe, as an individual, and the police, as an institution, defined the situation, the rapist, is clearly a product of the level of abstraction within which institutions versus individuals operate. At the level of the individual, concerns are relatively circumscribed in time and space. In any particular situation, we tend to assess elements within the immediate temporal and spatial proximity and make judgments as to our security based on these assessments. At the level of the institution, however, time and space are less circumscribed, with institutional assessments of security going well beyond the immediate situation. The orientation of institutions is such that the immediate temporal and spatial circumstances become less important relative to that which is temporally and spatially more broad and inclusive. Organizations tend to look at the big picture. While the rapist himself is a threat to the individual, that is, the person who operates within a circumscribed proximity, the arrest and detention and, ultimately, the closing of the case were central to police concerns that go beyond the immediate situation. What each level or party considers to be worthy or useful information varies substantially.

What does this say for security? Doe's lawsuit called into question the type of policing that the Toronto police had used in the summer of 1986. In Doe's case, being categorized as a woman worked to her disadvantage, given the way in which women were viewed by police and the choices police make with respect to releasing certain types of information. The police and Doe viewed the relevance of certain information in different ways. Doe's case revolved around the fact that she did not identify a threat in her immediate vicinity, either through her own access to information or through the police provision of such information, which did not allow her to exercise choice with respect to preventing a future negative outcome. Although Judge MacFarland indicates that Doe would have taken measures to prevent herself from being raped (Ontario Court of Justice: *Jane Doe v. Board of Commissioners of Police for the Municipality of Metropolitan Toronto*, 1998), a seemingly plausible assumption, the central issue revolves around the fact that Doe's ability to choose her course of action with respect to the threat was foreclosed. Doe argued that if she had been properly informed, she would have had a choice: to do nothing or to change her behavior in some way to lower the probability of assault. In reconstructing her case, Doe's argument made use of a retroactive probability model to explain the outcome. In the end, it is impossible to say that the rape could have been prevented had Doe been provided with information and had she taken subsequent action to deal with it. It is equally impossible to argue that the rape occurred because there was no information and hence no choice. Appropriate information allows for choices to be made in the face of danger, but this does not preclude making wrong choices. When information is inappropriate or absent, however, choices are restricted.

Profiling Routines, Spaces, and Places

The increased use of intelligence in policing has encouraged the analysis of crime and related events in the contexts of identifiable patterns of repeat

Figure 3.2   Crime Prevention?

events. In the discussion of these patterns, there have been two trends of analysis: One has been to look at the clustering of crime using density models, identifying hot spots as spaces in which opportunity for crime coincides with the actions of motivated offenders. The second has been to examine how areas change to become places where crime is more likely to occur. In the identification of crime locales we account not only for the crime behavior but also the change in social context that occurs both to stimulate and to encourage crime.

An important part of this equation is the action taken by individuals in managing their own vulnerabilities and contributing, through prevention strategies, to their overall safety or danger in an area. This action is nested within a larger context where agents of social control, whose actions are intended to deter the risk of crime, supervise the environment. In the analysis of crime risk, some interesting aspects of risk balance have emerged. The most significant rests with the realization that crime clusters in certain areas and around certain groups. This observation has led to important work on crime risk aided by crime mapping and is informed by classical work in criminology concerning the development of crime places.

Pattern analysis has encouraged researchers to acknowledge that crime may be matched to the routine activities of victims and offenders. While it does not explicitly reference risk balance, pattern analysis suggests that certain areas have a greater tendency toward the occurrence of crime. In this research, focused primarily on the density of crime or hot spots, there has been a failure to recognize that pattern analysis focusing on hot spots tells us about spaces in which crime occurs, but does not really address the issues related to the formation of crime places. For example, knowing that drugs are sold in a certain location is important for addressing police resources. What do we know about these areas that would lead us and others, specifically offenders, to see them as drug markets, however? The behavior not only repeats itself, but also changes the character of the neighborhood in which it takes place. In other words, as crime victims and offenders manage their environment, it responds to their actions, transforming in a way that creates security or insecurity for its occupants, either facilitating or deterring certain types of behavior.

Preventing Crime?

We are led to believe that crime is pervasive, and we are told to secure our windows, lock our doors, and be wary of strangers; the precautions we might take are those that primarily address that which is detectable. We are not advised to protect ourselves from indirect threats posed by price-fixing and embezzlement, nor are we advised to protest the conditions that may contribute to and motivate criminal activity. These crimes and their solutions are too abstract—and are certainly deemed as less worthy of attention by the public and policymakers—to garner the attention that more personal crimes have received. Having said this, a focus on the proximate threats to security may be one of the few ways that individuals, institutions, and states are able to maintain some sense of control in an insecure world. While the busy work of taping one's windows in the case of bioterrorist threat may do little to actually secure oneself against biochemical harm—a threat where harm may be realized independent of any actions individuals or institutions may take—such behavior may relieve some insecurity by its very action, and, at the least, result in a sense of doing something.[5]

Doing something about crime points to prevention: risk balance involves anticipating future harm and reducing it through deterrence measures today. Prevention strategies and, in particular, situational prevention, targets immediately proximate threats and seeks to neutralize them. The current emphasis on crime prevention differs substantially from the past positivist focus on identifying causes of crime. As O'Malley (1992) explains, the focus of positivist orientations has been, first, to identify or to create a specific norm or standard of behavior through a process of normalization. Second, the focus has been to identify individual uniqueness according to that standard of normalcy, and subject that uniqueness to correction, often under the guise of rehabilitation. O'Malley indicates that this positivistic orientation has been rejected in the late 20th and early 21st centuries for an orientation today that is more in line with the classical school of criminology: "In situational crime prevention, one of the fastest growing techniques of crime control, concern is with the spatial and physical aspects of crime, thought out in terms of the opportunities for crime rather than its causal or biographical origins" (p. 253). Situational crime control models assume that actors are rational and essentially the same (O'Malley) and act according to the logic of maximizing gains and minimizing costs (Cornish & Clarke, 1987).

The management of crime according to a situational crime model does not manage the individual, but rather manages the population through the control of situations and opportunities, in terms of, for example, target hardening (Clarke & Newman, 2006) This model is not unique to managing crime: the health management model, for example, has similar characteristics. Both the crime prevention and health management models emerge as forms of population control rather than a form of individual disciplinary control. These models are "concerned not with the individual's deviation from the norm, but with managing populations at an aggregate level" (O'Malley, 1992, p. 253). These actuarial models, according to Simon (1988), increase the efficiency of crime control because attempting to change individuals is difficult and expensive. The universal threat underlying situational crime prevention or health management edifies the notion that we must all take responsibility to prevent even what we are unable to detect. The concept of security becomes a matter of individual conformity, and deviation from the norm is viewed as threatening. By focusing on universality and rational choice rather than on causation, responsibility for outcomes becomes more diffuse—offenders and victims share responsibility for crime outcomes.

The result is that the individual and his or her social context are mined with increasing technical sophistication. Details that might have once gone unnoticed or undetected now become identified as relevant to security. As Reichmann (1986) explains,

> By transforming the meaningless (i.e., sound waves) into the meaningful (words), by joining what was heretofore unjoinable (matching previously disparate data), and by making what was hidden (body chemicals) apparent, these new techniques have increased the intensity and scope of what can be exposed and analyzed. (p. 156)

That which can be exposed and analyzed is subsequently named as threatening. Levidow (1994) makes a similar observation:

> A measurable thing called objective risk becomes attributed to a particular apparatus or substance [or person or situation], whose properties must be scientifically assessed by experts. In deferring to such expertise, we are complicit in reifying risk, in naturalizing potential harm as a technical property of things [or persons or situations]. (p. 441)

The future, in other words, is not only foreshadowed by particular characteristics, but is realized in the response to them.

Situational approaches rely on an understanding of various factors that are included in making a judgment about risk balance. Reducing the probability of crime, for example, cannot be achieved by focusing only on one particular aspect of the crime event, such as offenders. At an individual level, rational decisions can be made to prevent harm either by choosing not to offend or by protecting oneself. Yet individual choices, as we saw earlier with respect to Jane Doe, may be either undermined or supported at the institutional level. Situational crime prevention includes calculations at a more aggregate or institutional level that considers risk balance calculations, which do not unfold in the same way at the individual level.

While we may have success in detecting potential dangers in controlled facilities such as airports, detection is much more difficult in more diffuse and uncontrolled environments, such as mass transit systems or city streets. We are left to rely on low technology systems, using techniques such as random checking of backpacks or random road checks as a way of identifying threats. This process, however, introduces new difficulties. Where technology can be used to scrutinize everyone equally, the massive task of checking everyone entering the mass transit system means that decision rules have to be developed to identify hazards. In implementing their bag checking scheme after the London transit bombings, the New York Police Department stated that checks would be random and not subject to any discriminatory or profiling practices. In addition, they indicated that people who chose not to have their bags checked would be free to leave the stations.

As reasonable as this sounds, the practice of random checking creates some dilemmas for police. While customs performs random checking of individuals at border points, they acknowledge that they only catch a certain number of all individuals who are actually smuggling goods into the country. The consequences of smuggling, however, are less dire than the consequences of train bombings. Should the police ignore the characteristics of what appears to constitute a bomber in setting out a strategy for surveillance and search? If the policy is to perform random or nondiscriminatory checks, do suspicious grounds allow for setting aside the policy in favor of these suspicions? If suspicions are a product of both past experience and stereotyping, the decision to engage in checking is far from clear. There is no easy answer, although it could be argued that deterring the bombers at the doors of the subway may be much more difficult than getting the communities where bombers live to give the bombers up to authorities long before the bombs are made. This is a point not lost on community leaders who have joined together to denounce the use of violence and supported action against extremists operating within their communities ("From Muslims in America," 2005).

Crime Events and Risk Balance

Our risk balance model assumes dynamic movement consisting of balancing hazards against resources over time. Hazards vary, emerging and receding on the security radars of individuals, institutions, and the state, due to a number of factors—contingent and long term, political and otherwise. Similarly, the resources available to deal with identified harms also vary: other harms impinge on the assets available to deal with them, coupled with the reality that resources are often limited at any particular level. The risk balance perspective draws attention to the various parties to security, and the respective means that each party (individuals, institutions, and states) brings to bear regarding particular dangers.

The criminal event also identifies various parties to crime—for example, offenders, victims, and witnesses—each of whom responds to criminal behavior in ways that are often dictated by the respective position that each plays. Prior to a criminal exchange, future victims may be characterized by particular features and experiences that make them more or less vulnerable to a possible criminal exchange. The same can be said for offenders: offenders may have had particular experiences that increase the likelihood of them interpreting certain situations as conducive to taking advantage of others. While background or pre-event factors work to set situations up in particular ways, the actual criminal transaction may be influenced by contingent factors beyond the control of those directly involved. Offenders, for example, may misjudge the physical strength of those they have decided to attack, or witnesses might come on a crime scene causing a criminal transaction to derail. Finally, the aftermath of the event consists of responses to particular transactions, as well as, perhaps, a rethinking of the characteristics that each party may or may have not identified as signs of either weakness or strength in others, or opportunities or hazards within particular situations. The aftermath may also involve institutional actors, such as the police or the courts, determining punishments.

An important element of the criminal event is the context in which various crimes are played out. Certain situations, for example, are simply more likely to result in a criminal transaction than are others. Bars, for example, illustrate this nicely: alcohol, often coupled with young unattached males, increases the probability of criminal transactions. In other situations, the presence of an alarm system or dog in the house may result in an offender moving to a different residence that is less protected. The difference between the criminal event and risk balance revolves around the concept of balance, which takes into consideration more than one hazard at a time, and not simply crime, as well as the recognition and acknowledgment of the integration of particular perspectives (individual, institutional, and state) and the attendant resources brought to bear on identified hazards. Risk balance includes consideration of crime and other hazardous events, but goes farther by recognizing the varying levels of resources applied to hazards depending on the perspective from which such hazards are viewed.

Conclusion

There are certain things that we know about crime that relate to routine practices: many crimes are committed by a few offenders; many crimes occur in a few locations; proximity to residence of victim and offender correlates with crime occurrence; those who have been victims once are more likely to be victims again than are nonvictims likely to be first-time victims; and social disorder is often accompanied by crime.

In our discussion of community policing, we considered the police as information brokers, retrieving information from a number of sources about crime and crime potential. Community policing assumes a focus on low policing issues—issues with a more local and proximate orientation. The police themselves, however, have also been frustrated by the lack of information that they receive from above, or from the realm of high policing. National and international players who request information often fail to provide local policing agents with a context into which these information requests might be placed. Demands for access to information at the local level are often met, whereas similar demands are often not met at the national level.

Clearly, one of the most important impediments to security as it relates to crime is jurisdiction—which jurisdiction harbors information, what kind of information is held, and who is allowed access to it. The botched police investigation with respect to the murders committed by Paul Bernardo and Karla Homolka was a product of jurisdictional noncooperation. Two years prior to the first murder, police had DNA evidence from Paul Bernardo linking him to rapes committed in Scarborough, an adjacent district. Bernardo was, in fact, the entity known as the Scarborough Rapist. Once the rapes stopped in Scarborough, however, the push to continue the search for the perpetrator fell flat, despite the ready-made links to what was occurring in a nearby jurisdiction.[6]

Although the Bernardo-Homolka story highlights the territorial definition of jurisdiction, with the exercise of authority limited to certain geographic regions, the meaning of jurisdiction also refers to the "power or right to exercise authority," and "the power, right, or authority to interpret and apply the law"(Merriam-Webster OnLine Dictionary, 2007). Clearly, in the case of Jane Doe, the police perceived that their interpretation of law was paramount. They exercised authority in a manner, however, that compromised the safety of the citizens for whom they were responsible. The institutional jurisdiction perceived by the police compromised Jane Doe's power to exercise authority on her own behalf. Ownership of information and obligations and responsibilities with respect to such information are paramount considerations in the security arena. In modern society, at every level—individual, institutional, and state—the willingness to share information may require change. On the one hand, the threats that are most potentially harmful may be those that require both collaboration and the breaking down of traditional jurisdictional boundaries. Bayley's (2005) observation regarding pressures on policing may be particularly apt in terms of the pressures applied to jurisdictional boundaries as well. For instance, in order to address organized crime, jurisdictional boundaries between the federal and state levels may have to become more fluid. Similarly, if individuals, institutions and states are becoming increasingly responsible for their own security, the jurisdictional boundaries between these levels—whether perceived or real—may also need to shift. At the same time that there is pressure to break down jurisdictional boundaries, individualism suggests an opposing pressure in the pursuit of self-preservation. If security is seen as a zero-sum game—your security comes only at my expense—the likelihood of jurisdictional reconfiguration is much reduced.

Notes to Chapter 3

1. Karla Homolka, with her partner and eventual husband, Paul Bernardo, was involved in the sex slayings of two teenagers, Kristen French and Leslie Mahaffy, and was implicated in the death of Homolka's younger sister, Tammy.

2. Although Homolka was charged with manslaughter in exchange for information leading to the first-degree murder conviction of Paul Bernardo, videotapes of the murders that were revealed after her plea bargain suggested Homolka played a far more central role in the crimes than she had claimed.

3. What is little known about the color-coded security scheme used by Department of Homeland Security, which will be discussed in Chapter 4, this volume, is that there are clear statements about the freedom of movement that people have under the higher codes. For example, under code red, no one other than authorized law enforcement officials and their designees are allowed to leave the location that they are in when the alert is called. This type of restricted movement would be strictly enforced, with exceptions made only in the cases where key personnel is needed to take care of utilities or to manage an emergency facility.

The imbedded force of the color-coded scheme would be a great surprise to most Americans, yet the program was put into place with little understanding of its implications. Of greater debate, derived from a deep-seated anxiety about the reach of government, was the renewal of the terms of the PATRIOT Act in March, 2006, which renewed the power of law enforcement to identify, pursue, and prosecute terrorists.

4. This fear is echoed by police officers in their commentary following the decision in the Doe case. A representative of the Ontario Chiefs of Police indicates his fear that the ruling against the Metropolitan Toronto Police Force would place police officers in a no-win situation:

> If we are not protected from liability with respect to everything we do—even those things that we do in good faith according to the highest standards of the profession—and later on, we're second-guessed and found liable, you can see the dilemma for police. ("Police chief wants appeal of Doe case," 1998)

5. Hollway and Jefferson (1997) refer to such behaviors as "outlets of expression" for more generalized anxiety that has few forms of redress.

6. In his 473-page independent inquiry into the police investigation of Paul Bernardo, Justice Archie Campbell concluded that "'there were times during the separate investigations . . . that the different police forces might as well have been operating in different countries.'" The police basically stopped their investigation into the Scarborough rapes because no new attacks had occurred, without warning police in Bernardo's new location that Bernardo had been a prime suspect in these attacks (Jenish, 1996).

4

Modern Terrorism

Although the images of the falling towers of the World Trade Center can scarcely be forgotten, two well-televised terrorist incidents have since crowded our memories with haunting images of the suffering that terrorism creates. In September 2004, images from Beslan, Russia, showed bloodied school-children and adults and, for those lucky enough to have survived, their expressions of pain, anguish, and palpable fear. Media headlines in the immediate aftermath of the event began to change. Although initially stunned into silence by the magnitude of the situation, Russia's response quickly transitioned from grieving, to outrage, to laying blame: "Grief in Russia now mixes with harsh words for government" (2004), and "Russia's grief turns to anger" (2004).

Since referred to as "7/7," July 7, 2005, marks the date of a more recent terrorist event. In London, England, morning rush hour commuters were met with the detonation of three bombs discharged by suicide bombers on London's Underground. A fourth bomb was detonated nearly 1 hour later, on one of London's famous double-decker buses that was itself in the process of being rerouted around damage from the earlier blasts. Images of stunned and bloodied commuters and mass pandemonium prevailed on newscasts immediately following the blasts.[1] As with the attacks in the United States and Russia, the attacks in England were characterized by early reports that reflected fear of subsequent attacks, followed quickly by reports that asked more pointed questions related to blame, responsibility, and liability.

In each of these terrorist incidents, issues with respect to the harsh reality of terrorism in the 21st century appear to revolve around two central points: first, the history of terrorist activity that preceded the events and the political environment that may have played a role in the attacks;[2] second, the (lack of) information provided to the public during these events. From these central points critical questions emerge: First, was the event predictable, given the history of past encounters and intelligence regarding such activities? For example, unlike the prevailing situation prior to the attacks in the United States, London's Home Office was operating in a context of heightened awareness of the threat of terrorism. Second, if the event was predictable—and information was available—was it preventable? Third, if the event was not entirely preventable, were there safeguards in place to reduce the devastation? And if not, why not? And finally, in what ways do external threats differ from internal threats? How is information relayed about internal versus external threats, and how do responses to these respective threats differ?

While the difficulties that London now faces in this most recent terrorist incident are in certain ways unique, the issues that have surfaced and come into play are increasingly familiar in a post–9/11, post-Beslan, and now post–7/7 world. Terrorist events bring to the fore questions regarding information (who has it, who does not, and what should be done with it), as well as questions with respect to the even-more elusive concept of knowledge and what knowing consists of. These events also point to the difficulties surrounding precursors to terrorism and the role that globalization, for example, has played and will continue to play as both background and foreground to past and future terrorist events. Will efforts to respond to terrorism reverse the impact of globalization as border security tightens to address security threats? Or will international cooperation in the name of fighting terrorism allow more countries into the "globalization country club"? The association of globalization with terrorism suggests that there are winners and losers in global society, but determining which group is which is not at all straightforward, much less predictable.

Security efforts associated with terrorism also bring resoundingly to the fore the problems of individual rights and collective security. In establishing risk balance, how can responding to terrorist threat navigate the tension between individual rights and collective security? Does the tension between these two apparent poles result in a zero-sum game, with greater collective security only possible at the expense of individual rights, or vice versa? Our discussion of terrorism, then, derives from an emphasis on values, choices, and resources that are available to anticipate and respond to threats. Within the context of terrorist threat, an examination of the tension between the individual and the collective requires consideration of power and control—who wields it and who aspires to it.

Terrorism and Security

Despite its frequent usage, it is far from clear what is meant by the word "terrorism." Calhoun (2002) identifies some of the difficulties in attempts to define *terrorism* and *terrorist activity*. Record (2003) explains that the current definition of terrorism is simply "premeditated, politically motivated violence against innocents" (p. 6) yet the identification of political motivation and innocents is unclear. Furthermore, definitions of terrorism often suggest that terrorist acts are nonstate phenomena, perpetrated by those outside the state, often for political ends. Yet terrorism may not necessarily involve illegal activity: many regimes of ill repute, from Germany's Third Reich to the more recent regimes in Rwanda, the Congo, and Sudan, could be said to have committed and continue to commit terrorist acts within the parameters of self-made and self-serving legality. Calhoun notes that moral definitions of terrorist activity are similarly problematic. While democratic governments may condemn terrorist activity, the notion of a just war may also be used by terrorists in support of their activities: "Violent attacks upon strategic targets can be understood straightforwardly as being permitted by a 'just war' rationale, at least as interpreted by the killers" (Calhoun, p. 86). Rather than irrational activity, terrorist activity may instead be seen as strategic, with actors believing their actions to be just and justifiable and well within the domain of rational activity that might bring recognition and provide some measure of voice to their concerns. Furthermore, the suggestion that those who perpetrate terrorist activity are evil ignores the political context to which terrorists are responding (Record, p. 8).

The initial response of President Bush to the events of September 11, 2001, was to pronounce that the attacks were acts of war. Subsequently, he declared a war on terrorism. The absence of a flesh and blood enemy with which this type of conflict could be waged meant that the focus was on a method rather than on an entity (although al-Qaeda and rogue states came to personify the terrorist method). As Record (2003) explains, political administrations in the United States have favored the war analogy to suggest the seriousness with which they perceive the associated problem—the 1980s war on drugs is one such example. The language used to describe events or problems also frames our understanding and confers status on certain actors as experts. Hills (2002) notes that experts formulate the problem in ways that make them the experts; declaring this event a major conflict makes both state and military personnel the experts, rather than those who might define terrorism in other terms. The other strategy associated with terms of war and warfare is that these references pull the unfamiliar and unimaginable back into the realm of the familiar and imaginable. War, despite its infrequency, is something that has been previously dealt with and, presumably, can be managed again. It was exceedingly difficult for people to comprehend flying airliners into symbols of America without transforming these events into something that could be imagined: war.

The terrorist events in the United States, Russia, and Britain suggest that terrorist activity is not something that only occurs elsewhere, nor is it a problem that can be strictly viewed as the purview of the uncivilized alone. Furthermore, the rhetoric stemming from these events suggests that things are not always as they seem, thus the presumed need for vigilance against potential danger. President Bush, for example, suggests that Americans ought "to go on living their decent, honorable, free American lives and also to be ever-vigilant for the slightest signs of incipient terror, which might be anywhere" (quoted in Harpham, 2002, p. 576). The facade of normalcy and "decent, honorable, free American lives" against the apparently new reality that citizens must be vigilant for signs of incipient terror gives rise to questions about knowledge and prevention, as well as fallibility in the quest for security and protection against terrorist threat. The reality of human fallibility coupled with uncertainty regarding the identification of, and motivations for, terrorism contributes to terror and reproduces insecurity. As Harpham notes, "perhaps the surest symptom of terror is precisely the paralyzing inability to determine whether we have entered onto a new reality or are merely confronting for the first time the reality we had been living all along" (p. 578). In other words, should we have seen something? Is it only in hindsight that we recognize that we should have seen these events coming? Was the information flawed or simply nonexistent? What role have we played in the dramas that unfolded and the drama that vigilance is meant to identify or, at the least, mitigate? Will hypervigilance as a response to these events prevent further events?

Who Are the Terrorists and What Threat Do They Pose?

An excellent way to make sense of who the terrorists are and the threats they pose is to visit the Web site of the National Memorial Institute for the Prevention of Terrorism (MIPT), which hosts a major database for the analysis of terrorism groups and their actions.[3] The MIPT Terrorism Knowledge Base contains information on more than 20,000 incidents, the groups that were involved, and trials that took place. This information can be sorted by characteristics such as group, location in the world, type of attack, perpetrator, and victim characteristics. This site provides an up-to-date public inventory of what is happening in the world.

If we look at the various elements of the database, we find that in 2005 the most common type of action was an armed attack followed by bombings, while in 1998 bombings outnumbered armed attacks by almost five to one. Also, the groups that are active in attacks have changed over the years. In the five years from 1993 to 1998, the most active groups in terms of incidents were Anti-Castro Cubans and Basque nationalists. In the time frame from 1998 to 2003, the Revolutionary Armed Forces of Colombia committed the most incidents. Al-Qaeda and Hamas were involved in the most incidents in 2005. In terms of location, from 1968 to the middle of 2006, most acts of terrorism were in the Middle East, followed closely by Asia. A high number of events also occurred in Europe during that time.

The ability to assess changes in location and changes over time provides us with a vital tool in understanding how terrorist groups evolve and where terrorist threats are located. This enables individuals and agencies to conduct a more informed assessment of risk over time.

Globalization

> Ways of living cannot be sustained as 'national' only. The whole world is now the unity; the setting is global: there is one 'world' in the phenomenological or experiential sense, one world in the geo-political reach of power and communication, one earth as a bio-social environment. But this unity is both complexly divided, *and* [italics in original] interrelated in its differences, in many different ways. (Johnson, 2002, p. 212)

> There is no question that the drive to increase the security of national borders runs counter to the very forces that propel globalization. It is difficult if not impossible to address the demands for greater security and scrutiny of cross-border movements of goods, people, information, financial capital, even snailmail without some setbacks to the drumbeat of faster, cheaper, less red tape that drove productivity gains in the 1990s. (Brainard, 2002, p. 235)

There has been a voluminous expansion of research on globalization in the past decade. On the one hand, globalization has been likened to a runaway train, wreaking havoc on cultures and peoples by bulldozing everything in its path in pursuit of freer markets and capital acquisition. On the other hand, some maintain that globalization has indeed generated opportunities for capital expansion, at the same time creating opportunities for exchange and advancement in terms of health, technology, and movement across borders, as well as facilitating transparency and cooperation. Evidence for either vision seems readily available: globalization harbors both dark and bright sides.

A central component of globalization is the breakdown of national borders. Opportunities for market expansion, for example, are no longer limited to one's own country. Rather, technology such as the Internet allows for the sale of goods to bypass geographic boundaries. But it is not only the sale of goods that transcends these geographic boundaries—it is also the transmission of cultural capital, including ideas, beliefs, and values. Just as business may no longer require a state base from which to operate, associations of individuals with particular beliefs also do not require a state base. As Young-Bruehl (2002) notes, drawing on the work of Arendt (1951), the terrorism that brought down the World Trade Center's Twin Towers was not terrorism within a state for the purpose of rectifying a national injustice, nor was it terrorism in the service of a national liberation front, although some members of the network might also see this as a side goal. Rather, the *World Islamic Front,* which Osama Bin Laden and his colleagues accept as their name, involves "men of many nationalities, living in their own or other states, united by a supranational purpose that is anti-political" (Young-Bruehl, p. 573). Supranationalism involves the dissolution and erosion of the boundaries of the nation-state "into an amorphous bonding of a people" (Young-Bruehl, p. 574). It is from the basis of supranationalism that totalitarianism may grow. As Young-Bruehl further explains, "The aspiration of their Islamic movement [the World Islamic Front] is to bring down the governments that betrayed their Muslim populations by collaborating with the secularizing infidels of the West and to wage a Holy War upon those governments and peoples of the West—combatants and civilians without distinction—who have assaulted Muslims and desecrated Muslim holy sites and lands" (p. 574). While globalization is not the cause of supranationalism, it has inadvertently contributed to it by opening up borders—both physical and social.

In this context, Ang (2002) asks us to think about the global city, where she suggests that the erosion of nation-state boundaries can be clearly observed. At the same time, the global city is also the "key location of immigration-led cultural diversity and cosmopolitanism" (Ang, p. 161). While living together on a global level is problematic, the difficulties are played out at the local level. In global cities such as London or New York, individuals harboring a variety of beliefs and values interact on a daily basis. While conflicts and instances of "interracial or intercultural antipathies and incompatibilities" emerge, the global city at the same time and by necessity is a space where the "modern experience of 'togetherness in difference' is a central reality" (Ang, p. 162). The global city mirrors Beck's analysis of the global risk society. In the global risk society, as in the global city, multilateralism is compelled and unilateralism is meaningless. Because the most potentially devastating threats are common to all, everyone has a stake in the solutions to those threats. As Beck (2003) points out, however, "the everyday sphere of experience of the 'global risk society' does not emerge as a love relationship of everyone with everyone" (p. 258). Just as individuals and states recognize the globality of their own life contexts, so too do they have differing perceptions of what threatens security, the priorities such threats are given, and what might constitute perceived solutions to threats.

The erosion of borders as precursor to transnational terrorist threat plays into the very idea of risk society and the democratization of risk that Beck refers to in his earlier work (1992). Beck (2003) uses the term *globality of danger* to suggest a recognition by the world community that as class, nation, and government break down as sources of security, new forms of association and communality emerge that would have once been considered impossible. Specifically, Beck (2003) notes that "the terror attacks have brought states closer together and have sharpened the understanding of what globalization actually is: a worldwide community of destiny" (p. 258). Recognizing common dangers will force associations between unlikely comrades due to the perceived urgency of terrorist threat which is clearly an equal opportunity source of harm. If nothing else, there may be the realization that future terrorist attacks have repercussions for all—every party could be potentially caught in the (literal and economic) crossfire.

The state no longer monopolizes power: power now comes in the form of technological advance and, more importantly, the acquisition of knowledge. *Technological advances*, advances that are often outside the realm of state control, facilitate the extent and reach of terrorist threat. Individuals, for example, can produce knowledge-based weaponry in the privacy of their own facilities. Beck (2003) explains that unlike atomic weapons, which require the acquisition of rare materials which are often controlled by international agreements, the most threatening weapons today are those that require technical expertise and knowledge, not rare materials. This means that individuals or groups of individuals can wage war against states. As technology advances, terrorist threat also advances and the power of individuals in relation to the state grows. The individualization of threat— the reality that each and every one of us could possibly be harmful—has ominous results for society: "The citizen must prove that he or she is not dangerous, for under these conditions each individual finally comes under the suspicion of being a potential terrorist. Each person must thereby put up with submitting to random 'security' controls" (Beck, p. 261). As everyone becomes a suspect, distinctions between good and evil, citizen and noncitizen, become meaningless. In the same way, the distinction between civilian and combatant fades into the background.

Beck (2003) explains that globalization has gone hand in hand with neoliberalism, in that the neoliberal maxim has been to "replace politics and the state with economics" (p. 262). The neoliberal view has been that too much state involvement and bureaucracy have caused global problems such as poverty and the economic collapse of nations. Yet in the face of disasters such as 9/11, Beck suggests that a simple reliance on economic power is ill-equipped to provide answers to central questions regarding security that have heretofore been "repressed by the neo-liberal victory march" (p. 263). Critical questions are left unanswered: how economics can be decoupled from politics; how security can exist without the state and public services; how one can have a state without taxation or, for that matter, how one can have education, health care, and social security without taxation; how there can be legitimacy without democracy, civil society, or the public sphere; and how there can be security without legitimacy (Beck, p. 263). A global economy cannot exist without the safeguards of a state, Beck argues. The global economy, or globalization, requires state action, although perhaps not in the same form as we now know it.

Globalization in a risk society provides context for the issues surrounding terrorist threat, and the perhaps more onerous transnational terrorist threat. As Brainard (2002) observes, "globalization proved very fragile and heavily dependent for its survival on international rules and institutions and national commitments to maintaining open borders" (p. 234). The issue of borders, and the more expansive notion of naming, categorizing, and classifying people and behaviors will continue to figure prominently in our discussion as we turn to the difficulties in defining terrorism, and the issues terrorism raises and implications for dealing with it.

Who "We" Are

Let no-one be in any doubt, the rules of the game are changing. (Blair, 2005)

In the aftermath of 9/11, much was made of the fact that the terrorists involved were outsiders, people who were born and raised outside

North America. Yet far from being strangers to American soil, many of the 19 members of al-Qaeda who perished in these attacks had been in the United States periodically for some years in advance of the attacks. Federal security systems had failed to identify these persons as threats and allowed them both to enter and stay in the United States for some time prior to September 11, 2001. They were hardly the outsiders we might imagine. The subsequent U.S. effort to halt the infiltration of terrorists into the country has resulted in a great deal of effort and dollars spent on enhancing border security. The idea seems to be that if borders are simply made less permeable than they were prior to 9/11, terrorists will not be able to enter through conventional border points and the threat of terrorism will subsequently be reduced. The drive to reduce threat through technological means is voracious: if the right technology can simply be found, and with cost being no object, then outsiders can be kept out.

As the United Kingdom's Prime Minister Tony Blair suggests, however, one of the most recent terrorist attacks had little to do with securing borders. Rather than an external threat coming from outside of England, the events of July 7, 2005, were perpetrated by those already within the country's borders: enhanced border security would have done nothing to stop this attack. Of the four suicide bombers involved in the 7/7 attacks in London, three were born and raised in England, with the fourth raised in England since childhood. Furthermore, of the four would-be bombers in the failed July 21, 2005, effort to detonate an additional four bombs,[4] all were British citizens and had been in England for many years prior to this event. While debate continues with respect to where to draw the line between the protection of civil liberties and measures to enhance national security, Blair has suggested that certain Islamic groups will be banned from Britain, and a list is to be drawn up of individuals "whose activities or views pose a threat to Britain's security" (Blair, 2005) who will be kept out of Britain (assuming, of course, that they are coming from outside Britain). Responding in part to critics' suggestions that Britain has become a safe haven for extremists, Blair's response has, at the same time, drawn criticism from civil rights advocates and various Islamic groups who view this response as a slap in the face to the vast majority of law-abiding, nonextremist Muslims.

In his analysis of the migration-security nexus, especially post–9/11, Faist (2002) elaborates on how it is that international migration has often been linked with concerns with immigrant others—in terms of taking jobs, housing, and potential income; disloyalty to the host country; and to the more recent concern that immigrants may be part of nationalist movements who use terrorism in their global militant operations. As Faist points out, however, the links between migration and security threats are tenuous. Nevertheless, the anxiety and insecurity caused by legitimate migration is reborn in full-blown fear when migrants are believed to be linked with terrorist activity. Clearly, this is the situation in Britain today, with efforts being made to mark as outsiders those who have been insiders for quite some time. Terrorist activity reifies the dualisms that globalism had in some ways weakened: references to "us" versus "them" reinforce the notion of the inner circle that may be trusted, and the outer circle that is feared (Faist). The security narrative, as Faist observes, means that fear and anxiety, and more importantly, their sources, have to be controlled or, better yet, eliminated.[5]

Faist's observations point to the idea of an *emotion premium:* fear and anxiety as social costs. Fear and anxiety may be costly to individuals, in that these heightened emotions may result in energy expended or redirected in ways that may do more to undermine than to enhance overall security (including, for example, health complications from stress). Wilkinson (2001) distinguishes between fear and anxiety in terms of associated levels of knowledge. He suggests "the key to explaining the difference between fear and anxiety is represented as amounting to a difference in the amount or quality of knowledge we possess as to the objective dimensions of an anticipated danger" (p. 20). An anticipated danger or threat produces anxiety when we know little about it—in this situation anxiety is created because of the individual being in a state of uncertainty. On the other hand, when we have information about the anticipated danger or threat, we may instead experience fear. The difference is that fear may give us an object on which to focus. Just as knowledge may reduce anxiety, but potentially increase fear, belief may relate to anxiety in a similar way. What is believed to be true or factual likely works the same as information, potentially reducing generalized anxiety, but possibly increasing fear. Beliefs may run contrary to information, but their importance in establishing security is huge. Changing what people believe, or even emphasizing what they believe in, clearly can reduce the emotion premium and allow people to get on with their lives.

A system of beliefs was brought to the fore in the management of the crisis situation that immediately followed the 9/11 terrorist attacks. The government was unable to give the public the types of information that would have allowed for anxiety to be reduced. President Bush and his advisers chose a strategy to mobilize and calm the public that asked Americans to renew their efforts to believe in (and participate in) in the "American way of life." The crisis was managed by shifting attention toward what individuals were familiar with and what they believed in. Shifting focus to resume everyday life not only allowed the government to put on a face of calm, but also bought some time before the hard questions having to do with what really counted as information and knowledge were brought to the fore. This strategy—shifting focus to other issues or other beliefs—also allowed for intelligence gatherers to determine how costly fear levels might be: how much information is transmitted or withheld depends on how it might affect fear.

In the context of globalization and global partnerships, there are substantial roadblocks to coming to terms with security threats that emerge from within borders. First, there are political difficulties. This comes from the loss of trust by other international players that may result in actually having to admit that there are difficulties in one's own backyard. If nations are seen as needing to deal with internal threats, these nations' ability to deal effectively with external threats may be perceived by other nations, as well as their own citizens, as compromised. Rather than losing face on the international scene, some nations are more likely to concentrate their security efforts on external terrorist threats and to join the war against terror, therefore enhancing perceptions of being team players in the struggle against terrorism. No country is willing to appear weak in the context of international relations. Second, demands for enhanced security measures may be more easily realized against foreign others—noncitizens—than against one's own citizens. As described above, while Bush's response to the 9/11 attacks and Blair's response to the 7/7 attacks have been criticized by civil rights advocates as breaches of the civil rights of citizens of their respective countries. Measures taken to enhance security have been brought to bear more forcefully and consistently against citizens from other nations. For example, globalization involves global travel and crossing borders. The U.S. demand for biometrics, including fingerprints, face recognition, and iris scans, has been more easily imposed on foreigners than it has on American citizens. In fact, given that most terrorism in the United States originates domestically, as with many other countries that are currently focused on fighting global terrorism, there has been comparatively little biometric information on U.S. citizens due to concerns about U.S. citizens' civil liberties. More recently, however, all new and renewed passports for U.S. citizens will be issued electronically, meaning that passports will include an integrated circuit chip that stores biometric information on the passport bearer (Department of State, 2007).

The quest to gather biometric information on its citizenry has been advanced by the UK's Home Office, which introduced the Identity Cards Bill in May of 2005 (BBC, 2007). Those in favor of such a system suggest that identity cards would not only help to prevent illegal working and illegal immigration, but that the cards would aid antiterrorist measures by making it harder for terrorists and terrorist groups to use false or stolen identities. Those in opposition suggest the cards would do little to stem illegal immigration or illegal working, let alone seriously affect terrorist efforts due to the ease with which the cards could still be fraudulently obtained. Still others point to the invasion of individual civil liberties, and the possibility of function creep—the potential misuse of the data stored in the cards. In the United States, President Bush recently attached a Real ID program to an $82 billion military spending bill introduced in 2005. The Real ID card would require, in 2008, all those living or working in the United States to have a federally approved ID card in order to perform functions such as "travel on an airplane, open a bank account, collect Social Security payments or take advantage of nearly any government service" (McCullagh, 2005).

Intelligence: Information and Knowledge

When the ship had sunk, it was as if the village woke up halfway down a precipice. (Laxness, 2002, p. 216)

How we respond to the world around us is guided in part by past experience, and in part by what we wish, hope, and expect things to be. With respect to terrorism, Harpham's—as well as Bush's and Blair's—suggestion that the world may not be what we thought it was seems much like waking up and finding oneself in a precarious position. Information may enhance security by enabling prevention, amelioration, or mitigating action to reduce and limit damage. On the other hand, information may cause or reinforce insecurity because of perceived vulnerability and recognition of one's weaknesses.

"We Have Some Planes . . ."

In the "9/11 Commission Report" (National Commission on Terrorist Attacks Upon the United States [National Commission], 2004), it appears that the processing of information on the morning of September 11 by critical decisionmakers was seriously impeded by a lack of imagination. This failure to imagine was not, however, characteristic only of that particular morning, but appears to have been a widespread difficulty that greatly contributed to processing information in the months and years prior to this date. As the "9/11 Commission Report" plainly states, "The conflict did not begin on 9/11. It had been publicly declared years earlier" (National Commission, p. 46). But as has been made clear in the reports and accounts post–9/11, information does not readily translate into knowledge. So-called warning signs may only reveal themselves as warnings in hindsight.

In their study of terrorism insurance, Cummins and Lewis (2003) note that the failure to imagine is evident in that terrorist attacks were seen as a possible risk of doing business overseas, but terrorist events were not part of the realm of possibility in North America. To use insurance terms, the North American terrorist event generated significant *parameter uncertainty*, or event-induced uncertainty, applicable to the social world more generally. The cause of parameter uncertainty, however, is that a terrorist event such as 9/11 was simply not believed possible—it was outside the events set of those both inside and outside of positions of authority and therefore not imagined in the calculation of risk balance. As Viscusi and Zeckhauser (2003) observe, "much of the uncertainty created by the event is the realization that the events set that we previously thought was possible was incomplete and that the future may contain many other severely adverse events that are currently unanticipated" (p. 100). If an event is unimaginable, the event can scarcely be prepared for, a lament repeated by the police in London when confronted with the unanticipated acts of suicide bombers.

The "9/11 Commission Report" details the grim reality that the information transmitted to decisionmakers took some time to process. Even when transponders were turned off and aircraft disappeared out of radar range it was perceived as an extreme mechanical failure or, possibly, a hijacking in the traditional sense. The North American Aerospace Defense Command (NORAD), for example, apparently perceived that threats to security would come from outside the country. After all, NORAD was a response to the cold war between the former Soviet Union and the United States. "The threat of terrorists hijacking commercial airliners within the United States—and using them as guided missiles—was not recognized by NORAD before 9/11" (National Commission, 2004, p. 17). Furthermore, the Federal Aviation Administration (FAA) had no training policy that might have dealt even remotely with the situation as it unfolded that morning. While trained to deal with hijacking situations, the FAA presumed that hijacked aircraft "would be readily identifiable and would not attempt to disappear" (National Commission, p. 18) contrasting markedly with the experience that morning, when the planes in question radically departed from their flight paths and three of four planes had their transponders turned off. It was also presumed that a hijacking event would be accompanied by enough time to ensure that communication protocols between the FAA and NORAD could be followed. In the case of the first aircraft under siege, there was only 32 minutes between the first signs of trouble and the aircraft hitting the World Trade Center. The final presumption was that the hijacking would take a more traditional form—"that is, it would not be a suicide hijacking designed to convert aircraft into a guided missile" (National Commission, p. 18). Again, this presumption proved terribly wrong. Clearly, the experts, let alone the public, did not perceive vulnerability in terms of this kind of event nor were they prepared, despite the information that they had in their possession (which, perhaps only in retrospect, seemingly foreshadows the impending disaster). The summary of the first chapter of the "9/11 Commission Report" concludes,

> NORAD and the FAA were unprepared for the type of attacks launched against the United States on September 11, 2001. Under difficult circumstances, they struggled to improvise a homeland defense against an unprecedented challenge they had never before encountered and had never been trained to meet. (National Commission, 2004, p. 45)

The Report goes on to note, however, that these events were predated by information that clearly spelled out terrorist threat. Nevertheless, an event has to first be imagined before it can be prepared for.

Dealing With Vulnerability

Registering threat is dependent on, at the very least, acknowledging vulnerability. In his discussion of vulnerability, Mitchell (2003) explains that vulnerability is the "human capacity for responding to loss as well as the potential for experiencing loss" (p. 61). Individuals, institutions, and states differ in terms of vulnerability, with different factors and processes playing into vulnerability at each of these levels, as well as between individuals and among institutions and states. Not all individuals are equally vulnerable, nor do the same factors contribute equally to individual variability; these are points we discussed in our review of heuristics and mental shortcuts in Chapter 2, this volume. Vulnerability to terrorist threat, for instance, may

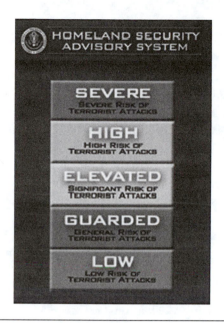

Figure 4.1   The Homeland Security Advisory System

be greater for those in crowded urban centers than for those in sparsely populated rural areas. Similarly, individuals in urban areas may be differentially vulnerable to terrorist threat because of variations in education, wealth, demographics, status, and power: some may be able to fend off certain attacks because of being able to afford protective gear, such as hazmat suits. The same goes for institutions, ranging from families to markets and public institutions. Not all institutions are equally vulnerable to particular terrorist threats. Institutions that provide critical infrastructure capacity may be more vulnerable to terrorist attack than institutions that are less critical to everyday societal operations.

Although the processes that contribute to vulnerability are wide ranging, Mitchell (2003) argues that the greatest opportunity for reducing vulnerability is found in "changing knowledge, behavior and societal impediments to protective action" (p. 62). Mitchell's suggestions for improving information include the following: (1) identification of vulnerability and vulnerability-producing mechanisms; (2) raising awareness of vulnerability; and (3) providing vulnerable populations with accurate information (p. 62). What is critical to Mitchell's explanation is that vulnerability is not a given, it is not "a hidden state of passive fragility that has just recently been rendered visible by unforeseen events" (p. 64). Rather, vulnerability is a process that is subject to revision and is not a concept that applies simply to "things," such as critical infrastructures, including airports, bus terminals, and power systems, but it is also, as we pointed out earlier, a social construction that is pervious to "emotions, symbolism, ideas and values" (p. 66). Referencing the newly created Department of Homeland Security in particular,[6] Mitchell suggests that security strategists must take into account the "expansive dimensions of socially constructed vulnerabilities" (p. 66). Vulnerability to terrorist threat ultimately varies between individual and institutional levels, and among individuals and institutions.

In the sections that follow, we build on Mitchell's insights with respect to the four parameters he has identified, using specific examples from the U.S. Department of Homeland Security as illustrative of the multiple dimensions (and multiplicity) of security from terrorist threat.

Identification of Vulnerability and Vulnerability-Producing Mechanisms

Since 9/11, terrorism has been presented as the most pressing threat to American security. Given the emphasis on airport and aircraft security, it might also seem as though the major terrorist threat stems from air traffic–related sources, as well as borders and the infiltration of others into the homeland. Furthermore, one might consider that the focus on air travel has made Americans less vulnerable to this realm of terrorist attack than previously.

Given experiences around the globe, it is clear that terrorism threat is real but that it constitutes only one part of an overall set of harms that we face in society. The most difficult challenge going forward will be to manage all of these dangers making decisions about priorities for response, reflecting our matrix of values, choices, and resources. Politicians and public policy planners need to be ready to deal with the dangers posed by hurricanes and public health problems, while maintaining vigilance against terrorists. Sometimes, this balancing act might require allocating more resources to certain types of terrorist threats over others. But, in doing this, planners confront the real dangers of the public's scorn from lack of preparedness, as demonstrated most clearly in the aftermath of 9/11. Critics of the current plans related to terrorist response (for example, Ripley & Frank, 2004; Johnston, Schmitt, Sanger, Stevenson, & Weisman, 2004; Greider, 2004; Mueller, 2006) draw attention to how it is that terrorist threat, or perceived terrorist threat, is diverting both money and attention away from more pressing vulnerabilities, a point underscored by the apparent lack of preparedness in dealing with the ravages of Hurricane Katrina. These authors worry that the funding currently funneled toward counterterrorist measures is drawing money away from areas where funding is clearly lacking, but also where increased funding would reduce vulnerabilities, especially in the realms of health and education. As Greider observes,

> wasting money on faddish concerns is not the worst outcome. I would go further and assert that the 'war on terrorism' itself will produce random injury and death—inadvertently, of course—because the spending will deform and undermine the country's other priorities. (p. 16)

This is not a debate that is going to be easily resolved; it reflects the constant struggle that we face as a society in establishing risk balance.

A great deal of money has been provided for technological innovations in the pursuit of reducing vulnerability to terrorist threat. Mitchell (2003) elaborates on the attraction of the government to technological fixes, such as the development of protective equipment, chemical and biological detection systems, protection of databases, identification systems, and so on. The significance of this orientation is that it provides "greatly expanded opportunities to secure lucrative contracts for research, development, production, installation and operation of new technology systems" (p. 67). The identification and determination of vulnerability is therefore propelled by technological expertise. Similarly, establishing power is also a product of technological expertise. Flying passenger planes into the World Trade Center capitalized on media technology in New York City and brought the event to worldwide attention, even as it was happening. The images have been played and replayed. Technology not only facilitated the exposure of this event to the world community, but it also played a role in masterminding and carrying out this event. We similarly saw the use of technology in the home videos of the Beslan hostage-taking aired on public television, which were apparently produced by the terrorists themselves and provided to the media. The provision of such information to the public plays a central role in perceptions of security with respect to terrorist attack, as well as perceived threats to national security (both internally and externally).

The difficulty with technological identification of and response to threat is the assumption that there is a straightforward relationship between the causes of terrorism and its outcome, and that vulnerability to terrorism can be reduced by the use of such technologies. Technological answers to social threats seem to have found a comfortable home in the realm of security against terrorism. The factors that contribute to and affect terrorism vulnerability may, in fact, be separate (in time and space) from their outcomes. In other words, it is not always possible to suggest that a certain event or cluster of events can be definitively attributed to a particular outcome; there is often a great deal of distance between the cause of a terrorist event and the outcome (Lum, Kennedy, & Sherley, 2006). Similarly, threats may remain relatively constant as background features, without necessarily being realized as a discrete event. This is counter to the assumptions that appear to be made with technological fixes, which suggests that technological fixes can somehow immediately circumvent factors that may have been years in the making. In addition, rather than focusing on the wide array of factors that contribute to terrorist threat, technological fixes ignore the social dynamics that play a role in creating vulnerability to terrorism, such as national and international foreign and immigration policies. The identification of vulnerability to terrorism therefore requires a strategy that investigates a wider range of influences, and does not simply limit the investigation to elements that are most amenable to technological solutions.

Notwithstanding this caution, the advances in certain types of technological innovations have helped in deterring and responding to terrorism. The failures of communication devices during the 9/11 attacks have been central to improving police and emergency response communications. During the London attacks, the police radios worked and facilitated the quick response and rescue of victims, even though cell phone technology was overwhelmed and effectively failed to function during the crisis. In the response phase, closed-circuit television in buses and trains proved to be an essential tool in reconstructing the events and identifying perpetrators. This became particularly important in the pursuit of the offenders in the second set of failed attacks. The offenders were quickly rounded up and arrested before they could either disperse or regroup and attack again.

The attention and funding applied to particular forms of terrorist threat may not significantly alter our vulnerability to terrorist threat. For instance, measures that address personal safety in the home may not be realistic in the face of an actual terrorist event. Arguments about the effectiveness of these measures in addressing the public's fears about exposure also challenge whether this form of information increases perceptions of security, or underlines perceptions of insecurity. A major criticism of the Ready Campaign, for example, a public awareness effort by the U.S. Department of Homeland Security, is that there has been a misidentification of vulnerabilities.

Advice is provided to the public with respect to securing homes against possible terrorist attack, with directives ranging from stocking food, water, and batteries, to behavioral guidelines in case of a chemical attack. One of the most significant findings of workshops held in 2002 by Partnership for Public Warning (PPW) was that the Homeland Security Advisory System (HSAS) served as little more than "America's mood ring," failing to provide any specific information that would be useful to reduce potential harm (PPW, 2004). As the editors at the *New Republic* point out, "it's not homes we need to worry about most. According to counter terrorism experts and past history, terrorists target densely crowded urban areas—subways, office buildings, malls and other places where people won't have flashlights and Poland Spring at hand" (*New Republic*, 2003). The attention paid to unlikely targets potentially results in greater exposure to terrorist activity of other less-protected venues, such as train stations. The 2004 bombings of commuter trains in Spain and 2005 London bombings should suggest that the apparent lack of attention to these venues in North America, often in favor of airports and targets of biochemical threat, may have increased rather than reduced vulnerability in certain venues, although this situation is rapidly changing with new initiatives introduced by transit agencies in major U.S. cities.

The difficulties in identifying vulnerability, specifically exposure to terrorism, are large and are complicated by the reality that vulnerabilities emerge over space and time. In determinations of vulnerability, the notion of risk figures prominently. In their examination of the formula for funds for terrorist reduction across the United States, Ripley and Frank (2004) explain that each state was allowed a certain minimum funding level. However, the minimum funding level means that states with greater risk of terrorist threat, based on factors such as population density, infrastructure, and so on, may be inadequately funded in comparison to states characterized by less vulnerability. The arguments that the overfunded states have made is that relative worth is as important as relative vulnerability as the primary consideration with respect to funding. Seemingly less exposed states argue that, "'our citizens deserve the same kind of protection that they're afforded in other places in the country'" (Ripley & Frank, p. 36). Vulnerability depends in large part on social factors that technology, for example, cannot begin to address.

Vulnerability-producing mechanisms involve factors having to do with choice, on the one hand, and coercion, on the other. The relationship between the individual and collective realms complicates the notions of choice and coercion. What becomes critical is the extent to which individual rights are sacrificed in the name of collective security, or collective security in the name of individual rights. According to Seligman (1998), the core of civil society is the relationship between the "private and the public, the individual and the social, of public ethics and individual interests, individual passions and public concerns." The question of civil society is how "individual interests [can] be pursued in the social arena and, similarly, the social good in the individual or private sphere" (p. 29). Is collective security and individual freedom a zero-sum game? Among others (e.g., Wells, 1999), Short (1984) suggests that individual and institutional security and vulnerability are intertwined. As Wells notes, "risk is privatized and becomes a matter for individual judgment. This brings a tension, because individual situations are, of course, also institutional: 'the liberated individual is dependent on a series of secondary agencies and institutes.' This tension between the individual aspects of risk decisions and determinations of risk by social institutions produces profound and troubling issues of trust, accountability and personal responsibility" (p. 8). These issues figure prominently as we turn our discussion to the matter of global risk.

Supply chains. The demand created by globalization has opened doors to markets and regions once considered closed. China, for example, whose borders were previously impenetrable to Western investment, has begun to entertain the possibility of allowing such investment in, just as the rest of the global market has begun to negotiate with Chinese investors. Yet it is not only in terms of new markets that globalization has created vulnerabilities. Globalization has also created permeability in the boundaries between public and private industry. Business and trade partnerships in a global world undermine distinctions between national and international trade, but distinctions between public and private business are also undermined in a global setting. Rather than being seen as separate or even parallel entities, globalization has forced interconnections and partnerships—permeability—between national and international entities and between private and public industry. For corporations that are large enough, permeability and interconnections may be somewhat offset by a process known as vertical integration, defined as buying particular parts of the production process so that a company may control lengths of the supply chain or even the entire supply chain, from production to retailing. Alternatively, parts of the supply chain may be controlled by partnering with one or another company to integrate processes.

While various nodes (partnerships and integrations) exist that control large parts of particular supply chains, even these must eventually face the reality of commerce in a post–9/11 world. The reality of trading, at least of trading with the United States and many of its allies, is that each link of the supply chain must be secured against terrorism. For example, the U.S. Customs and Border Protection have developed a program entitled Customs-Trade Partnership Against Terrorism (C-TPAT). Hailed as a partnership between government and private industry, the program is geared to "protecting America and the global supply chain while moving commerce across our borders even more efficiently—more efficiently than before 9/11" (C-TPAT, 2004, p. 2). C-TPAT's primary goal is to secure supply chains in accordance with C-TPAT criteria—partnership, efficiency, and security. The idea is that local as well as international partners who have agreed to C-TPAT criteria are responsible for the implementation of specific security criteria and agree to submit themselves to intense scrutiny to "validate that supply chain security meets C-TPAT minimum security criteria and best practices and that procedures used are reliable, accurate, effective and meet the agreed upon security standards" (C-TPAT, p. 8). Although membership in C-TPAT is now voluntary, the advantages to becoming a member are clear: trade with a major global partner, the United States, is facilitated. Failing to become a C-TPAT partner will no doubt result in economic hardship, as supply chains will be beset with cumbersome security criteria through which membership helps to navigate.

Various forms of power can be realized in securing the supply chain, at the same time that weaknesses are exposed. Those who participate in programs such as C-TPAT, for example, are promised efficiency and expeditious trade with the United States. Participation, however, requires exposure to a centralized authority: the program demands particular information from its partners and requires adherence to predefined best practices along with inspections and validations that specific security criteria are being met. The independence of trade and movement that globalization heralded is overlaid by the quest for security embodied in programs such as C-TPAT. On the one hand, this may not be a bad thing, because experts on terrorism maintain that supply chains are sources of huge vulnerability. Efforts to bolster overall supply chain security therefore make sense. On the other hand, vulnerability to terrorism, which may actually be a remote threat, especially for some U.S. trade partners, may be traded for vulnerability to a centralized authority—the United States government—in the case of C-TPAT.

Support for C-TPAT has been mixed. Clearly, it is to the advantage of businesses worldwide to be able to secure their goods against outside threats. As one corporate executive notes, "our business would be finished"

Figure 4.2   Ocean Links of the Supply Chain

if one of their corporation's product containers was found to inadvertently house explosives planted by terrorist factions (anonymous, personal communication, 2005). On the other hand, there are huge expenses associated with the program and delays in bringing procedures up to the standards of the program's best practices. The costs and delays incurred are also undertaken in a situation where it is difficult to say with any certainty that terrorist threats will ever be realized or, perhaps worse yet, prevented. Participation in such programs is therefore undertaken on the basis of fear— fear of terrorism, and fear of being left out of the marketplace because of failing to conform to these new standards. Membership is also likely to move from voluntary to compulsory if businesses expect to be able to maintain their market share.

Despite some reservations, the C-TPAT program seems to address the fundamental tenets of institutionally based risk balance. This is not a conventional program of risk assessment, but is rather an integrated system that matches security costs against risk, keeping in mind the values that promote commerce to flow quickly through the supply chain. All partners in this program understand that something needs to be offered to enhance security, which is the reward of expedited movement of goods coming from this exchange.

Raising Awareness of Vulnerability

> Secrecy and centralization are useful watchwords in a conventional war. In this shadowy new one, it is citizens who are going to have to calculate the odds, both individually, as they decide what risks to run in the quotidian decisions of life—whether to take the bus or tube, say—and collectively, as they decide how much a society should be willing to sacrifice in order to secure itself against new dangers . . . if the war against terrorism is going to last for years, governments need to mobilize their people. The way to do that is to treat them as adults and give them as much information as possible without compromising sources of intelligence—even if this does cause a few sleepless nights. (*Economist*, 2002, p. 11)

Individuals and institutions differ markedly in terms of their vulnerability to particular terrorist threats, and vulnerability does not remain constant for any particular individual or institution. Mitchell (2003) explains that commuters, for example, are located in different regions, with different schedules and different destinations. Times and places are characterized by different levels of vulnerability, but vulnerability also varies with knowledge about threats, as well as the "degree to which [individuals] can avail themselves of protective resources; their access to alternatives, and the willingness of society to facilitate different choices" (Mitchell, p. 65), in particular, about where one lives and works. Every individual is also subject to the vulnerabilities that distinguish his or her membership in particular social categories. Awareness of vulnerability and the ability to calculate risk balance, requires that unique circumstances are taken into consideration. Individuals are not equally exposed to terrorist threat, nor are institutions equally exposed.

Awareness of vulnerability requires specific information—not only with respect to particular threats, but also with regard to the variations among individuals and institutions to which such information is directed. Global warning systems about broad-based threats may do little to heighten awareness. Individuals or institutions may not see themselves as facing threat due to the assortment of other factors that characterize their particular circumstances. The problems with distributing information regarding terrorist threats to individuals and institutions are the same as the problems that prevail with crime warnings: individuals may not see themselves as being those to whom particular messages are targeted.

Further complicating the issue of vulnerability, individuals and institutions operate at much different levels of abstraction. On the one hand, individual concerns are circumscribed in time and space. In any particular situation, as the availability heuristic predicts, individuals assess elements within an immediate temporal and spatial proximity and make judgments about security based on these assessments. On the other hand, an institution's time and space is less circumscribed with institutional assessments of security going well beyond the immediate situation. General warnings are better suited to the less circumscribed context of institutions, while the circumscribed contexts of most individuals require specific directives in order to have meaning.

The issues of liability and responsibility also figure into any advisory system. Given the difficulties faced in terms of defining specific terrorist threat along with the recognition that there are differences in vulnerability (for example, between institution's and individuals, as well as between geographic regions), the HSAS can be said to be doing its job by virtue of the fact that the system draws attention to and creates an awareness of terrorist threat. It could be suggested that because the HSAS applies to all Americans, including those at different levels of government and private enterprise, the existence of the warning system itself reduces state liability should terrorist threat ever be realized. The HSAS implies that a "no threat" condition does not exist. Rather, the scale bottoms out at "low threat." The threat of terrorism is therefore construed as ever-present. A *Washington Post* article in 2003 posed a similar question: "What would a green day look like?" ("How green was our warning?", 2003). If the threat of terrorism is omnipresent, Americans already operate in a heightened state of awareness because terrorism is always on the radar, thanks to the existence of both the Department of Homeland Security itself and the HSAS. In other words, Americans, by virtue of being American, already perceive (or should perceive) a general threat of terrorism. The DHS can therefore not be held as responsible or liable for future negative occurrences because of failing to issue warnings to Americans who are already in effect warned by their status as American. This argument should sound familiar: As we discussed in Chapter 3, this volume, the Toronto Police Service argued that women do not need specific warnings about rapists as they are already prewarned of the danger by virtue of being women.

The liability and responsibility issue could be managed far more effectively with a greater emphasis on a bottom-up approach to vulnerability. Mitchell (2003) promotes the participation of lay populations in the determination of vulnerability, rather than simply leaving the issue in the hands of federal experts who may be unaware of local circumstances. Local participation would facilitate individuals and institutions being more likely to sensibly address their own vulnerabilities. Furthermore, issues of vulnerability may be wrested from experts and other groups who might be forwarding their own agendas, and might instead engage a broader section of the population. "Such a strategy requires a far greater level of shared knowledge about terrorism threats and vulnerabilities— and an openness to voluntary lay inputs—than presently exists" (Mitchell, p. 68). PPW suggests that existing emergency plans and practices need to be taken into account: effective plans start at the local incident level, rather than from the top down (PPW, 2004). This strategy may also help to define threats in communities where the dangers may come from within. The delicate job of communicating with the Muslim communities in England, for example, from which the bombing suspects emerged, highlights the problems of information gathering and risk assessment. For these communities which fall victim both to the bombers' actions and authority's reactions to these attacks, it is vitally important that they find a way to communicate known threats to those empowered to prevent or deter these actions.

Providing Vulnerable Populations With Accurate Information

Terrorism, as defined in the FEMA (2004a) publication "Are You Ready?" is

> the use of force or violence against persons or property in violation of
> the criminal laws of the United States for purposes of intimidation, coer-
> cion or ransom. Terrorists often use threats to: create fear among the
> public; try to convince citizens that their government is powerless to pre-
> vent terrorism; get immediate publicity for their causes. Acts of terror-
> ism include *threats of terrorism; assassinations; kidnappings; hijackings;*
> *bomb scares and bombings; cyber attacks (computer-based) and the use*
> *of chemical, biological, nuclear and radiological weapons* [italics added].
> High-risk targets for acts of terrorism include military and civilian gov-
> ernment facilities, international airports, large cities, and high-profile
> landmarks. Terrorists might also target large public gatherings, water
> and food supplies, utilities, and corporate centers. Further, terrorists are
> capable of spreading fear by sending explosives or chemical and biolog-
> ical agents through the mail. Within the immediate area of a terrorist
> event, you would need to rely on police, fire and other officials for
> instructions. *However, you can prepare in much the same way you*
> *would prepare for other crisis events* [italics added]. (p. 148)

According to the Department of Homeland Security, preparing for a
terrorist event would mean embracing the protective measures as specified
by the HSAS. The government further advises in its "Ready" campaign,
"We can be afraid. Or, we can be ready" (Department of Homeland
Security, n.d.). Being ready is different from being afraid, but both readiness
and fear may have as their basis information or the lack thereof. The above
definition of terrorism suggests that not only are the types of possible terrorist activity broad, but so too are the types of measures that might be used
to prepare for such an attack. Furthermore, the measures that individuals
may take will diverge substantially from the measures that an airport
authority may take. The "Ready" campaign provides partial advice to individuals with respect to unlikely scenarios. For example, the directives that in
the event of a chemical attack individuals should get away and then wash
with soap provides limited information. Getting away, for example, is not
good enough (one has to move upwind, not downwind). Practical advice on
the more likely scenario of having to navigate mob behavior and avoid
getting trampled is not available.

As noted above, the "Ready" campaign defines terrorism as threats of terrorism, assassinations, kidnappings, hijackings, bomb scares and bombings, computer-based cyber attacks, as well as the use of chemical, biological, and nuclear weapons. Despite the circularity in defining terrorism as threats of terrorism, the remaining activities included in the definition of terrorism are wide ranging—assassinations to chemical weapons. Chemical weapons, as the anthrax scare a few years ago suggested, may come in the form of anthrax-laced envelopes. As Harpham (2002) notes, this type of letter does not, in fact, have to reach "its destination in order to communicate itself: we are all the proper, but horribly improper destinations of its ghastly message" (p. 574). The types of precautionary measures that might be taken in response to terrorist threats are therefore vast, and require vigilance in response to many possible events.

The nature of the threat to which citizens are to respond—terrorism—is too wide ranging and nonspecific to allow for concrete action that must be specific to be meaningful. The conditions do not specify what type of terrorist activity should be on the collective radar, but instead simply suggest that the risk of nonspecific terrorist attack is more or less severe. The determination of threat level also raises the issue of transparency. It is not clear what kind of information informs the determination of danger levels, and what kind of information might tip the scales in favor of either lower or greater levels. What information does government have that warrants the determination of a yellow versus an orange threat level, for example? Do calculated probabilities of realizing certain perils substantially increase or decrease between levels? As has been noted by the Partnership for Public Warning (2004), "public credibility will be significantly enhanced if there is a well described and understood process for changing the threat level and releasing information" (p. 5).

Much of what we believe in and maintain to be true about terrorism is not the product of direct experience, but is rather the result of limited information uncritically gleaned from and provided by experts and expert systems. The experts identify threat and the citizenry is asked to follow their directions. Most of us have no information from direct experience about terrorist activity that would enable us to make a decision contrary to these directives. For example, American citizens trust, or at least are being asked to trust, the experts—in this case, the Department of Homeland Security and the president—to accurately identify harms. The citizens expect that experts will not only respond to such threats, but will also provide information needed in the face of such threats.

American citizens are told that the Department of Homeland Security establishes threat levels based on four questions: (1) Is the threat credible? (2) Is the threat corroborated? (3) Is the threat specific and/or imminent? (4) How grave is the threat? While citizens may be aware of the questions the HSAS has used in determining threat levels, the answers to these questions are unknown. What, for example, makes a threat credible versus incredible? Is a threat more or less credible depending on the corroboration associated with it? Are dates and times attached to specific threats? Is assessment of gravity based on possible loss of life, or possible monetary damage? What is important about these questions is that there is no procedure or forum for questions to be asked and answered. This absence of information again centers on the issue of trust. First, the HSAS is clearly a top-down system—the Department of Homeland Security provides the information, and those further down the line receive it. Little attempt has been made to involve citizens in the HSAS; therefore their concerns are not likely to be addressed. Second, while the apparent expectation of the Department of Homeland Security is that the recipients of the HSAS information will simply trust the information put forth, trust may be a one-way street. While much information used to determine threat levels is classified, the process by which threat is assessed is obscure and does little to bolster the public's trust.

The provision of information in the face of terrorist threat is further complicated by the varying demands for information on those in possession of it. In addition, as we suggested earlier, there are complications with respect to what counts as information. Imagination becomes critical to identifying the signs in front of us. As the "9/11 Commission Report" (National Commission, 2004) also makes evident, the management of information— what to do with the information once it becomes available—is critical. Beyond management, issues surrounded determination of responsibility: Who should be responsible for the identification of and subsequent action taken with respect to responding to information? Who is responsible for the relevance and pertinence of information? General information is useless in the face of specific threats (Greider, 2004; Bobbitt, 2004).

The rationale behind the provision of information (or lack thereof) from those in the know is often premised on the argument that warning systems need to strike a balance between increasing awareness and causing panic.[7] As Bobbitt (2004) points out, however, the time when citizens were able to "trust their leaders to decide when, from a strategic point of view, information could be safely released" (p. A19) is now over:

On the one hand, no official wants to neglect giving a warning to the public that might save lives; on the other, such action awards the terrorists a costless if minor victory by terrorizing the population and using government channels to do it. If officials then try to minimize the impact of the warning with suggestions that the public go about its business as usual, they dilute the effectiveness of the announcement and encourage a complacency that they were trying to pierce in the first place. (Bobbitt, p. A19)

Bobbitt (2004) suggests that the answer to this apparent conundrum is to differentiate between informing, alerting, and warning. He suggests that informing would amount to simply putting into the public domain as much information as possible "without compromising intelligence sources and countermeasures" (Bobbitt, p. A19) Alerting, on the other hand, would be directed to specific public officials or infrastructure specialists who would take necessary precautions based on specific information. Finally, warnings would include cautioning the public at large with respect to specific threats coupled with specific advice that can be acted on. The gist of this differentiation is more than semantic: general warnings cannot be issued for specific threats. Warning systems must be specific if they are to make a difference in terms of public protection. Information that is specific will allow for better management of space and time. General information may do nothing other than heighten anxiety, or worse, fail to protect either individuals or institutions in meaningful ways.

Readiness and Response

If, as Hunt (1999) notes, "anxiety is a general feature of the human condition it is important to consider under what conditions anxieties manifest themselves in overt social action" (p. 514).[8] When fear and anxiety are viewed as social costs, there is motivation at both the individual and institutional levels to reduce it. It is critical to get back to normal in order to reduce anxiety; returning to normal also may work to enhance the policies that government puts in place to reduce threats. In a context of fear and anxiety, as Keohane and Zeckhauser (2003) observe, individual responses to collective threats may undermine the effectiveness of policies that are meant to reduce those threats. For example, the call to hypervigilance may generate a raft of meaningless leads, with suspicion taking precedence over evidence.

Anarumo, in research completed in 2005, examined the views that U.S. local law enforcement officials shared concerning the imminent threat of terrorism. He conducted a nationwide survey of police leaders and asked what they viewed as immediate dangers, the extent to which their agencies were prepared for these incidents, and the likelihood of being able to prevent them from happening. The groups that were considered imminent dangers ranged from environmental groups to international terrorists. In the minds of the police, the most serious threat radiated from the actions of domestic terrorists. These groups had acted in the past and, it was felt, they would strike again soon. Interestingly, the police responses about who to fear varied by region of the country, with threats from environmental groups appearing in the West and threats from antiabortion groups and international terror groups appearing in the East.

As for preparedness, the police indicated that they felt that their agencies were not as fully prepared, in terms of training or equipment, for a major disaster as they should be, although this varied by size of agency and by the type of threat. Their concerns also included knowledge of what they needed to do to prepare for these incidents. The implications of this research are that there is no single global threat that the police fear; rather, there are distinctly different threats depending on local experience and opportunity. Weighing out the risk balance for local agencies depends a great deal on the extent to which these agencies are able to take these local conditions into account in their planning and preparations. We will return to these themes in Chapter 6, this volume, where we discuss prevention and preparedness.

Conclusion

Attempting to find ways to reduce the possibility of future terrorist attacks is a rational course of action. Certainly, every effort must be undertaken to ensure that these types of events will not happen. At the same time, navigating a course through the multitude of factors and issues identified above is a challenge of major proportions. Despite these challenges, more fruitful avenues in the quest for security against terrorism can be explored and would contribute to preventing similar occurrences.

First, emphasizing the notion of terrorism, rather than concentrating on terrorist activity, would help to avoid the difficulties associated with reification, and the focus on ever more particular components of potential terrorist threat. By focusing on the range of activities and behaviors comprising the category of terrorist activity, a shallow approach is traded for an approach that may go farther to reduce the likelihood of terrorism. Rather than simply asking "how," a more useful avenue of enquiry would be to use a deep focus on "why" such events occur in the first place. One implication of focusing on terrorist activity rather than on terrorism is the tendency to seek answers through technological advances. Instead of seeking social answers to terrorism and asking the difficult questions about the relationships of various nations to each other, the impact of Western globalization, the significance of cultural differences, the implications of foreign policy, or the relationships of various groups to each other within nations, and so on, an exclusive focus on terrorist activity instead leads us down the garden path of high-tech responses. Mitchell (2003) suggests that focusing on technology to reduce terrorist threat and to prevent or minimize damage simply misses the point. Rather than developing and supporting technology that proposes to identify potential terrorists through computerized assessments of gaits, for example, as the Information Awareness Office's Terrorism Information Awareness Program proposes, we would do better to take seriously the more difficult social questions that are central to understanding and ultimately preventing future terrorist events. As Mitchell notes, it is much harder to assess and change ideas and behaviors than to develop technological efforts, but the former efforts are more likely to prevent terrorist acts.

Second, governments must give careful consideration to their positions as knowledge brokers. Just as we do not necessarily expect the police to be able to prevent crime, it may also be unreasonable for the government to eliminate terrorist activity. Rather, we expect that the police—and the state—will act as knowledge brokers, and will provide us with information that we can use to protect ourselves. Information that can be effectively used by individuals is absolutely necessary: general protective measures do not provide individuals with information that can be usefully employed against specific threats. There are difficulties associated with issuing general warnings against a range of terrorist threats, at the same that there may be difficulties associated with issuing specific warnings. Issuing general warnings against specific threats not only amounts to a dummy down process, but also reflects a lack of trust in the citizenry to act responsibly with specific knowledge. Although warnings that are too specific may potentially increase vulnerabilities in other respects, warnings that are too general increase the likelihood of apathy and noncompliance. A business as usual message along with heightened threat levels provides little guidance and begins to undermine expert credibility.

There is little doubt that assessment of terrorist threat is fraught with murkiness. Tom Ridge, formerly the secretary of the Department of Homeland Security, is quite right when he suggests, for example, "We have to be right several thousand times a day. The terrorist only has to be right once" (OnLine NewsHour, 2003). And yet, this view assumes that the terrorist threat is constant and discernable. The difficulty with the information that governments possess is determining whether security is enhanced or undermined by divulging information. As it now stands, the state must straddle an untenable position in terms of trust relationships—ensuring safety at the same time providing little or no information to those whom it is expected will simply trust the government. There is a level of moral responsibility borne by those who are asking to be trusted. Trust without responsibility is like asking the citizenry to have faith—a request that wears thin in the face of elevated levels of fear and anxiety. At the same time, while the American public could be described as generally lacking trust in their government, there is also a deep-seated faith in all things American (HarrisInteractive, 2005). Perhaps paradoxically, there is also a belief that democratic governments will act in the best interests of the citizens of their countries. Not only is there moral responsibility, but there is also tangible liability. Who is responsible for preventing terrorism? From a legal perspective, the more information provided to the public, the less liable the state is. As with crime and health prevention, the onus lies with the consumer or potential victim.

Just as regions within countries may vary in terms of vulnerability, so too is there variation in global vulnerability to terrorism. Although terrorism is a relatively new concern to North Americans, other regions of the world have learned to deal with terrorist threat for some time. Perhaps the response of Londoners to the events of 7/7 is demonstrative. Rather than becoming immobilized, the day after the bombings Londoners were making their way back to work, even riding the public transportation system. Similarly, in Israel, the damage due to terrorist attacks tends to be cleared within hours. How is it that certain regions of the world have come to terms with terrorism, and built this possibility into everyday life? Is the terrorist threat that the United States faces so different from the terrorist threats that, for example, Britain, Northern Ireland, or Israel face? Considering how other countries have responded to terrorism may not only help to forge a working relationship between the state and its citizenry, but it may also help to reveal common ground among the international citizenry, especially in terms of the categories of the haves and have nots, and to work toward balancing the threat of terrorism with the present reality of everyday life.[9]

Notes to Chapter 4

1. The death toll in the London attacks stands at 56, of whom 52 were civilians and four were suicide bombers.

2. For example, in the seven months prior to the Beslan attack, Russia had experienced at least seven terrorist incidents. In February 2004, a female suicide bomber blew up a Moscow subway car, killing 41 morning commuters. In May 2004, a bomb planted in a stadium grandstand killed Chechnya's president as he watched a Victory Day parade. The next month, insurgents stole uniforms of the local police in order to seize the capital of the Ingushetia region and opened fire on actual police officers who believed they were running to the aid of their uniformed colleagues. Nearly 100 were killed in this incident. On August 21, 2004, a similar raid was carried out in Grozny, leaving 22 people dead. On August 24, 2004, Chechen women suicide bombers blew two passenger airliners out of the sky with bombs strapped to their bodies, killing 90. A week after that, another woman suicide bomber targeted a subway station in Moscow. Ten people died. Within hours, the Beslan attack began, ultimately killing 331 people, 187 of whom were children.

3. From the MIPT Terrorism Knowledge Base Web site (www.terrorism knowledgebase.com/Faqs.jsp#who_is_MIPT): "The National Memorial Institute for the Prevention of Terrorism (MIPT) is a non-profit institution dedicated to deterring and preventing terrorism on U.S. soil or mitigating its effects. MIPT was established after the April 1995 bombing of the Murrah Federal Building in Oklahoma City and is funded through the Department of Homeland Security's Office of Grants and Training (G&T). MIPT actively supports emergency responders from around the country in an effort to honor those who performed so bravely in Oklahoma City."

4. Only the detonators actually exploded, and no one was hurt.

5. As Faist notes, efforts to control immigrants have had the effect of making them even more visible as aliens. The increased visibility is used by some to suggest that even tighter controls are warranted.

6. On March 12, 2002, assistant to the president (who was to become Secretary) of the Department of Homeland Security Tom Ridge announced the formation of the HSAS. It was claimed that the system would "provide a comprehensive and effective means to disseminate information regarding the risk of terrorist attacks to Federal, State, and local authorities and to the American people" (White House, 2002). The HSAS would serve as a national framework for a number of alert systems, although the primary emphasis would be to communicate the nature and degree of terrorist threats. Furthermore, the HSAS would suggest "appropriate levels of vigilance, preparedness and readiness in a series of graduated threat conditions" (White House). Associated with each threat condition would be a corresponding set of protective measures to help both government and citizens determine the actions they might take to "help counter and respond to terrorist activity" (White House).

7. This is true despite evidence to suggest that panic is only one possible response and a relatively rare one; see the discussion of Quarantelli's (1989, 2003) work in Chapter 5, this volume.

8. It is important to note that while Hunt (1999) suggests that there are differences between fear and anxiety, he maintains, as do we, that the distinction between fear and anxiety are ultimately difficult to sustain.

9. There has been important work that has studied the origins, etilogy, and spread of terrorism that can be referenced to obtain a much more detailed view of this issue. See, for example, Deflem, 2004; Hamm, 2007; Hoffman, 2006; Kushner, 2002; Riley et al., 2005; and Shields, Damphousse and Smith, 2006.

5

Landscapes of Security

Health and the Environment

The Physical Landscape: Health

> Severe acute respiratory syndrome (SARS) was first recognized in
> Toronto in a woman who returned from Hong Kong on February 23,
> 2003. Transmission to other persons resulted subsequently in an out-
> break among 257 persons in several Greater Toronto Area (GTA) hos-
> pitals. (Wallington et al., 2003)

Characterized by pneumonia-like symptoms, severe acute respiratory syndrome (SARS) made a world tour in 2003. First detected in a farming
village in China in late 2002, the infectious disease quickly spread to a
nearby city from where it launched its journey around the world (Beck,
2004). On April 22, 2003, the World Health Organization (WHO) issued
a travel advisory recommending limited travel to Toronto, Canada. In May
2003, WHO officials reported 6,234 cases of SARS in 25 countries (Beck).
By the end of 2003, 689 deaths had occurred as a result of SARS, with 43
deaths occurring in Toronto alone.

The spread of this disease has been linked to globalization and the permeability of borders, as well as to communication failures. Attempts to learn
more about the outbreak in China were hampered by the Chinese government hiding evidence of the disease and blocking access to outside attempts
to access infected areas. Reports that the disease was under control were

Figure 5.1   SARS and Other Threats

SOURCE: www.CartoonStock.com.

coupled with doctors revealing that patients had been loaded into ambulances to wait while inspections were eventually conducted at particular hospitals. The disease could have been contained much earlier, but the fact that WHO officials did not receive accurate information undermined their ability to provide details to a global society that depends on cooperation. As Beck (2004) points out, "globalization may be what makes a worldwide epidemic possible; but lack of cooperation between governments is what makes it likely" (p. 65). Global communication systems such as WHO are only as good as the information on which they rely.

The SARS story provides a useful vignette for introducing security as it relates to health. First, there is the intersection of individual health concerns and how those concerns may be undermined by actions at the national and international levels. Second, jurisdictional questions arise with respect to who is held accountable for spillover effects which are the result of decisions (causes) far removed from disease outbreaks (effects). Can threats to health security in a global society really be contained within a particular setting? Third, SARS illustrates the political brakes and accelerators that surround health issues at both the local and global environments. These are influenced by the respective degrees of power and influence wielded at any particular level.

In the first half of this chapter, we consider the intersections of individual and institutional risk balance regarding health; the jurisdictional issues with respect to accountability and health security; and the relevance of power and influence in determinations of health and sickness. We begin our discussion of health as it relates to security by first considering what it means to be sick. If an individual or group of individuals is determined to be sick, what does that mean for the individual, for the group, and for the rest of society? Recognizing differences in resources helps to reveal how it is that sickness and health may be a matter of perspective. An individual exposed to a rare, untreatable disease will view his or her security differently than will those who see themselves as healthy; also, the ill individual's view will be much different from the views of those in charge of controlling sickness.

In Sickness and in Health

> The living body seems to be now the only thread on which the otherwise scattered and disparate episodes into which life in the fluid world has been sliced can be strung together. The mental and emotional energy once expended on the care for immortality or eternal causes now converges on the body, a solitary rock amidst quicksand. (Bauman, 2002, p. 63)

> Under the health promotion banner, the distinction between healthy and unhealthy populations totally dissolves since everyone is "at risk." (Petersen, 1996, p. 49)

The world existing outside the body consists of opportunities and hazards, simultaneously making the body the site of pleasure and of pain. As Bauman's (2002) quote suggests, a great deal of anxiety surrounds the physical body. Because the body is "a solitary rock amidst quicksand" (Bauman, p. 63), efforts are typically taken to secure the body against harms posed by the ever-changing environment. These efforts may become normalized and routine, such as going for yearly medical checkups.

The influence of actuarial thinking in the realm of health has ensured that there is no such thing as "healthy"; rather, there are degrees of healthiness, and, by default, degrees of illness. In what has been referred to as *surveillance medicine* (which is the blurring of the lines between health and illness where everyone becomes a target for potential medical intervention)

Greaves (2000) refers to *partial patients* as those who may not feel unwell, but who have been "informed medically that because of certain personal characteristics, they have or may have a disease or other medical condition or are at risk of acquiring such a disease or medical condition" (p. 23). Partial patients are the result of a process that has taken place over the course of the past century. An epidemiological transition occurred in the early 20th century that was characterized by the decline of infectious disease coupled with the rise of noncommunicable, degenerative disease, such as cancer or heart disease, as the primary causes of mortality. Greaves notes that with "this new epidemiological pattern the traditional uni-factorial model of disease gave way to the multi-factorial model" (p. 25). Rather than looking for one specific causal mechanism, this orientation widens to identify multiple risk factors. Influenced by the availability of statistical models and large data sets, statistical regression analyses paved the way for the identification of multiple factors that seek to predict disease. For example, while we may not know exactly what causes lung cancer, it has been determined that factors such as smoking contribute to the onset of this disease. Smoking may not *cause* lung cancer—some smokers never get cancer—but the probability of getting cancer increases if one smokes. A multitude of factors are therefore related to (correlated with) ill health without necessarily causing sickness: because of the range of factors related to ill health, few individuals are invulnerable, with sickness always a possibility, however remote or likely.

The impact of technology and the development of screening techniques have also meant the discovery of more and more illnesses, increasing the likelihood of finding risk factors for more diseases, but not necessarily finding more disease itself. Furthermore, this statistical modeling capacity allows for the identification of various health risk profiles so that individuals can be scored in terms of probable disease or illness acquisition. Not only the sick are profiled; rather, there is now

> the potential for every citizen to become the subject of medical attention, there being a gradient of concern from patients with identifiable diseases, through patients at high risk, medium risk and low risk of developing certain diseases in the future. (Greaves, 2000, p. 25)

The result of this gradient is that health and illness are only relative and never absolute.

The degree or gradient of illness and health has implications for monitoring the individual and his or her characteristics, as well as implications for intervention. An individual considered by his or her risk factor score to be high risk might become increasingly subject to monitoring because of that score. Such risk scores are probability scores and do not reflect the acquisition of the disease or condition under consideration. A risk profile, however, may take precedence over the more subjective component of health. Medical tests or test scores that suggest some probability of ill health has been identified may undermine individual claims to good health. Of course, in the realm of health and other realms such as crime, risk profiles often take on a life unto themselves, and scores reflecting probability may be misinterpreted as reflecting a present condition—or an identity—itself.

Jurisdiction and Spillover Effects

> The highly publicized emergence of new diseases and the re-emergence of others, combined with the increased speed and volume of international travel, have made countries aware of their vulnerability. (Heymann, 2002, p. 179)

The danger of infectious diseases such as acquired immunodeficiency syndrome (AIDS), smallpox, SARS, and bovine spongiform encephalopathy (BSE; also called "mad cow disease"; see Food and Drug Administration [FDA], 2004b) have garnered a great deal of publicity and have raised concerns that public health is not simply an individual or national issue, but rather is a global issue. Of particular note, a common feature of headline-grabbing diseases such as these is that they are contagious. As observed earlier with respect to Greaves's (2000) analysis of partial patients, it had been assumed for some time that contagious, plaguelike diseases were a thing of the past. However, as Heymann (2002) notes, the "resurgence of infectious diseases have been viewed as a factor that can undermine national and international security" (p. 179). In the new security era, noncommunicative, chronic, and degenerative diseases, despite the fact that these are potentially more deadly, are often given short shrift over contagious diseases. It seems fair to characterize chronic as the realm of the everyday, whereby those who deal with chronic pain, for example, must come to terms with their pain on a daily basis—it becomes something one has to live with—routine, in fact. Contagion is outside the everyday, however, found more often in the realm of the spectacular. While contagion may also be relatively mundane, as in the case of colds, coughs, and some forms of the flu, the types of contagion now appearing on the health-threat radar often emanate from far more exotic sources (i.e., China in the case of SARS, England in the case of mad cow disease) than the common cold. Contagion has gone global.

Contagion, a form of impurity, threatens by making boundaries vulnerable and permeable. Not only are individual bodies vulnerable, but so too is the body of the larger community. Perceptions of the body go hand in hand with perceptions of community—whether local or global. Douglas and Calvez (1990) identify four different attitudes with respect to contagion: First, the body is porous, open to invasion and unprotected. Second, the body is strong because it is able to cope with infection and is self-restoring. Third, the body is strong because of two protective layers, one consisting of the physical skin of the body that allows as well as denies access, and the other consisting of the community, which also allows and denies access by codifying acceptable behavior. Fourth, the body is a machine covered with a protective envelope, but one that requires undertaking appropriate precautionary behavior. The attitudes that one holds of the body will be influenced by one's membership in particular communities or cultural enclaves and the perceptions associated with those communities. Contagion then becomes a matter of perspective, and what to do with those who are contagious is dependent on the social and cultural understanding of victims of contagion and of the disease itself. At various times and in various settings, contagion has been dealt with through means such as quarantine, separation, or even elimination.

In his discussion of AIDS, Brandt (1987) notes that Western society has not had a great deal of experience in dealing with spectacular or contagious health issues:

> The fact that as a society we have been fortunate not to have had to address any major infectious disease on an epidemic level since polio accounts for our relative lack of social and political experience in dealing with such problems. (p. 200)

Although Brandt wrote this nearly 20 years ago, his observation applies to the 21st century. This inexperience in dealing with contagious disease has two implications:

1. A lack of experience in dealing with contagion is manifest in the application of actuarial or categorical thinking to those who have been deemed at risk of infection, or those who are at risk of infecting others. While a particular individual may not have a disease, that individual's

membership in a group deemed as risky will result in treatment as though he or she actually has the disease, rather than as simply characterized by a particular probability of acquiring the disease. Williams (2001) refers to this as epidemic stigmatization characterized by suspicion and fear of those who are thought to belong to the carrier group. Young (1996) raises a similar issue with respect to those who have AIDS, and suggests that the infection itself becomes conflated with a particular identity. In the case of AIDS, the stereotype is that AIDS is the disease of homosexuality, making AIDS the marker of a homosexual identity. While other contagious diseases may not be associated with an identity as specific as that associated with AIDS, contamination may be associated with individuals who have chosen particular lifestyles and have presumably willingly exposed themselves to harm. If exposure to harm is by choice, it is a short step to unfairly blaming those who acquire particular contagious diseases.

2. The second implication of little experience with contagion has to do with the advice given to those who feel themselves to be (or those who are) vulnerable to a particular contagious threat. Often, the questions surrounding protection are left unanswered and are derailed by efforts to establish blame. As Hamre (2002) notes with respect to the anthrax scare of 2002, "Everybody in Washington was preoccupied with the question, 'who did this?' What the public really wants to know is, 'What can I do to protect myself?'" (p. 14). Clearly, the orientations of government may differ substantially from the orientations of individuals with respect to perceived health threats. Related to this is the fact that public health capabilities around the globe are uneven, with vulnerabilities and responses to these similarly unevenly distributed (Kahn, 2003/2004, p. 57).

Brakes and Accelerators in the Local and Global Health Environments

It is difficult to escape societal pressures to lead a healthy lifestyle. In the media, at work, and at school, we are bombarded with messages to stay fit, exercise, quit smoking, stop drinking, eat healthy, drink plenty of water, and get enough sleep. Advice about healthy living is often couched in terms that are readily understood: prevention today will be rewarded tomorrow. In some ways, health prevention is trading futures—what we give up now (that extra dessert or glass of beer, for example) will reap benefits for us in the future (a healthy heart and trim waistline).

Frohlich, Corin, and Potvin (2001) explain that, despite some definitions of lifestyle incorporating elements of both individual choice and structural determinants, researchers in health promotion and public health tend to use the term *lifestyle* primarily with reference to "individual behavioral patterns that affect disease status" (p. 783). They note that when lifestyle is conceived of as a cluster of behavioral choices, such as choosing to smoke or drink, it can be pathologized and reduced to a variety of risk factors. Lifestyle then becomes a conglomeration of risk factors that are disengaged from the social and environmental contexts in which these choices are made. Altering pathological lifestyles is therefore the obligation of individuals who are expected to practice self-regulation, regardless of the contexts in which they operate.

The promotion of healthy lifestyles through self-regulation goes hand in hand with individual responsibility. Petersen (1996, p. 45) describes the emphasis on preventative techniques involving "self-management of risk and self care" as a "subtle and sophisticated form of individualism that involves everyone in the task of tracking down and controlling or eliminating sources of risk from their own lives." As we noted in Chapter 2, this volume, self-governance—taking care of and governing one's own affairs and oneself—amounts to self-surveillance. We keep watch over ourselves in order to maintain control. The entrepreneurial self creates the self, reflexively, with relatively little direct help from the state, although with much indirect coercion. Furthermore, individuals are assumed to be rational, exercising choice in establishing their health biographies. Those who become ill may therefore be seen not only to have failed to protect themselves, but also to have failed society by posing a threat to others.

The strict utilitarian calculus underlying health prevention fails to adequately address the contexts in which individual choices are made. It is assumed that information, education, and communication will ensure that informed actors make rational choices. What is not taken into account, however, is the context to which information and education strategies are targeted. Chan and Reidpath (2003) explain how, in the case of individuals having been identified as contagious, these strategies often involve self-imposed restrictions, such as when individuals reduce their exposure to others whom they might infect. But not all actors can equally exercise agency, because not all are equally free to act. Agency differs not only in terms of who is identified as contagious, but also with respect to health prevention advice more generally. The burdens of these self-imposed restrictions are not equally borne, and traditional public health assumptions often fail to recognize these differences (Chan & Reidpath). Clearly, risk position affects the types of restrictions one might be able to impose on oneself: removing oneself from harm's way often

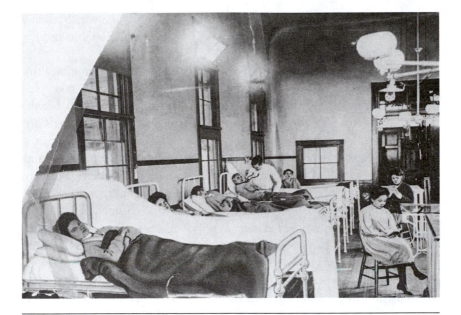

Figure 5.2   Typhoid Mary

requires resources that are not equally available. These authors highlight the case of Mary Mallon, or Typhoid Mary. Mallon was an asymptomatic carrier of typhoid bacilli in New York, in the first decade of the 20th century. Mallon was employed as a cook in a household whose members subsequently contracted typhoid. When suspicion fell on Mallon as the carrier, she was detained in hospital for a period of three years. She was released on the condition that she would not work with food. Although she made a living for a short period washing clothes, the insufficient income forced her to return to the food industry under an assumed name. During her short time under the assumed name, Mallon infected a number of fellow staff members, two of whom died. When Mallon was subsequently identified, she was returned to quarantine, where she spent the last 23 years of her life.

   Mallon's case highlights the disparities in agency and life opportunities that might befall those who are considered contagious and the social response to such individuals. Mallon had only two choices after losing her first job: live in poverty or return to the only profession she knew to provide a survival income under a false name (Chan & Reidpath, 2003). Chan and Reidpath note, "Social responsibility and economic insecurity are not easily reconciled" (p. 42). An extreme measure of surveillance—incarceration—was followed by an even more extreme measure: life imprisonment. Mallon's imprisonment was a form of punishment not only for contagion, but also for the possibility of contagion.

We see parallels here to health prevention and the promotion of healthy lifestyles more generally. While individuals are encouraged to take precautionary health measures and to pioneer themselves into good health, individual liberties may be at stake. At the same time that individuals are responsible for fashioning healthy selves, certain preventive health measures may invade personal liberty. Measures such as vaccination, quarantine, and mandatory reporting of disease may interfere with personal liberty, but may also be justified under the rhetoric of personal responsibility, as well as of economic efficiency. The individual is obligated to keep him- or herself in good health so as not to pose a danger to self or others—despite the impingement on individual liberties—and is expected to contribute to society, or earn one's keep. Petersen (1996) observes, "the disciplinary self-improvement demonstrated in the pursuit of health and fitness has become a key means by which the individual can express their agency and constitute themselves in conformity with the demands of a competitive world" (p. 53).

If we consider the measures through which surveillance is brought to bear on the general public, front-line health professionals frame the meaning given to any particular health issue in certain ways. Just as the street constable may simply be following orders dictated by the police administration, the degree to which front-line health professionals accommodate the medical institution also has implications for surveillance. For example, recent threats with regard to bioterrorism have left some front-line health professionals questioning the utility of preparedness for low-likelihood events that demand their personal exposure to hazards. In December 2002, President Bush announced that the bioterror threat of smallpox would be initially dealt with by the vaccination of about 1 million workers—healthcare professionals and military personnel. The lack of cooperation by health professions was obviously unanticipated, and "hundreds of hospitals and thousands of health professionals have refused to participate in pre-event vaccination until liability and compensation issues have been resolved" (May, Aulisio, & Silverman, 2003, p. 26). Questions remain with respect to the safety of the vaccination, with tests on young people finding that up to one-third missed work or school as a result of the vaccination. More serious, however, is that vaccinated professionals may expose vulnerable patients to infection, and therefore compromise the health of a large proportion of patients. The government has since devised a compensation plan to reimburse workers who might have negative reactions to the vaccine—a vaccination that can result in death for some—but questions remain as to what types of negative reactions are eligible for compensation. The potentially deleterious effects of the vaccine, effects that are well known to the medical profession, have resulted in a failed initiative, with few health-care professionals cooperating with the vaccination plan.

May and colleagues (2003) explain that health-care professionals' refusals to be vaccinated against smallpox presents a classic conflict between individual versus public goods: "how much risk should an individual health care professional be required to assume in order to attain a public good" (p. 28)? The authors argue that, in fact, health-care professionals do not have a professional obligation to put themselves at risk because of the hypothetical and small risk of a bioterrorist attack involving smallpox. Essentially, their argument rests on the notion of emergency circumstances and how that condition is subverted in the case of legislation requiring vaccination of health-care professionals for bioterrorist threats. Health-care professionals are typically professionally obligated to subvert their own interests (in this case, their own health) only in the event of emergency circumstances. The vaccination legislation amounted to asking health-care professionals to subvert their own interests for a hypothetical circumstance, not an emergency circumstance. Therefore, "pre-event vaccination of health care professionals clearly does not meet the conditions of emergency circumstances precisely because there is no such immediate threat" (May et al., p. 28). While the vaccination of health-care professionals may be argued on the basis of national security interests, May and his colleagues suggest that such an argument requires that health-care professionals assume a responsibility to the state over and above that of the average citizen (p. 31). These authors argue that, while members of the military have agreed to subvert their own interests for that of national security, health-care professionals have not made a similar agreement, having instead agreed to treat the sick as their obligation to their profession.

There is more to the refusal of health-care professionals to be immunized against smallpox than the conflict between the individual and public good. The refusal to participate in this vaccination program also highlights the flimsiness of expert models, and the often-problematic integration of politics with the determination of health and health policy. The front-line health professionals see the possibility of bioterror attack as small and have chosen not to expose themselves because of the small risk of attack and the potentially onerous (if not dangerous) consequences of such inoculation. This suggests that experts disagree—health matters are not as clearly based on scientific evidence as we may have assumed. Politics figure prominently, not surprisingly, in the determination of threat. Furthermore, the refusal of these professionals to acquire the vaccination is a clear sign that the state and the medical profession view differently the bioterror threat; in other words, institutional perspectives may define differently the same hazard.

A similar argument may be made for the obligation of citizens to protect themselves against threats to ill health, as well as against threats more generally. To whom is the duty to protect oneself owed? In the context of current societal norms, the duty to protect oneself is owed to the self, first, and only secondarily to the state. In the context of emergency situations such as that posed by terrorist situations, one might argue that the first duty is owed to the state. However, protecting the self in the context of non-emergency situations may be the purview of individual choice. Individual choice, though, is subject to surveillance. The rise of surveillance medicine may actually coerce individuals into making particular choices for the collective good.

Armstrong (1995) suggests that surveillance medicine is characterized by the problematization of the normal. This refers to the widening of potential targets of medicine to include entire populations. The inclusion of entire populations is facilitated by attempts to determine what "normal" consists of. Armstrong suggests that problematizing the normal was first directed toward children, and is evidenced in technologies such as growth charts tracking height and weight. He notes that, while individuals may be plotted along the chart in order to track individual growth, the standard of comparison is the general population with the goal to determine how the individual child fits into the larger population. Individuals can only be more or less normal against a broader standard based on averages. Similarly, distinctions between health and illness began to be replaced by gradations of health. Health by degree meant that, rather than the medical profession simply focusing on the body of the patient, medical surveillance expanded the medical profession outward, beyond the confines of the hospital into the realm of lifestyle (Armstrong, p. 398).

The notion of lifestyle breathes new life into the former distinctions between sign, symptom, investigation, and illness. A headache, for example, may be a sign of high blood pressure, but high blood pressure may be a sign of some other affliction, such as impending stroke (Armstrong, 1995, p. 400). Signs, symptoms, and disease may all be used to calculate probabilities of other illnesses and disease. Armstrong explains that the notion of lifestyle is used to represent the precursors of future illness: "Symptoms, signs, illnesses and health behaviors simply become indicators for yet other symptoms, signs, illnesses and health behaviors . . . each illness is simply a nodal point in a network of health status monitoring" (Armstrong, p. 401). The more information there is at hand, the greater the possibility of uncovering degrees of sickness.

Terrorist Events as Health Events

It is increasingly recognized that, with few exceptions, all terrorist events become health events of differing scale. There are inevitably casualties that need to be treated. Hospitals and other medical facilities are tested for their quickness of response during these situations. Sometimes, these facilities may be overwhelmed with the surge of demand, both from those directly affected by the attack and others who may have suffered secondary effects. The 9/11 World Trade Center attack tested the medical response of New York City in terms of dealing with initial victims. Prior to 9/11, Congress instituted a program known as TOPOFF (Top Officials), which sought to improve the capacity of those in positions of authority to respond to terrorist and other attacks and threats. Results of these tests, which began in 1998, continue to reveal substantial difficulties: ineffective communication, deficient coordination among leadership, flawed command structures, and flawed decision making, as well as "a lack of antidote availability to treat even basic toxic emergencies at healthcare facilities" (Dudley & McFee, 2005, p. 420). Hurricane Katrina, discussed in detail later in this chapter, provides further evidence of these specific problems.

Health officials recognize that their scope is moving beyond the obvious efforts at fighting disease to being pushed increasingly into a public health mode, which demands that they prepare for unforeseen disastrous events. Increasingly, governments have acknowledged the importance of this response through efforts to grant suprapowers to health officials in times of emergency, powers that would previously have been the purview of law enforcement or emergency management officials. In 2003, President Bush announced Project Bioshield, which provides resources for medical countermeasures to protect against terrorist attack involving biological and chemical weapons, or "other dangerous pathogens" (White House, 2003). According to the White House Web site, resources will be available through Project Bioshield to pay for improved vaccines and their development, especially for smallpox, anthrax and botulinum toxin, as well as countermeasures for "other dangerous pathogens, such as Ebola and Plague, as soon as scientists verify the safety and effectiveness of these products" (White House). Furthermore, the Food and Drug Administration would be provided with the authority to make new and various treatments available quickly in the event of a crisis. Initial estimates were that the program would cost $6 billion over a 10-year period (Food and Drug Administration, 2004a).

Signed into law in July 2004, Project Bioshield faces what may be insurmountable difficulties. Although funding is available for the development of vaccines, drug companies are, in general, hesitant to put resources and time into their development. As Dudley and McFee (2005) note, the barriers to vaccine development include the reality of corporate liability, and lack of sufficient funds to protect against liability, as well as constraints related to human safety. Unlike clinical trials among those who might already have a disease or illness, testing vaccines against biological weapons poses unique challenges: it is ethically unacceptable to expose individuals to the types of harms that these sorts of trials might involve. While product liability issues remain a deterrent to developing vaccines against possible biological terrorism, the reality of the cost effectiveness of these projects also impinges on the willingness of companies to pursue their development. Effectiveness aside, drug companies want to be able to sell their products—vaccinations that will be purchased only in the event of a crisis situation of unknown proportions and (potentially) low probability may not bolster the bottom line.

An example of the difficulties associated with Project Bioshield is evidenced in the tale of VaxGen Inc. The federal government contracted with this company to provide a vaccine for anthrax by the end of 2006. Due to contract changes between the federal government and the company, as well as delays resulting from questions regarding the drug's safety, the expectation is that the drug will not be available until late 2008, with final delivery in 2009. As reported in the *Washington Post* (Gillis, 2006), problems associated with VaxGen have been

> a political embarrassment for the Bush administration, which awarded VaxGen some $1 billion in contracts to produce what was supposed to be a modern vaccine that could protect as many as 25 million people from exposure to deadly anthrax spores in the event of a terrorist attack.

The *Post* cites sources indicating that the company is expected to seek compensation for changes to their initial contract. In a case such as this, the ability of health officials to respond to particular health threats is compromised by the realities of the safety and political factors that influence how vaccines develop.

There are some who argue that Project Bioshield has had positive spin-off effects for other realms of public health beyond those that deal exclusively with biological terrorism. Dudley and McFee (2005), for example,

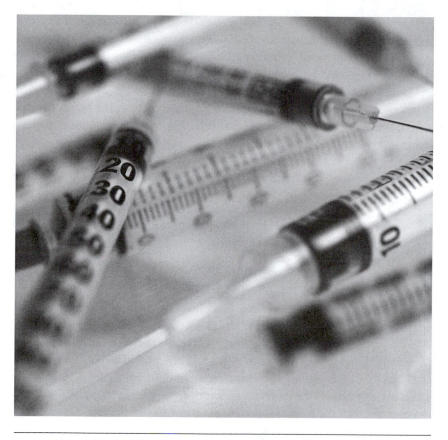

Figure 5.3   Bioshield Projects

argue that the clear emphasis within Project Bioshield on collaborative efforts between government, public health professionals, and private agencies will benefit all parties. These authors argue that the use of funds to protect against biological terrorism will "enhance attention to other public health issues, such as influenza, human immunodeficiency virus, tuberculosis and food- and water-borne illnesses" and that attention to "weaponized biological agents will also aid against naturally occurring global illnesses" (Dudley & McFee, p. 422). Attention to one particular aspect of the health realm does not leave other realms unattended: it is not a zero-sum game. Others, however, beg to differ and maintain that infectious diseases more broadly must be specifically addressed within Project Bioshield.

In April 2006, the Infectious Diseases Society of America (IDSA) presented a statement on the reauthorization of the Project Bioshield Act (Blaser, 2006). In this statement, the IDSA argued that the reauthorization of the Bioshield Act must specifically include and extend the statute's scope beyond the development and acquisition of vaccinations and treatments specific to "bioterrorism-related pathogens and apply current incentives to products to be used against naturally occurring infectious diseases, including anti-microbial resistant infections" (IDSA, 2006, p. 1). In effect, the IDSA points to disease itself, regardless of the source, as the target toward which weapons of defense must be aimed. The IDSA points out that policymakers should be concerned:

> While concern about bioterrorism is appropriate, it is important to keep things in perspective. Not one American has died from bioterrorism since President Bush first announced Project Bioshield in February of 2003, but drug-resistant bacterial and other infections have killed hundreds of thousands of Americans in hospitals and communities across the United States and millions of people across the world during that same short period of time. (p. 2)

The statement also supports the argument that incentives for research and development in the realm of antibiotics is difficult to sustain and is diminishing in favor of more profitable drugs such as those that treat "chronic, life-long conditions and lifestyle issues" (IDSA, 2006, p. 4). The IDSA argues that national security is undermined by inattention to infectious diseases, and that the burden to promote industry attention to anti-infective research and development lies with the federal government.

The arguments of the IDSA are persuasive and speak to the issues of communication and information. As the IDSA points out above, safeguarding against bioterrorist threats makes sense. What makes less sense, however, is failing to address the health threats that have not disappeared in the wake of these more recent concerns. Given the remote probabilities associated with bioterrorism, in contrast to the known record of destruction associated with infection, to ignore an established threat that has gone out of vogue, is to potentially undermine security, more broadly conceived. Terrorism, as we have pointed out in earlier chapters, is but one threat that the state, institutions, and individuals must deal with; other threats to security are often more prevalent and far less abstract.

Furthermore, the funding behind Project Bioshield may mask in simplicity what is in reality a complicated set of factors. The public may perceive that federal dollars flow to that which the state defines as most threatening. In the case of health, because of the exorbitant amounts available for research and development against bioterrorism, the message is that the greatest threat to health is bioterrorism. As the IDSA points out, this is clearly not the case. The federal funding behind what is perceived by many as an obscure threat undermines the concerns that are, in fact, local and are far more real in their everyday consequences. Any individual in the United States may be much more likely, in terms of probabilities derived from past incidences, to die from the flu or from AIDS than to die of bioterrorism. As Glass and Schoch-Spana (2002) note, this high-level agenda setting in the health realm distances the public even more from the state and from the medical profession. These authors note that the effort behind bioterrorism responses "has not, to date, defined a role for the public in disease surveillance, even though the general public historically has been an accurate source of reports of infectious disease outbreaks" (Glass & Schoch-Spana, p. 220). On the one hand, infection is something the public can understand because it is within the realm, for many, of everyday experience. Citizens already possess some form of common knowledge of this threat, having learned about germs from a very early age. On the other hand, bioterrorism resides well within the realm of the unfamiliar, and citizens are once again asked to hold hands with health professionals and other experts through the thicket of unimaginable health threats, at the same time that they are dealing with the realities of health threats that actually are easily imaginable and recognizable in their everyday occurrences.

Information regarding these obscure health threats may well have little resonance. Glass and Schoch-Spana (2002) indicate that the delivery of information about health threats is as important as the delivery of medicine and vaccinations (p. 220). The public may become even more distanced: the arguments for protection against bioterrorism are seen as usurping what the public may feel are the more credible and familiar threats to health. The ability of authorities to engage the public in protection efforts against bioterrorism will require familiarizing the public with such threats and making these threats as real as those they face more often from less spectacular sources of disease and injury in the realm of the everyday.

Summary

AIDS. Anthrax. Smallpox. SARS. Mad cow disease. Reading like a failing report card on health, it would be difficult to deny that there is indeed a pressing need for health security measures at the individual, institutional, state, and even global levels. What becomes increasingly evident, however, is the degree to which individual health no longer remains a personal issue. Given the contact that increasingly occurs on a regular basis between individuals, as well as among citizens worldwide, individual health has potentially complex and far-reaching consequences. Further decisions made at the institutional and state levels affect the health choices and resources available to individuals at any given time.

While our tendency has been to consider health a personal issue, many of the factors that influence health and illness lie outside the realm of individual control. We note the role that politics play in the determination of health threats, and the impact that various political choices have both for public health and for motivation for research and development in less lucrative domains of health research. While political factors outside individual control may be consequential for individual health, individuals are increasingly being asked to assume responsibility for their own health. In and of itself, personal responsibility for health makes sense, but only in situations where the choices are not haltered by structural constraints. Very early on, disease was linked to losses in productivity that motivated public health initiatives. While it is evident that disease and ill-health are linked to losses in productivity, therefore making a healthy population a desirable standard, public health initiatives are motivated by much more than a healthy economy, and are increasingly linked to security in a global world. Again, we note the importance of risk position and risk balance: certain factors may exacerbate vulnerabilities, while other factors serve to bolster immunities to various forms of health hazards. As with our discussion of terrorism, states and governments also inhabit various risk positions. Protection against SARS, for example, is very much a global issue, with vulnerabilities affected by respective degrees of power and insularity at the international level.

At various points in this volume, we have referred to the landscape of security, and how it is that certain issues come to the fore while others recede, depending on the perspective one assumes. Undoubtedly, physical bodies play a role in that landscape, with the health of physical bodies an issue at each level of analysis—individual, institutional, and state. The geographic landscape also plays a role in how it is that security is perceived, with risk balance playing out differently depending on the physical environment with which one is dealing. Most obviously, those who reside in Kansas and Nebraska, for example, spend less time worrying about tsunamis than they do about tornados. Likewise, urban dwellers on the East Coast may perceive the likelihood of terrorist attack much differently than do farmers in the Midwest.

Our consideration of the physical landscape of security continues in the next section. We begin with a quote from a relatively well-known radical environmentalist and continue our examination by reflecting on various approaches to, and definitions of, environmental security. We consider definitions of disasters, and then move to a more deliberate and measured examination of Hurricane Katrina and how this event clearly illustrates risk imbalance, in this particular case, and the impact that this imbalance has had for the security of various stakeholders.

The Physical Landscape: The Environment

In my lifetime I have witnessed an onslaught against the inhabitants of this world lead by the greed of industrialized nations. It is my belief that the oppression of people is rooted in the oppression and exploitation of nature. A fundamental disrespect for life that began with the conquest of Mother Nature and has lead to the conquest of humankind.

I struck back. In an act of resistance designated to raise awareness and draw attention to a problem that affects every human being, every animal, every plant, and every form of life on this planet. I am speaking of global warming, air, soil and water pollution. We are in the midst of a global environmental crisis.

On June 16, 2000 I ignited a fire that would forever change my life. I torched 3 SUV's. I took extra care and used specific fuels to ensure no one would be injured. (Luers, 2007)

Jeffrey "Free" Luers, among others, views the natural environment as a victim in need of protection. The crimes Luers committed in defense of the Earth were meant to draw attention to the fact that the Earth's security and integrity is threatened by the very sources that others would define as evidence of progress. Environmental security, according to this perspective, can only be achieved by minimizing the anthropogenic threats that the Earth now faces. The pursuit of wealth from this view has undermined the foundations of the planet, with little apparent political will to reset the course of destruction on which we now find ourselves. In the absence of political will, radical environmentalists such as Luers argue that individuals must take up the environment's cause independent of state or corporate support and do whatever is necessary to stop this so-called progress.

Concerns with environmental protection, however, cannot be viewed as simply the hobbyhorse of a limited number of radical environmentalists. While few may feel that torching SUVs (sport-utility vehicles), widely criticized for their high fuel consumption, is an appropriate means by which to stop the oppression and exploitation of nature, protection of the environment has increasingly found itself on the radar of individuals, corporations, and states. Recycling facilities exist throughout urban centers and residents in many locales are encouraged to "reduce, reuse, and recycle," in order to limit the amount of waste produced (in some cases, through threat of fine

Figure 5.4   Environmental Damage

for too much trash). At the corporate level, for example, the New Source Review program in the United States is an effort to reduce emission levels associated with manufacturing, not withstanding the loopholes that allow many corporations to avoid installing environmentally sound, yet costly, technologies. At the international level, the Kyoto Protocol (formerly the Kyoto Protocol to the United Nations Framework Convention on Climate Change) was structured to ensure that its signatories guaranteed limiting greenhouse gas emissions to a predetermined formulaic level, among other guarantees, in order to limit ozone depletion.

While recycling and various acts with respect to limiting harmful emissions may constitute environmental protection, what exactly is meant by environmental security? Does the protection of the environment ensure security? Furthermore, what or who is the referent object when referring to environmental security? Is the protection of the Earth itself, for itself, at issue, or is it simply one aspect of national security? In the discussion that follows, we begin to explore these questions. Security and the environment consist of a varied range of images, from specific harms such as dealing with contaminated soil in particular geographies due to oil and gas extraction, to rainforest clear-cutting in South America and its global impact.

Defining Environmental Security

Concern with environmental security has focused on the distinctions between natural and man-made disasters. While such distinctions might have once been clearer, it is difficult to label, for example, flooding in dammed areas as being either natural or man made. Equally, the distinction between the private and public realms begins to disintegrate in the context of environmental security. A corporation's choice to dump contaminated water into local streams, for example, is a decision that cannot be considered private any more than individuals dumping paint thinner into sewers could be considered as such. Finally, disasters have different effects on the rich and on the poor. Hurricane Katrina provides an example of how this works. Perhaps in contrast to Beck's (1992) assumption that risk has a democratic effect on the poor and the rich, other observers suggest that environmental issues disproportionately affect the poor or minorities. Those with access to resources are far better able to protect themselves against hazards associated with the environment than are those without.

There are two primary perspectives on environmental security. First, environmental security is viewed as a branch of, and matter for, national security. This definition focuses on the ways that environmental degradation and scarce resources play into and intensify the potential for conflict. This view has more recently been challenged by a second view that sees environmental security as distinct from national security having to do, instead, with environmental degradation and its related causes as by-products. In this view, environmental degradation may include national security interests, but the focus remains on the ecological component—the environment itself. Broadly speaking, global change, including issues such as deforestation, depletion of the ozone layer, and loss of biodiversity, to name a few, is the focus of this approach. These two approaches to environmental security clearly have different referent objects: in the first case, the nation is the referent object, and in the second case, the environment itself is the referent object.

Concerns with environmental issues as a national security matter (the conflict approach) emerges from the observation that "ecological stress can lead through several social mechanisms to armed conflict and/or to political instability" (Dimitrov, 2002, p. 681). Population growth, for example, coupled with unequal access to resources and environmental change, contributes to both national and international conflicts. Conflict concerning the physical environment is central to this perspective on environmental security. Dimitrov cites the example of water scarcity: Egypt and Ethiopia have had disputes over the Nile River, whereas Jordan and Israel have fought over the Jordan River. Further examples include securing food supplies where agricultural demands outstrip production and refugees fleeing their home countries because of ravaged environments or environments insufficient to support the people dependent on it. Because water use and land use issues may involve conflict, this perspective tends primarily to involve military establishments as the key institutions by which these concerns can be addressed.

The second major approach to environmental security derives from an ecological perspective. Although issues such as food or water scarcity may come to the fore, "the primary entity to be protected is no longer the state but the ecological environment" (Dimitrov, 2002, p. 684), or, as Eddy (2004) notes, "environmental degradation of the global commons" (p. 23). In contrast to the view maintaining that environmental factors can be the source of conflict and stress, this approach upholds the notion of universal harm and the idea that human health is inextricably linked to the ecosystem. As Soroos (1995) points out, rather than environmental security involving various nations attempting to position themselves in advantageous positions relative to each other, the ecological approach downplays competitive endeavors and instead focuses on cooperation in order to address the cumulative effects of the threats now facing the environment. Rather than simply seen as a surface on which various interests and conflicts are played out, the environment is seen as being one with its inhabitants, both human and nonhuman.

Given that these two perspectives define the referent object of environmental security in such different ways, the identification of and responses to environmental issues will also differ. In the conflict approach, for example, rather than protecting the environment per se, the goal is to maintain some degree of balance between fractious parties, or some degree of balance with respect to human use and the environment so as to avoid conflict. For example, rather than protecting the environment, the conflict approach would suggest that the answers to particular issues lie in restructuring or reformulating an equilibrium, say between users of particular waterways, or between food production and population growth (Dimitrov, 2002, p. 683). In these sorts of measures, human needs are prioritized and environmental protection refers to the protection of the environment for human needs. The approach would be similar to treating the signs and symptoms of environmental stress, such as land-use issues, rather than treating the illness itself.

On the other hand, the ecological approach to environmental security maintains a more holistic approach, giving more regard to securing the environment itself: "Because environmental stress itself is a threat to security, regardless of whether it eventually leads to violent conflict, allowing critical decline of hydrological systems would already be a de facto security failure" (Dimitrov, 2002, p. 684). Whereas the military might be called on to respond to environmental security issues in the conflict approach, in the ecological approach, nongovernmental organizations, other institutional actors, and individuals would be called on to establish security. This approach to environmental security encourages a bottom-up approach and is more likely to involve local, as opposed to national, organizations. The manner in which environmental security is addressed therefore depends on what is believed to be threatened, which in turn has implications for whether unilateral or collective security strategies are undertaken.

The conflict approach to environmental security has tended to favor unilateral responses to threats. As Eddy (2004) explains, in the post–Cold War period, the fallibility of borders to nonmilitary threats was recognized. At the same time, these threats "provided rationales for military and other interventions in other nation states as a 'defensive action'" (Eddy, p. 24). Threats that are environmentally based, such as changes in water basins that might lead displaced peoples to cross borders, are increasingly seen as threats that require defensive, unilateral, action. The ecological approach to environmental security, on the other hand, views unilateral efforts as damaging and insufficient to protect the global commons. Rather than promoting and acting on self-interest, the ecological orientation maintains that environmental security can be better sought through multilateral cooperation. "Protection of the global commons would necessarily involve extra-national cooperation of some kind between nation states" (Eddy, p. 24).

Power and Knowledge

Whether one takes a conflict or ecological approach may be influenced in different ways by one's respective access to resources (power). This brings us to consider risk balance in terms of the ways in which individuals are able to reduce the negative effects of environmental disasters and dangers on their health and well-being. Those with greater access to resources may wish to maintain the status quo and undertake unilateral action that might preserve that position of power; alternatively, they may consider themselves to be duty-bound to lead by example in the realm of environmental protection and participate in multilateral action. The litigation process or the threat of litigation may also serve as a means through which to persuade those of varying degrees of power and knowledge to undertake specific types of actions to prevent disaster. Litigation processes determine the knowledge base at the time of the disaster (that is, what various parties knew in advance of litigation claims being heard); they also determine the resources that were available to avoid being found responsible for damages. Establishing what is known in advance of disasters involving large-scale environmental damage is a particularly thorny question when it comes to establishing cause and effect. Environmental damage (the effect) may be removed in time and space from the source of such damage (the cause). Furthermore, what is maintained as being safe at one time may be identified as harmful only much later, at a point far removed from when the damage was done.

One of the most infamous cases of environmental harm of the past century was the case of Love Canal, New York. It illustrates the convergence of a number of the key factors central to establishing security—power, knowledge, control, and vision. Lois Marie Gibbs, known as "housewife and mother turned activist," describes the situation at Love Canal:

> The Love Canal crisis began in the spring of 1978 when residents discovered that a dumpsite containing 20,000 tons of chemical wastes was leaking into their neighborhood. The local newspaper ran an extensive article, explaining that the dumpsite was once a canal that connected to the Niagara River five miles upstream of Niagara Falls. This canal, 60 feet wide and 3,000 feet long, was built by William T. Love in the 1800s in an attempt to connect the upper and lower Niagara River. Mr. Love ran out of money before completing the project, and the abandoned canal was sold at public auction, after which it was used as a municipal and chemical dumpsite from 1920 until 1953. Hooker Chemical Corporation, a subsidiary of Occidental Petroleum, was the principal disposer of chemical wastes at the site. Over 200 different chemicals were deposited, including pesticides such as lindane and DDT (both since banned from use in the U.S.), multiple solvents, PCBs, dioxin, and heavy metals.
>
> In 1953, after filling the canal and covering it with dirt, Hooker sold the land to the Niagara Falls Board of Education for one dollar. Included in the deed was a "warning" about the chemical wastes buried on the property and a disclaimer absolving Hooker of any future liability.

The board of education, perhaps not understanding the potential risks associated with Hooker's chemical wastes, built an elementary school near the perimeter of the canal in 1954. Home building around the canal also began in the 1950s, and by 1978, there were approximately 800 single-family homes and 240 low-income apartments, with about 400 children attending the 99th Street School next to the dump. (Gibbs, 1998, p. 1)

After her kindergarten-aged son was constantly ill, and finding inexplicable maladies among her neighbors, Gibbs (1998) petitioned residents to shut down the local school. Her efforts prompted two eventual emergency evacuations of the area, as well as a government-sponsored permanent relocation of all families who wished to leave the area. The government recovered its $60 million in costs through a lawsuit eventually paid by Occidental Chemical. Gibbs writes that part of the initial hesitation to evacuate the area was the expense incurred by the evacuation and relocation costs. Initially the government refused to evacuate the area, not wanting to set an evacuation precedent because of the many other sites across the United States facing the same difficulty, and not wanting to evacuate due to the supposed lack of scientific evidence to support the indications of illness and the incidence of miscarriage resulting from exposure to chemicals.

Love Canal illustrates some of the difficulties in establishing responsibility, the impact of power and knowledge, and the establishment of cause and effect. It seems clear that Hooker Chemical was aware of the possible issues associated with Love Canal. Selling this land for $1 with the warning regarding the buried chemicals suggests that Hooker was aware of (had knowledge of) the possibility of serious complications associated with this waste. While the disclaimer was meant to absolve Hooker of future liability, the specifics of the dangers associated with the area had not yet been spelled out. In other words, although a specific link between cause and effect had not been established at that time between chemical exposure and health difficulties, Hooker had enough knowledge to try to protect itself from whatever the future held, although their efforts ultimately failed. Lack of specific knowledge, Hooker had anticipated, would not equate with responsibility for future damages. Part of the argument against having to compensate residents (or, technically, compensate the government) was that the connection between cause and effect was tenuous. The government, which eventually did pay for the costs of evacuation and moving, was loathe to point a finger and betray corporate interests. While Hooker's bid to protect itself against future financial liability may have failed, it seems apparent that the big losers at Love Canal were the residents, whom Gibbs (1998) described as "a blue-collar community" in a "David and Goliath struggle" (p. 1).

The Blurry Boundaries Between Natural, Man-Made, and Other Disasters

Norris (2001) found that technological disasters are more stressful than natural disasters to victims. At least part of the reason for this has to do with the moral character of man-made or technological disasters, and the perceived intentionality or negligence associated with the evolution of these types of disasters. In their article on corrosive communities, Picou, Marshall, and Gill (2004) explain that the litigation process that follows particular man-made disasters can exacerbate the stress associated with the disaster. Rather than being able to recover on their own terms, victims of such disasters often endure an extended period of negative effects associated with the litigation process. Ironically, the process that is meant to recover losses and provide some degree of relief for victims is also the process that exacerbates the stress that it is designed to alleviate.

The litigation process associated with disasters and other events is a formalized method of laying blame and responsibility on particular parties and determining methods of redressing or compensating economic, psychosocial, and environmental damages. As noted in the previous chapter, being relieved of responsibility and laying blame elsewhere can potentially reduce anxiety, at least in some instances, and to a certain degree. Part of the litigation process, however, is establishing the type of event that best characterizes a particular disaster. Disasters are, essentially, nonroutine events. However, Picou and colleagues (2004) suggest that there are certain types of disasters that can be labeled as consensus-type events or consensus crises, with emergency personnel working in a coordinated effort to quickly and effectively relieve victims' suffering. All involved parties are working toward victims' timely recovery. Disasters that are not acts of God and would instead be viewed as man-made are often viewed differently, with a resulting lack of coordination. Some stakeholders, such as corporations, potentially do not act in the best interests of the harmed parties but rather act according to self-interest. The litigation process often highlights the disparities among parties and the ways in which various types of disasters are viewed.

The litigation process involves establishing responsibility for disaster. However, there is often a combination of pressures that make distinguishing man-made from natural difficult. As Picou and colleagues (2004) explain, "the severity and duration of disaster impacts may be ascribed to anthropogenic factors, even though a disaster itself may be perceived as an 'act of nature' or 'God'" (p. 1498). The inability of dams, for example, to hold water loads is an example of this difficulty. When a dam fails due

Figure 5.5   Controlling Environmental Damage After Hurricane Rita

to heavy rainfall, should it be considered a natural or a man-made disaster? Depending on the perceived source of the disaster, determinations are then made regarding who is to be held responsible and for how much. In the 2005 spring flooding in Calgary, Canada, city residents blamed the city for allowing houses to be built too close to the river's flood plain. While no dam failed in this case, urban planning itself was perceived as the problem, evident in waterlogged basements. In addition, while there are a combination of factors that may underlie particular disasters, an oft-held view is that because so many "elements of the environment are befouled by the spoils of human endeavors, [then] all disaster events may be perceived as rooted in anthropogenic forces" (Picou et al., p. 1498), or rooted in forces that are the result of human influence on the environment. The question then becomes, "Is the environment really natural any longer?"

Adding a further barrier to the supposed simplicity of defining disasters as either natural or man made is the phenomenon of terrorism and the resulting disasters associated with such acts. The terrorist attacks on the United States in 2001 were immediately characterized by a consensus-type approach, with caring for victims and reducing harm to victims as the first priority in the hours immediately surrounding the attacks. Despite the reported lack of coordinated effort between the police and fire departments, the goal of emergency services was to save lives and address injuries. In the early days after 9/11, and since that time, however, consensus evaporated. Instead, the same factors that tend to be associated with technological disasters came to the fore: responsibility, blame, and compensation. Questions came into focus such as why the government was not able to avert this disaster, why the targeted buildings were not better designed to withstand these sorts of forces, and why communication systems failed began to surface, along with big-picture questions having to do with the errors made in international relationships by the government. Litigation, according to Picou and his colleagues (2004; see also Marshall, Picou, & Gill, 2003), has come to be a defining feature of the response to September 11, establishing a connection between terrorism and technological disasters of other descriptions.

In contrast to the view that the environment can be owned is the view that the environment essentially owns us: that our relationship with the environment is a force over which we may have little choice and control. In her book on risk, Lupton (1999) recounts the story of a couple who were warned by experts that their home was lying in a particularly dangerous location, given the probability of future landslides. The couple's reaction was to say that they understood the risks, but they were willing to forfeit some security in the face of a threat that had yet to be realized and might not be realized in the immediate future. Their attachment to their home and surrounding environment overruled any impetus to move from the area. Similarly, since 1906, the year of the San Francisco earthquake that killed 700 people and set off a number of large fires, urban development along the San Andreas Fault has continued to grow. Despite the prediction by experts that another major earthquake is likely to occur, businesses and residents appear unwilling to respond to this threat by moving out of the area, although more recent acknowledgment of the likelihood of disaster is evidenced in the use of certain building materials that might better withstand shocks.

These examples assume that choices are being made. While some individuals who have the means to live elsewhere choose not to do so, others clearly do not have a choice and live in certain areas because of circumstances that are not of their own choosing. The nature of environmental threat as it relates to security and relative positions of power and influence (risk position) has most recently been stunningly evident in the coastal U.S. states of Mississippi and Louisiana. As we discussed earlier, in August 2005, Hurricane Katrina whipped the residents of these southern states with anywhere from Category Three to Category Five hurricane conditions.[1] Residents of New Orleans appeared to have expected the big one to happen one day, as local newspapers and other reports had detailed the likely damage in the event of such a hurricane years earlier, while hurricane experts predicted that it was only a matter of time. Ill-prepared for the magnitude of water accompanying Katrina, many of the levees were unable to withstand the hurricane-induced pressures, leaving many parts of the city all but completely submerged.

The Evolution of Disaster

Disasters occur when natural, technical and human-induced phenomena impact on vulnerable socio-economic systems. Vulnerability to disasters is a function of objective hazards and human activity in a constructed environment. Human behavior patterns can be influenced; therefore, vulnerability can be reduced. This makes disaster reduction not a random choice but a moral imperative. If communities need not suffer, they should not suffer. In addition, there are important socio-economic benefits of disaster reduction. Insufficient investment in disaster reduction leads to much higher costs for humanitarian assistance and reconstruction following natural disasters, and to a widening development gap between rich and poor communities. The cost-effectiveness of disaster reduction thus makes it a strategic imperative as well. (United Nations [UN], 1999, ¶ III. 14)

The United Nations declared the 1990s as the International Decade for Natural Disaster Reduction (IDNDR). The mandate of the IDNDR program was to focus on "disaster reduction through the scientific understanding of natural disasters, the assessment of their damage potential, and the mitigation and reduction of damage through technical assistance and technology transfer, education and training"(UN, 1999, ¶ I. 1). Following a review in 1994, the IDNDR redefined their focus and

placed greater emphasis on social sciences and economics; focussed on the development of public policy, including legislation and national policies for disaster reduction; intensified regional and sub-regional approaches, and shifted from emergency preparedness to the reduction of vulnerability and risk. (UN, ¶ I. 3)

The refocused mandate was formal recognition that, while science and technology may help to identify natural hazards, social policy would allow for the circumvention of the evolution of hazards into disasters.

The IDNDR report lists a number of factors that account for the substantial increase in economic costs and losses associated with natural disasters over the past decades. Some of these factors include

- population concentration in high-risk areas, without adequate efforts to reduce risk and vulnerability;
- global disregard in the realms of "socio-economic planning, risk assessment and monitoring, early warning and disaster preparedness" (UN, 1999, ¶ II. 7[b]);
- vulnerabilities created in modern industrialized societies due to overdependence on complex infrastructure systems;
- degradation of the natural environment, "leading to negative synergies between the occurrence of natural phenomena and increased risks for communities exposed to natural hazards" (UN, 1999, ¶ II. 7[d]);
- indications of global climate change, including aggravation of climate disparities ability;
- increasing episodes of compound disasters, such as natural-technological disasters; and
- the impact of large-scale poverty and potential for economic collapse, especially for developing countries and countries in transition, thereby increasing vulnerabilities to disasters.

This list of factors includes factors that precede disasters, as well as factors that make a difference during and after a disaster event.

How can a risk-balance approach be used to understand disasters? It is important to note that hazards are not disasters, but rather, hazards can become disasters. For example, living along the San Andreas Fault is hazardous. The San Andreas Fault is so named because tectonic plates (the North American and Pacific Plates) meet well below the Earth's surface at this particular location. When these plates shift, earthquakes occur. Some of the hazards associated with earthquakes include ground motion, ground rupture, aftershocks, fire, landslides, flooding, and, in some cases, tsunamis (Nelson, 2004). In order to compensate for the probability that tectonic plates will shift, various procedures can be taken to minimize the probability of earthquakes turning into full-blown disasters. Strict building codes, for example, specify standards for enabling buildings to withstand ground motion.[2] Individual homeowners may prepare their homes for earthquakes by strapping their water heater tanks, securing large appliances, anchoring bookcases and cabinets, removing hazardous cleaning fluids, and securing objects such as pictures, plants, and so on. Individuals may also circumvent disaster by taking up various emergency preparedness measures, such as practicing drills, developing evacuation plans, securing important documents, and preparing emergency supplies. Government, either at the state or local levels, may facilitate preparedness, for example, by providing appropriate and timely information and by developing emergency plans that involve producing written disaster plan documents and ensuring that these documented plans work.

The motivation to circumvent disaster, however, is often not straightforward, with various factors impinging on the ability and willingness of individuals and organizations to prepare for disaster. In his overview of major findings from social scientific disaster research, Quarantelli (2003) observes that individuals tend to have little interest in disaster preparedness in advance of disasters. Often, the low probability of particular hazards or disasters means that individuals tend to focus their attention on more immediate, everyday concerns. Second, individuals tend to take seriously explicit warnings of impending hazards and will respond rationally. It has been found that one of the greatest impediments to evacuation, however, is that individuals fail to leave if the location and safety of their loved ones are in doubt or are unknown (Quarantelli). Third, individuals tend to help each other should disasters occur: prosocial behavior tends to predominate, especially in terms of initial search and rescue efforts.

At the community or local level, research findings indicate that local areas tend to give low priority to community-level mitigation plans (Quarantelli, 2003). Quarantelli notes, however, that the level of preparedness has improved over the past few years, primarily due to the mass media and the reporting of disasters to the larger world community. Second, preparedness at the community level is often uneven and problematic. Often there are stresses among local agencies, such as between the police and fire departments, preventing the cooperation required among various agencies to prepare effectively. Disaster preparedness, it seems, is often snagged by pre-existing political cleavages between various public, as well as private, agencies. Partnership for Public Warning indicates that "perhaps the single most important recommendation [with respect to advisory systems] is the need for cooperation and partnership" (2004, p. 14). Third, the coordination of various agencies is problematic: some organizations are well established, such as the police and fire departments, whereas other organizations may emerge out of the disaster itself, including organizations set up in the wake of emergencies to handle disaster functions, such as search and rescue efforts and triage. Different groups with different functions create major coordination issues. Finally, Quarantelli observes that community issues emerge in the aftermath of disasters, with remaining problems, such as poverty, often re-emerging and made worse. Other issues are, for instance, whether—and how—to rebuild.

At the organizational and government levels, the research findings that Quarantelli (2003) examines indicate that disaster mitigation is rarely on the agenda of organizations. With the exception of the banking, chemical, and nuclear industries, disaster is often unplanned for and measures are rarely instituted to respond to disaster. Although this has begun to change in the post–9/11 period, especially with the recognition that lack of preparedness constitutes a liability, disaster mitigation tends not to be a high priority. Quarantelli further observes, "to the extent that non-emergency organizations undertake preparedness planning—and until recently few did—they often plan incorrectly" (p. 6). It appears that written disaster plans do little in the way of actually mitigating disaster. Disaster preparedness requires actionable processes, such as public education campaigns; establishing links between groups; assessing and monitoring information; holding rehearsals, simulations, and drills; training campaigns; engaging citizens; creating non-emergency agencies; as well as changing laws and updating resources (Quarantelli). During the crisis period of disasters, Quarantelli notes that the question, "Who is in charge?" is often asked, but is also meaningless since a command and control model of reckoning with disaster is impossible. Associated with crisis management are three major issues (Quarantelli, p. 6): information flow between organizations and between citizens and organizations; decision-making problems resulting from either the loss of higher-level authorities (due to a variety of factors), or due to conflict regarding disaster tasks and jurisdictional control; and issues related to differing perceptions as to what constitutes coordination. As Quarantelli observes, at one plane crash in the United States, 439 groups appeared on the scene to offer their services (p. 4).

There are four stages of disaster-related behavior (Quarantelli, 2003). The first is the mitigation stage, which includes various measures taken well in advance of potential disasters including, for example, building codes, training and educational campaigns. This would be the stage where hazards and threats are recognized. The second is the preparedness stage, which involves behaviors that relate to an immediately pending hazard. Measures taken at this stage would include evacuations and warnings. The response stage involves actions that are taken during and immediately after the realization of the hazard or threat. Examples at this stage include search and rescue efforts and emergency medical services. The final stage is recovery, and includes responses taken after the crisis period is over, such as the restoration of power and the rebuilding of homes and infrastructure. Each of these stages prepares for the following stage, with the recovery period after one disaster preparing for the mitigation stage of the next potential disaster.

The Evolution of Hurricane Katrina

> That things have gone so badly so quickly after the storm in New Orleans has produced, beyond sympathy, feelings in Europe of disappointment, distress and even fear that a major city in the world's superpower could have fallen into something that looks, from this side of the Atlantic, like anarchy. ("View from abroad," 2005)

The stages of disaster-related behavior suggest that that there may be opportunities for averting disaster as the mitigation stage emphasizes. Importantly, however, the mitigation stage of one disaster may be the crisis stage in terms of other disasters. As we note below, the crisis stage of Hurricane Katrina for Floridians occurred at the same time as the mitigation stage for Louisiana and Mississippi residents.

The Mitigation Stage

On Tuesday, August 23, 2005, the National Hurricane Center registers Tropical Depression 12: the 12th depression of 2005, and the predecessor of what would become a hurricane of major proportions. The tropical depression was situated over the Bahamas, and the region issues a tropical storm warning with indications that the depression would be steadily intensifying. Forecasts suggest that the storm will hit Florida by Friday of that week. In anticipation of fuel shortages, oil and gas futures jump with the expectation that oil production in the Gulf Coast will be disrupted.

On Wednesday, Tropical Depression 12 surpasses wind speeds of 34 knots and becomes Tropical Storm Katrina. Katrina is the 11th named storm in 2005, doubling the number of tropical storms experienced in the region by this time in 2004. Hurricane warnings are posted in major southern centers of Florida including Miami, Fort Lauderdale, and West Palm Beach, as well as the southern tip of Florida and the Florida Keys. Forecasts predict very heavy rains along with 120 km/h winds. Predictions also suggest that after passing over Florida, the storm is likely to intensify as it crosses the Gulf of Mexico.

Later in the afternoon of Thursday, August 25, Katrina is upgraded to a Category One hurricane, after having flooded parts of the Bahamas. It is headed straight for Florida. Authorities in Florida recommend that residents leave the Florida barrier islands, while some southern schools close early. At 6:30 p.m., Katrina hits Florida—8 hours earlier than forecasted. It leaves 11 people dead from falling trees and weather-related traffic incidents, and more than 1 million people without electricity; Governor Jeb Bush declares a state of emergency in Florida. Meanwhile, the National Hurricane Center forecasts that Katrina is destined to hit the northeastern Gulf of Mexico in three days—Sunday.

After being briefly downgraded to a tropical storm on leaving Florida, Katrina recharges and becomes a Category Two hurricane on Friday, August 26. Drilling rigs and petroleum-producing platforms are evacuated in the Gulf Coast, yet gas and oil production remain unaffected. The governors of Louisiana and Mississippi issue states of emergency in anticipation of Katrina, which also makes the implementation of emergency procedures, such as evacuation, easier to implement. New Orleans Mayor Ray Nagin is quoted as saying, "this storm really scares me" (MSNBC, 2005). He is alarmed at how little time there is to prepare for what has become the inevitable arrival of Hurricane Katrina.

The Preparedness Stage

The director of the National Hurricane Center, Max Mayfield, indicates that Katrina is a "perfect" storm ("Bracing for Katrina," 2005). Katrina has become a Category Three hurricane. Saturday, August 27, residents of New Orleans begin to board up their homes, and in some parishes (districts), voluntary evacuations are called. In other coastal areas of Mississippi and Louisiana, mandatory evacuations are ordered. The evacuation calls prompt long line-ups at New Orleans gas stations and highways where, in some cases, both lanes are directed out of town. The Superdome (a large, covered sports arena in New Orleans) is opened as a shelter of last resort with residents encouraged, in the first instance, to leave town. In a city of 485,000, approximately 100,000 residents have no transportation to leave the city.

Katrina becomes a Category Five hurricane as it blows over the Gulf Coast on Sunday, August 28. The National Hurricane Center suggests that the hurricane will affect a large area and that "preparations should be rushed to completion"(Appleborne, Drew, Longman, & Revkin, 2005).With 300 km/h winds and expected 10-meter storm surges, the Superdome takes in its first 10,000 people of the estimated 100,000 who remain in the city: Mayor Nagin warns that it is not expected to be comfortable in the Superdome as power may be out for days. High-rise hotels choose only to house tourists, although they have offered shelter to local residents in the past. Mayor Nagin issues mandatory evacuation and an emergency order that allows state and local authorities to commandeer buildings and vehicles as they see fit. A Pentagon spokesman indicates that the Gulf States have adequate National Guard units to handle the impending storm.

The Response Stage

On Monday, August 29, Katrina hits land as a Category Four hurricane, with the eye of the hurricane missing New Orleans by approximately 30 kilometers. Although sparing New Orleans from the very worst of the rainfall and high winds, the windows of high-rise office buildings are shattered and a particularly poor district of New Orleans is flooded by up to 7 meters of water, while in another area 40,000 homes are swamped. The power fails at the Superdome at 5 A.M. Later that morning, the wind tears at the roof of the Superdome, leaving two gaping holes. Although search and rescue teams initially wait for the worst of the storm to pass before beginning their efforts, it is estimated that 80% of New Orleans residents had been evacuated.

A further estimated 80% of New Orleans is flooded following the break of two levees on Tuesday, August 30. The flooding brings even more people to the Superdome, where an estimated 25,000 are housed with no running water and no electricity. Rescue efforts are concentrated on survivors stranded on rooftops and in attics. The airport is opened for relief flights, and the Pentagon announces that it will send five ships. Reports of looting begin to surface. Some thefts involve necessities, but there are also reports of looting of guns, electronics, and other valuables. Some looting is said to occur in full view of the police.

The Recovery Stage

Reports of looting escalate on Wednesday, August 31, with thieves reportedly using a forklift to break through the walls of a pharmacy (MSNBC, 2005). Fourteen hundred police officers are ordered to discontinue rescue operations and restore order in the city and control the widespread looting. The mayor calls for a complete evacuation of the city, saying it may be months before residents can return, while emergency medical teams begin to set up triage support in trailer trucks and tents. Military planes remove the seriously sick and injured out of the city, while other people wander along Interstate 10, their belongings carried in bags or laundry baskets, or pushed in shopping carts.

Figure 5.6   Flood Damage in the Wake of Hurricane Katrina

On Thursday, September 1, Louisiana Governor Kathleen Blanco instructs members of the National Guard and other authorities to restore order and to shoot to kill. Efforts to remove people from the Superdome to Houston's Astrodome are disrupted due to gunfire ("Ex-FEMA Chief tells of frustration and chaos," 2005). Estimates are that it may take 8 or more days to drain the city. A $10 billion federal emergency aid package is prepared, and more than 20 countries offer to help the United States cope with the aftermath of the hurricane.

The Superdome continues to be emptied of people on Friday, September 2: emergency shelters in Houston are quickly opened because the Astrodome is filled to capacity. Helicopters drop massive sandbags on the broken levees and the first major supply of food, water, and medicine is trucked into the city. A major influx of National Guard troops arrive in the area, bringing the total to 20,000 troops stationed in Louisiana and Mississippi. A chemical storage facility explodes, sending acrid smoke into the sky. By Saturday, September 3, evacuations are nearly completed and few remain at the Superdome.

The Complications of Hurricane Katrina

The losses associated with Hurricane Katrina are many and wide ranging: from those who died due to the direct impact of the hurricane; to those who lost property, homes, and community; to the infrastructure damage that brought this region of the country to its knees; to the political football of blame lobbed between citizens and government, as well as between levels of government. As we noted in Chapter 2, this volume, our heightened sensitivity to insecurity, coupled with the increasing demands for self-sufficiency in the face of harm, makes the issues that arose with respect to Katrina all the more critical to understanding how it is that disasters unfold and how their effects might be minimized. The aftermath of Katrina is the precursor stage to subsequent hazards. The way in which damages are addressed—whether economic, structural, or social—will pave the way for responses to subsequent similar situations.

Our analysis of this event reveals three major themes, each of which emerges and recedes throughout the entire event, much like the water levels that engulfed New Orleans' Fifth Precinct. These three themes include vulnerable risk positions, communication breakdowns, and failed leadership.

Vulnerable Risk Positions

As we determined in Chapter 2, this volume, vulnerabilities to harm and danger are not equally distributed. Individuals are not equally vulnerable: certain characteristics of individuals may increase vulnerability—such as advanced age and reduced mobility—while other characteristics mitigate vulnerability—such as access to resources, including money and transportation. Hurricane Katrina, not unlike other hurricanes, was not an equal opportunity disaster.

New Orleans is located in Louisiana, the second-poorest state in the United States. Only Mississippi is poorer, and that state, too, was particularly hard hit by Hurricane Katrina. While Louisiana is comparably poorer than other states, in New Orleans income varies substantially. The 2000 census indicated that fully 23% of New Orleans' residents lived below the poverty line. Furthermore, African Americans' incomes were, on average, 40% lower than Whites' incomes. In the areas most affected by Hurricane Katrina, 67% were African Americans. Nearly 8% of residents in the hardest hit regions of New Orleans did not have access to transportation (Center for American Progress, 2005).

The implications of differential risk positions become evident in an event like Katrina. Those with fewer resources are affected differently than those with more resources. Certain residents were more likely to suffer the consequences of the hurricane, specifically those who were limited by a lack of resources to living in particularly vulnerable and undesirable areas, and were similarly unable to leave these areas in the face of danger due to limited assets and no transportation. Early directives to leave the city apparently failed to recognize that not all residents had the ability to remove themselves from harm's way. These directives not only exacerbated the distinction between the haves and the have-nots, but also reiterate how important it is for communications to be meaningful for particular audiences. Clearly, because of varying risk positions, not all residents received the message in the same way, if they received any communication at all. While some had the means to either shelter or remove themselves from harm, others clearly did not. Similarly, in terms of recovery, some will have the means to replace their lost property, while others will not.

Communication Breakdowns

Communication requires careful consideration of the audiences to which messages are directed and the nature of the messages transmitted. In the case of communication regarding disasters, the manner in which communications are received and interpreted are further influenced by the proximity of a particular disaster to those both transmitting and receiving messages. Well in advance of the development of Hurricane Katrina, reports such as that from the IDNDR constituted one of any number of forewarnings issued and ignored with respect to the likely failure of the levees. In a widely cited article in *Scientific American*, Mark Fischetti (2000) laid out in graphic detail the ways in which the levees would fail as the result of a Category Five hurricane. In 2000, however, despite the regularity of hurricane season, a hurricane of this magnitude was perceived as altogether too abstract, and existing only in the realm of possibility. While this and other articles might have served as advance warning, priorities obviously laid elsewhere.

In the last days of August 2005, the likelihood of disaster became far more tangible as Katrina became increasingly a reality and decreasingly a mere possibility. Communications between various levels of government, and between levels of government and citizens, were fraught with a sense of urgency that impending harm often provokes. In the specific case of Hurricane Katrina, there was much criticism with respect to the content of the messages between authorities and the public. The most salient issues with regard to communication between authorities and citizens included whether authorities were providing citizens with accurate information about the seriousness of the impending hurricane, and whether the authorities communicated what they knew about the disaster with appropriate timeliness. In terms of accurate information, there was criticism that the authorities did not anticipate and recognize the gravity of the situation that

Hurricane Katrina represented, and furthermore, that even if the gravity of the situation had been fully realized, that there was no effective plan in place to deal with the looming hazard or its consequences. With respect to time-liness of communications, criticism was leveled at the authorities that by the time directives to leave the city had become mandatory, it was simply too late—especially too late for those who had little access to transportation or funds to remove themselves from danger. Those who had remained had no means by which to leave.

Communication between various levels of authorities was also at issue. As Alberts (2005) points out, myriad concerns evolved, including that "officials with the Federal Emergency Management Agency, part of the Department of Homeland Security, failed both to grasp the scope of the dis-aster and to mobilize aid to rescue victims." Not only did it appear that no one was in charge, but the directives issued often seemed contrary to what might be expected in the face of this type of disaster. Mayor Nagin, for example, at one point in the early days of the crisis told the New Orleans Police Force to quit search and rescue efforts and to return to the streets to stop the looting. The deployment of police officers and media communica-tions that turned attention to looting over rescuing suggests a communica-tion failure, at least in terms of those waiting to be rescued and whose lives were imperiled. (We consider communications between levels of authority in the next section.)

The media played a significant role during the various stages of Hurricane Katrina, not unlike the role the media has played in other disasters. In dis-aster situations, the media facilitate communications among those directly involved in the disaster and communicate the event to the rest of the world. Although the role of the media varies during the stages of disaster, the media tend primarily to serve as a management tool in the preparedness and pre-paration stages, as well as to provide information about recovery in the postevent stage. As Perez-Lugo (2004) indicates, the media also play a role during the impact stage of the event. In her study of responses to Hurricane Georges in Puerto Rico in 1998, Perez-Lugo found that the media also served as emotional support and companionship, especially during the event itself. While many of the victims of Hurricane Katrina did not have access to tele-vision sets and newspapers, they did have access to reporters in the very early stages of the event. A number of dramatic stories were the outcome of reporters interviewing victims who felt that authorities were not listening to them. In one particular case, a female reporter, Christie Blatchford (2005), and her cameraman arrived from Canada a day before the National Guard arrived. They were met with tears of frustration and evidence of sickness and death. While many reporters were not able to provide the physical help that victims required, reporters were able to listen and provide emotional support to despairing victims.

The media use of technology meant that the pictures and stories associated with the flood were transmitted around the globe nearly instantaneously. International onlookers observed that the country that many perceive to be omnipotent failed to provide basic services to its own citizens. In a most unfortunate media moment for the government of the United States, it was reported that those in charge had no idea of the extent of the damage that had been caused along the Gulf Coast until they had seen the media images on the news.

The use of technology and the speed at which stories are created and distributed also plays into the reality that media stories of disasters are often incomplete and may focus on particular sensational aspects over aspects that are perhaps more important. For example, Quarantelli (2003) notes that the media tend to focus on the formal search and rescue groups, ignoring the fact that 90% of search and rescue is undertaken by citizens. Due to the immediacy of broadcasts, the media may play a greater role in defining the issues than is productive. For example, a splash of stories during the flooding event focused on the looting and criminal activity that was going on in the early stages of the disaster. These stories were accompanied by various captions suggesting that crime was an even greater threat than the floodwater itself. Later reports, well into the aftermath of the disaster, suggested that these early reports had been overstated and that looting may have been relatively rare.

Failed Leadership

Criticisms of the response to Hurricane Katrina focused primarily on failed leadership. The Federal Emergency Management Agency (FEMA) was held particularly accountable for the way in which the emergency response was handled, with perhaps the foremost criticism that of incompetence at the helm. The role of FEMA is to coordinate disaster relief, which includes the four areas focused on above: mitigation, preparedness, response, and recovery. The coordinator is also responsible for making things happen: bringing the right people to the table to ensure tasks are done, and done effectively, and ensuring a presence so that others are aware of the role of FEMA and what it is supposed to be doing. The logistics of evacuating people was a central issue that was inadequately prepared for. With regard to incompetence at the helm, Michael Brown, director of FEMA, was the target of much criticism. Regardless of President Bush's observation, "Brownie, you're doing a heck of a job" (White House, 2005), many critics suggested that losses could have been greatly reduced, had a leader been in place who was familiar with emergency preparedness and response. Ten days after the president's praise, Mr. Brown resigned, to be replaced by interim director, now Director David Paulison.[3] Although FEMA bore the brunt of criticism for the failed response to Hurricane Katrina, state and municipal governments were also criticized. Mayor Nagin, for example, issued a voluntary evacuation in advance of a mandatory regulation that, for many, was too late. State senators appeared to have a difficult time convincing FEMA officials that the hurricane was indeed as bad as it was. Because the levees did not fail straightaway, the urgency of the situation may have been assumed by some to have diminished with the passing storm. Yet in the aftermath of Katrina, most fingers pointed directly toward FEMA.

Summary

The lessons to be learned from Katrina are many. First, nature does not exact its toll evenly on the population: risk position matters. Those who are able to afford protection or who have the means to avoid hazards are obviously far less harmed by the challenges of natural hazards and disasters than are those who have no means to protect themselves. As has been observed in other natural disaster situations, from earthquakes to tsunamis, it is the poor who suffer the most. Second, risk position plays a crucial role with respect to the salience of messages communicated and the means by which individuals in various positions are able to respond. In New Orleans, calls to evacuate not only came very late to certain areas, but also assumed that particular residents had the wherewithal to evacuate. Given that public transportation had shut down, poor and elderly residents were physically unable to remove themselves from harm's way—they had no cars, no money, and no way of getting out of their homes. Communication is critical: As we have emphasized, information is a key component of security, as is the need for information to align with the contexts to which it is provided. Communication breakdown appeared part and parcel of the failed leadership evident throughout this disaster.

In its report, IDNDR presented a number of recommendations that speak to the notion of risk balance. More recently, the Department of Homeland Security has begun to recognize that a multidisciplinary approach is better suited to enhancing security in a variety of realms. Specifically, the

IDNDR suggests a "broader orientation on intersectoral approaches"; "a growing understanding of the human dimension in the occurrence of natural disasters, and of the relationships between socio-economic factors, risk factors and disaster vulnerability" (UN, 1999, ¶ II. 8[a], 8[b]); improvement in telecommunications systems and global monitoring systems; as well as increased study of global environmental change.

The observation that certain segments of the population may be at greater risk of exposure to environmental (and other) hazards is not new. For many years, criminologists have reported that certain populations are more vulnerable to crime than others: the young, minorities, males, and those with lower incomes and lower education. Not only do these characteristics describe those most vulnerable to criminal victimization, they describe those most likely to criminally offend. In the environmental security literature, there is a similar tendency regarding victims: those most vulnerable to environmental hazards are also young, minorities, with lower incomes and lower education. Unlike crime, however, where the perpetrators tend to have the same characteristics as victims, those who create the conditions of environmental degradation tend to be much different from those who are its victims. Those with far greater access to resources (owners) tend to be those who create and ignore the conditions of environmental degradation that most affect those with characteristics much different from their own.

In another parallel to the criminology literature, various elements of the environmental literature have focused on the notion of environmental justice, much like the notion of restorative or distributive justice in criminology. The idea behind environmental justice is that environmental hazards are disproportionately borne by particular segments of society, which requires fundamental redress. Pollution and environmental degradation disproportionately affect the poor compared to the wealthy. Dawson (2000) writes, "environmental justice movements build upon perceptions of prejudice and use the environment to graphically demonstrate their broader claims of injustice and discrimination" (p. 23). Whereas earlier grassroots organizations associated themselves with particular locales and concerns with specific sites that required solutions (such as the Love Canal, described above), Dawson observes that local concerns have more recently been replaced by a focus on identity and how it is that these identities become attached to the environment and its degradation.

The association of various subgroups with environmental injustice issues may be considered ether positively or negatively, depending on whether environmental security is viewed from a conflict or an ecological approach. On the positive side, the alignment of particular subpopulations with environmental issues often provides subgroups with exposure to and knowledge about environmental issues at hand. In the short term, as Dawson (2000) notes, drawing groups in on this basis "may provide an excellent tool for awakening a sub-group to injustices and recruiting people into the social justice crusade" (p. 24). While the initial stages of this process of drawing people in represents a boon to those who prefer a multilateral approach, the later stages are often characterized by power that is derived from an us versus them orientation. The later stages can become more characteristic of the unilateral approach, with gains registered in terms of the security of individual groups versus the security of the environment itself. As well, the links between subgroups and the environment may well be instrumental with little concern for advancing the others' platform.

Conclusion

Security with respect to health and the environment is clearly important for individuals, institutions, and governments. The corporeality and tangibility of bodies and environments—the centrality of space, in effect—creates greater immediacy for health and environmental security over concerns about crime and terrorism security.

As we have suggested throughout this book, these differences in perspective manifest themselves in terms of the balance that individuals, institutions, and states bring to bear on managing health and environmental issues. Risk positions vary among individuals, as well—healthy individuals view public health care, for example, much differently from how sick individuals who may rely on publicly provided health care view it. Furthermore, institutional risk positions, especially with respect to financial capacity, play a role in the determination of research and development applications for new drugs, for example. The importance of these developments obviously varies substantially between those individuals needing certain drug therapies, and the corporations that are able (but perhaps not willing) to provide these medications. Public health-care institutions, on the other hand, may acknowledge the importance of these drugs, but may be without sufficient funding to provide particular drugs to their clients, nor have enough resources to be able to convince government of the importance of motivating these developments through certain incentives.

Notes to Chapter 5

1. Hurricanes are classified on a scale of one to five. Category Five is the strongest and potentially the most damaging.

2. It is important to note, however, that the enforcement of these standards may not be especially strong and it is particularly difficult to enforce the retrofitting of various buildings to comply with new standards. Concrete construction is most susceptible to damage, while wood and steel structures are better able to flex and therefore withstand earth-shaking motion.

3. After an extended search to fill the position of director, President Bush nominated David Paulison as director of FEMA effective April 2006. Paulison is well known as an advocate of home emergency preparedness kits. He first came to national attention as the central advocate of the use of duct tape and plastic sheeting for protection in the event of a biochemical terrorist attack.

6

The Stages of Risk
Balance and Security

This chapter deals with themes that relate more directly to managing and addressing identified hazards. The actions taken at various times and in particular places may work to alleviate potential harm or perhaps work to circumvent the occurrence of harm altogether. On the other hand, opportunities for responding and planning may be missed, resulting in greater harm than might have been the case if opportunities had been taken advantage of, or had the radar been programmed to register alternative possibilities. The strategies employed by individuals, institutions, and states obviously vary, but so too does the weight that each accords particular hazards: demands on attention, time, and resources affect the prioritization and management of identified hazards.

To this point, we have examined the theoretical context of risk balance, and the ways in which associated issues play out with respect to the realms of crime, terrorism, and health and environmental threats. Our goal in this chapter is to operationalize some of this abstract overview into a more concrete discussion of what people, institutions, and states should do and actually do regarding preparedness and prevention, response, and recovery. In many ways, as we have seen in our discussion of environmental hazards, the traditional hazards literature has forged well ahead of the realms of crime, terrorism, and health, with the recognition that there are different phases to managing more traditional hazards, which are often associated with the

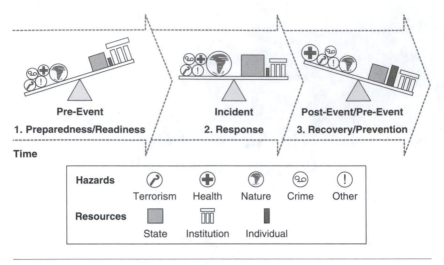

Figure 6.1   A Risk Balance Model

physical environment, and different responses required throughout the hazardous event. Our risk balance approach brings to the table an expanded all-hazards conceptualization of threats. This comes with the recognition that there are a number of hazards across a variety of spatial and temporal contexts, identified through specific values and choices, which vie for the attention (or application) of typically limited resources.

Figure 6.1 illustrates our model and highlights the focus of this chapter. The illustration suggests a three-stage model, consisting of the pre-event, incident, and postevent stages. Importantly, the last stage, the postevent stage, is also simultaneously the pre-event stage to future hazards; in fact, we could be said to be in a perpetual pre-event stage for a number of hazards. At Stage 1, we note that various hazards may be weighed differently, and that the resources applied to these hazards vary among individuals, institutions, and the state. At Stage 2, the incident stage, we note again that the weight of hazards varies, as do the resources applied by individuals, institutions, and the state. And finally, at Stage 3, the postevent stage, resources are differentially applied to hazards than in previous stages. The point of this model is that the balance and the ways in which resources are applied to hazards vary over time and space.

This model also illustrates that different approaches to addressing and managing hazards and threats emerge and recede over the course of time. The pre-event stage conforms to the preparedness and readiness steps that agencies and individuals need to follow to avoid harm in the first place.

If this fails and an incident occurs, we move to the incident (response) stage. Response involves direct reaction by, for example, individuals, law enforcement, public health officials, and disaster relief organizations. Finally, at the postevent (aftermath) stage, recovery and prevention will vary depending on the application of resources, and preparation may begin for the next incident, thus becoming the pre-event stage for the next incident.

As we mentioned in Chapter 1, this volume, there are other hazards that may be characterized as chronic rather than discrete. These types of hazard, along with more discrete hazards, can also be taken into account in a risk balance perspective that weighs various hazards in order to differentially allocate resources. Chronic hazards may get comparatively little attention and resources, while discrete hazards often tend to command attention, due to their flavor of the month appeal and often emergency proportions. For instance, although smoking is a chronic hazard in our society, the resources allocated to this threat as compared to the threat of terrorism (which may become a chronic threat someday as well) is relatively little, despite the loss of life that may be attributable to smoking.

We begin our examination of preparedness and readiness by taking a close look at insurance. While insurance is not the only form of preparedness, it deserves careful consideration because of its significance at the individual, institutional, and state levels, and for the ways in which insurance and the assumptions behind it affect security both within and across these levels.

Preparedness and Readiness

Insurance

> Insure today, secure tomorrow. . . . Your next accident could be forgiven. . . . You're in good hands. (Allstate, n.d.)

Understanding how individuals and institutions balance potential hazards with resources entails looking at a range of programs and products that are available to enhance security. Crime prevention strategies, for example, involve not only locking our doors to prevent burglary, but also insuring our goods in case of a loss. This form of protection relies on individuals negotiating with insurance vendors to cost out their likely exposure to hazards and prepare for possible harm in the event of such exposure. Private insurers contribute to our safety net, but their operations and vulnerability to economic, social, and political change also makes them important players in the over-all security landscape. In discussions of crime prevention, for example, sur-prisingly little attention has been paid to insurance despite its importance in shielding victims from loss. The increased attention paid to terrorism and natural disasters and the major impact that these events can have on insurers has brought this industry and its practices more closely into the debate about security. In terms of our approach to security, insurance demonstrates how agents, including institutions and states, mobilize resources to anticipate exposure to hazards and possible harm and to manage and cope with such exposure, should it occur, in the aftermath.

Insurance policies are sold and promoted as a means of securing tomor-row and providing peace of mind. The types of insurance policies that indi-viduals may purchase on the market are wide ranging: from life, vehicle, and disability policies, to long-term care. The insurance industry continues to grow at an unbridled pace, as more and more of social life appears to be captured by the security landscapes that insurers help to create and, subse-quently, hope to cover with their respective policies. Individuals are also increasingly amenable to purchasing and acquiring insurance coverage and there appears to be a growing recognition and acceptance that dangers or, for insurers "predictable contingences," are a part of daily experience. Although the future is not known, what is known, and therefore predictable, are particular types of negative outcomes that could characterize otherwise normal situations. Most of us recognize that accidents can happen, but these events are usually out of our control. We do not know, for example, if we might be involved in a car accident today or in the future, nor can we predict whether we might need long-term care as the result of injury or dis-ease. Insurance allows us to manage contingencies so that we are not caught unprepared to deal with these situations. Insurance is both a means of dam-age control in the aftermath of specific events and advance preparation for possible future events.

Importantly, however, insurance policies do not provide blanket forms of security but are rather geared toward particular, well-defined, and spe-cific contingencies that could occur. Life insurance policies, for example, do not cover death as the result of intentional activity, such as self-inflicted injury or participation in high-risk sports. Death as the result of suicide or sport participation falls outside the realm of contingent and within the realm of intentional (within one's control). Not only are intentional actions exempt from most insurance coverage, but so too are claims that may be the result of carelessness or negligence. Claims against one's home insur-ance, for example, may be declined if the insurer determines that the home was insufficiently protected. Leaving all the doors and windows of one's home open prior to a burglary may result in a failed bid to claim the costs or burdens of this event through one's insurance policy.

As this example suggests, insurance policies are not neutral security products, but they determine how the insured, whether individuals or institutions, must conduct themselves, or learn to conduct themselves, by virtue of the parameters of the insurance contract. By exerting pressure on the insured to conform to the insurer's expectations, both the insurer and the insured can expect to fulfill their expectations for security: the insurer may have fewer claims to pay out, thus securing the bottom line, and the insured can reasonably expect that claims will be paid in the event of specified contingencies. Insurers influence the costs of participation in risky activities, for example, by refusing to fully pay insurance claims. More importantly, the insured may simply be denied coverage if the insurance company decides that previous behavior or past experiences make the individual too high a risk. In this way, individuals' overall risk balance is influenced by the determinations of the insurance companies, which are able to dictate, at least to some degree, the types of activities that one might engage in.

The questions that are central to preparedness are, "Who bears the costs of life's misfortunes, or life's potential misfortunes?" and, "How do the costs of (potential) misfortune relate to establishing security?" The answers to these questions vary depending on a number of factors: most importantly, the types of misfortune or hazard under consideration, the parties to that misfortune, and how it is that costs are defined. Ill-health and its subsequent costs, for example, may be either collectively borne, as in the case of publicly accessible health-care programs, or may be covered by individuals themselves, in the case of private health-care plans for those who can afford them. Those with greater access to resources are in a position to purchase protection, either in the form of insurance policies in advance of misfortune or in the form of access to cash to cover misfortune as it occurs. Those with less access to resources will not only be less able to avoid misfortune, due to certain restrictions on their lifestyles as a consequence of fewer resources, but also will be less able to deal with misfortune, when and if it occurs, for the same reason.

There are a number of systems by which the costs of misfortune can be assigned. For collectively borne costs, such as those having to do with certain elements of the physical and social upkeep of the citizenry, the tax system is the means by which such costs are covered. For individual parties, however, tort law provides a means by which costs can be shifted from victims to offenders after the harm has been done. Insurance policies guard against the individual entity shouldering the full responsibility for particular costs, such as the cost of hospital care, should misfortune occur. This type of insurance is referred to as *first-party insurance*. Insurance policies also provide protection in cases where individuals may be found responsible for particular costs. Vehicular insurance, for example, is a form of third-party insurance, often referred to as a type of compensation scheme. Individuals purchase automobile insurance in order to protect other drivers from mishaps for which the insured may be responsible. Of course, acquiring third-party automobile insurance is not a choice that individual drivers independently make, because it is typically against the law to drive without this form of insurance.

Not only are tort law and insurance a formalized means of attributing and redistributing blame and blameworthiness, but tort law and insurance can also be seen as relief from anxiety and economic concerns. By redirecting responsibility from one's self or organization toward another, one may subsequently perceive anxiety to be reduced and responsibility to be diminished.

Those with the power to name and define hazards, such as experts, obviously wield much influence with regard to how particular elements emerge as dangerous or recede as benign. Individual actors may highlight certain elements of their own particular situations as hazardous or not. However, it is more often security experts, such as police, health officials, environmentalists, and particular government agencies and officials, who supply expert definitions of hazard and potential hazards. While private insurance agencies may determine whether they will or will not insure particular actors, individual or corporate, the idea of just desserts also rears its head in public insurance formats. While actors may have some choice about purchasing insurance, with the exception of liability insurance for car owners in most states, we have far less choice when it comes to social insurance programs. Public pensions and taxation, for example, are forms of social insurance (social security). Taxation, akin to paying insurance premiums, is pooled to offset the costs of social programs, such as public health insurance, as well as to offset the upkeep costs of such things as roads and highways, or to pay the costs of large-scale disasters, as has been proposed in response to the major hurricanes of fall 2005. In nations such as Canada and the United States, contributions made by many actors to a pooled fund are the means through which public assistance programs are funded.

Insurance connects directly to the social construction of hazard—insurance can only cover what insurers have defined, or can define, as hazardous based on what is known. Insurance does not cover as-yet-unspecified contingencies and some of the contingencies that insurance does cover may not be worth purchasing insurance for ("Insurance plans you can avoid," 2006). At the same time that insurance covers known contingencies, it has more recently attempted to address terrorism and the costs of terrorism. While types of terrorism activity can be named, estimating probabilities and damage associated with it is a matter of great speculation yet sidetracks the attention of government so that more tangible threats, such as the ill health of the population, are ignored.

Although many of the possible harms that individuals face are not class specific, insurance as a distribution mechanism may recreate divisions based on characteristics other than class, such as genetic predisposition. Technology can be used to identify and differentiate groups, which ensures a proliferation of new risk categories. The pace of technology prevails with ever-more ways to divide the population into increasingly narrow slices based on the latest technological findings, such as what might result from the Genome Project (Genome Project, n.d.). Insurance as a security distribution mechanism fosters the differentiation of populations into increasingly smaller units, which may work more to secure the insurers than the insured. The difficulties that such distinctions pose for social life are great: the distinctions that insurers make to characterize subpopulations often have little relevance for those who populate these categories.

The idea that technology can help to divide the population into increasingly smaller units is actively pursued by the company Risk Management Solutions (RMS) Inc., based in California (Gosselin, 2006). This company has built software that allows for insurers to learn as much as possible about potential clients in a bid to replace more traditional insurance coverage. The claim is that by acquiring increasingly fine-tuned data on clients, insurers will be able to offer a wider variety of policies to suit the needs of their clientele. The goal is to learn as much as possible about clients in order to predict future insurance coverage. Rather than looking back at what risk particular types of clients have posed in the past, the emphasis is on looking forward and basing policies on predictions that use as yet uncharted data in actuarial processes. The good news for insurers is that greater numbers of categories are produced, so that clients are placed in categories of people exactly like them. The bad news for clients, however, is that rather than having a larger pool from which to draw to offset the costs of insurance, smaller pools are created within smaller categories, which effectively increases the costs of insurance policies. For some, the costs of insurance may be close to the costs one might encounter if uninsured. Essentially, this development shrinks the protections that clients might have once obtained from acquiring insurance in the first place.

A Friend of Insurance: Anxiety

Many of us recognize that our social worlds are permeated by factors and contingencies that are beyond our control. Some of these contingencies may occur with some predictability, and we deal with these with relative ease, often through routines or scripts that we have developed out of experience or observation. Dealing with individuals who jump queues for example, may be handled through particular scripts that we have at our disposal ("The end of the line is right over there"), in the same way that we might learn to deal with traffic congestion by routinely avoiding major roadways on our way home.

Other contingencies are not as predictable. We cannot anticipate being hit by a truck, nor can we anticipate acquiring a virus at work. Nevertheless, both insurers and insured recognize this as a possibility and can buy insurance to address some of the financial hardship that might follow from predictably contingent events. But is motivation to purchase insurance entirely economically driven? On a daily basis, the newspapers tell of the latest findings that suggest that the foods we ate last week are carcinogens this week. Where some years ago a suntan was indicative of leisure and money, that same tan today is frowned on as a sign of carelessness and as a source of potential disease. From diets to terrorists, we are told to be aware and vigilant, if not hypervigilant. As Hubbard (2003) points out, we are required to "vigilantly monitor even the banal minutiae of our lives" (p. 52). The ever-increasing stacks of self-help books on bookstore shelves are evidence of the self-absorption that appears to characterize the 21st century. The obsessive monitoring of our selves and our surroundings takes its toll, however, with the result, often, of ambient fear and anxiety that things are slipping out of our control. The desire to exert some degree of control, therefore, may manifest itself in the purchase of insurance policies. Such policies may provide not only guarantees against future losses, including financial losses, but may provide a form of limited reassurance today by restoring or helping to restore confidence today.

In a recent example of this anxiety, we have witnessed a widely reported increase in the problem of identity theft. This elevated concern has emerged from an apparent spike in occurrences, although some have argued that these incidents are simply better known because of changes in laws that require financial institutions to report these types of security breaches. Recent statistics suggest that more than 9 million Americans a year are victims of identity theft (Federal Trade Commission [FTC], 2006). In looking more closely at the numbers, it is apparent that these include

Figure 6.2   Anxieties Then and Now

SOURCE: www.CartoonStock.com.

credit card fraud, which are primarily thefts; phone or utilities fraud, or the opening up of new accounts; bank fraud, such as tampering with existing accounts, and so on. The actual number of hijackings of identity appears closer to about 250,000 per year (FTC). Still, this is a high number, and the overall anxiety about this has resulted in legislators launching investigations on how to solve this problem. At the same time, financial institutions have found a new source of revenue: identity theft insurance. While the actions or inactions of financial institutions have increased the problems of identity theft, the costs of managing the consequences of this are handed back to consumers.

Risk anxiety is a social state at least partially engendered by a lack of trust in experts and expert knowledge. In their examination of risk anxiety as it applies to children, for example, Scott, Jackson, and Backett-Milburn (1998) suggest that parents are provided with conflicting advice with respect to, for example, immunizations: immunizations save lives and damage children (Scott et al., 1998). Individuals are left to determine which course of action they will take amid conflicting advice. What appears clear, however, is that responsibility for these decision lies with the individual. Although today there are many unknowns for which there is no insurance policy, the use of private insurance policies for identified hazards are evidence of the desire to provide self-protection in the face of these known contingencies, simultaneously reducing some anxiety as a result of perceived protection.

Rationalizing Risk

Formerly, the goal of placement or classification was to determine how particular individuals stood in relation to others. Testing, for example, allowed a school system to determine the ability of students in order to provide instruction that might best match their abilities. Ultimately, the goal was to ensure that most students were working at a normal or average level—students were normalized. In the case of poor performance, the goal was to bring the student closer to the overall average of the student population. As Simon (1988) points out, rather than attempting to normalize, individuals are now conceived of as locations in actuarial tables, which are tables that consist of a variety of categories, a point we made in the discussion of crime profiles in Chapter 3, this volume. Normalization has been traded for supervision: "actuarial practices seek instead to map out the distribution and arrange strategies to maximize the efficiency of the population *as it stands* [italics added]" (p. 773). Academic testing, for example, might once have been used to identify weaknesses with the goal of providing instruction to overcome those weaknesses, yet testing in the framework of actuarial practices is instead used to locate similar others for the purposes of efficiently managing—but not changing—particular groupings. Individuals are no longer compared to an average, nor are attempts made to make them average; instead, individuals are simply members of an actuarial location according to certain criteria.

Actuarial placement has implications for the future of similarly categorized individuals. The form of security offered through insurance may be based specifically on the qualities that are shared with those in a grouping (actuarial location) who may have little in common with each other, other than the shared characteristic for which they have been grouped—for example, renters versus owners. Employment is another means of grouping exposure to particular hazards: the likelihood of being hit by a truck is certainly greater for a highway construction worker than it is for a university professor. Victimization surveys show similar patterns for differential risks of crime depending on occupation (Sacco & Kennedy, 2002). Similarly, the likelihood of contracting a contagious disease is greater for health-care professionals than it is for construction workers.

Simon (1988) suggests that, despite their popularity in the contexts of insurance, actuarial practices fly in the face of the Western emphasis on individualism and the ideal of individual uniqueness. Resistance to actuarial practices, however, is often stifled not only by the subtlety of such practices and the preservation, often, of stereotypes and the status quo, but also by the prevalent idea that a contract should benefit all parties to it. In other words, individuals should get what they pay for. The fairness of the contract is at issue when both high- and low-risk individuals are grouped together. When grouped with individuals who are clearly at greater risk of acquiring illness, for example, low-risk individuals may pay more for their low risk than what is paid by those who are high risk. From the low-risk perspective, this may be seen as unfair, because the contract, which is one of mutual aid, with premiums paid for future claims, does not benefit the low-risk individual. Whether this is viewed as unfair depends on one's views with respect to entitlement and rights to protection.

The manner in which insurers view individuals will have clear implications for the types of compensation that can be claimed in the face of predictable contingencies, as well as the types of predictable contingencies that we might be subject to, as determined by the insurer. This may limit the opportunities we have to acquire security, in this case in the form of insurance, and also may limit what counts as hazardous. We are packaged with others who have similar characteristics, but the lack of a social basis to the actuarial groupings may do more to undermine security both outside and within insurance schemas than it may to provide security: "the more a particular dimension of socially recognized difference marks an actual difference in life opportunities, the more powerfully does that dimension stand out as a mark of identity and belonging" (Simon, 1988, p. 789). Similarly, insurers have the power to balance risk and create the security landscape in ways that are advantageous to them

The alternative model of insurance, risk pooling, recognizes this reality but deals with it not in terms of penalizing those at high risk through elevated premiums but instead accommodating those at high risk through equal contributions despite unequal need. The security that insurance provides is therefore dependent on the type of model underlying the insurance contract, and the models themselves rely on different assumptions with respect to responsibility for individual welfare and entitlement to protection and security, and whether welfare is an individual or a societal concern. In a risk-pooling, or solidarity, model, those whom an insurance contract is meant to cover generally recognize that their probable experiences of harm may differ significantly. At the same time, there is general agreement that funds will be pooled despite the unequal probability of need. The assumption underlying a risk-pooling model is that all claimants are equally entitled to compensation, despite the front-end inequality in terms of their risk positions.

A process referred to as underwriting determines individual responsibility in an actuarial model in market-based insurance. This process involves the investigation of an applicant in order to determine, first, if the applicant is indeed insurable and second, the risk classification and hence the cost of the contract that the insurer is willing to write (Stone, 1993). There are essentially three categories in which applicants may be placed (Stone, 1993, p. 306): First, there are those who are deemed insurable and who may range from low to high risk, with higher-risk applicants paying more for their premiums but whose coverage may be essentially the same as those who are low risk. Second, there are those who are substandard, which refers to high-risk applicants who are charged high premiums for lesser coverage. Finally, there are those who are simply uninsurable, or those with whom insurers fail to enter into contracts. The ability of an applicant to obtain insurance is therefore not equal, nor is the insurance that individuals receive equal. The insurer's willingness to underwrite an applicant is based on information that may be extremely wide ranging, from demographic factors such as age, sex, and race to social factors such as income, whether and how much individuals smoke and drink, type of work, familial responsibilities, and so on. All of these factors are then placed into an equation that determines the likelihood of particular negative outcomes and the type of insurance the insurer is willing to offer for the risk that such characteristics pose: risks also include the likelihood of future claims (Stone).

Complaints have been brought against the insurance industry for "redlining" (Stone, 1993, p. 310). Redlining refers to the former practice whereby red lines were explicitly drawn on maps indicating particular zones or areas where insurance contracts would be denied. The practice extended to preclude certain people as well as geographic regions. Redlining is an illegal discriminatory practice that amounts to withholding insurance coverage as well as other services from particular areas or groups of people because of poor economic conditions, or stereotypical

assumptions. While overt discriminatory practice is illegal, insurance protection (or lack thereof) has the effect of propagating negative social conditions (Simon, 1988). For example, there are certain factors typically
entered into actuarial equations that might influence home insurance policies, such as minimum property values and maximum property age requirements. These seemingly neutral policies, however, may disproportionately
affect particular areas and residents of cities, such as inner city residents
(Simon, 1988). If the losses incurred in those areas are thought to be higher,
then insurance in these areas may be higher, and residents there might not
be able to afford home insurance. If inner city residents happen to be poor
minorities, then it follows that these seemingly neutral policies are, in practice,
far from neutral in their implications: "Outside the middle classes, harsher
and old-fashioned methods of security prevail" (Simon, 1988, p. 75).

The formulaic basis of underwriting and actuarial insurance schemes
has implications for individual security, and depoliticizes what in reality
has grave social consequences. Actuarial underwriting relies on statistical
models that fragment individuals into increasingly smaller components
in order to determine their particular risk levels (Simon, 1988). Actuarial
scores for individuals may involve hundreds of factors. The effect is that
control is taken away from individuals and traded for complicated algo-
rithms produced by statistical programs. As Silver and Miller (2002)
point out, decisions regarding insurance and the security it can offer are
desocialized—taken out of social context—with statistical models
imposing the appearance of neutrality. Statistical formulas are then used
to determine probabilities for contingent events; these formulas have
also been used to predict behaviors that fall outside the realm of contingency. In particular, actuarial models have been used to predict future
offending, a behavior that may be either contingent or intentional. The
difficulty with these models is that they tend to generate a high number
of false positives, at the same time that false negatives are also produced.[1] Prediction of behavior based on actuarial models is problematic,
because these predictions affect the distribution of benefits and burdens
differentially throughout the population.

Coercion may also be found in the small print of insurance policies,
whereby policies may include more within the parameters of the contract
than simply the insurer and the individual signatory. In the case of policies
for individuals, the insured's family may also be subject to the constraints
dictated by insurers. For example, in the case of home insurance, the
insurer specifies that particular precautionary behaviors must be in place,
often prior to insuring or prior to claims being paid. If the insured or

members of his or her household fail to take precautionary measures as dictated by the insurer, then insurance or claims may be denied. Whether or not the occupants of a household are part of the formal contract, the policy works to establish parameters around their behavior as well. This has the effect of pulling a network of individuals into the net of insurance despite family or household members not being part of the formal insurance contract. Not only do insurance nets surround individuals and their networks, but insurance networks also include a number of informal and formal agents of social control. The police, for example, are drawn into insurance claims processes, as are health professionals. Attempts by insurers to validate or disregard claims involve verification networks, making certain that the insurer's assets are protected. This verification network draws together both formal and informal agents of social control: the verification network becomes a control network.

Moral Hazard

The product that is sold under the pretext of insurance shapes how it is that individuals come to define and view their social worlds, as well as how they view their individual security landscapes. If there is no insurance coverage, predictable contingencies becomes less real and therefore less threatening. Five years ago, terrorism was not insurable, but today it is. As O'Malley (2000) notes, insurance companies tend to extrapolate threats to property as threats to security. Even if individual safety and property security is more threatened by those inside than by those outside the home, the insurance product shapes and legitimizes what is defined as threatening. At the same time, insurance does seem to make more sense in the context of property than it might in the case of life insurance—life and death, although concrete, tend to be viewed somewhat more abstractly than tangible items such as televisions or stereo systems.

Moral hazard is the term used to refer to the chance that a contract will change the risk-taking behavior of one or the other party to the contract, to the detriment of the other party. In the case of insurance, this means that people with insurance may take greater risks than they would without it; the insurance contract has somehow changed their perceptions of danger to the detriment of the insurer. Insurers could also change their behavior, but the concept of moral hazard is an issue that appears primarily to concern insurers, not the insured. Moral hazards are threatening to insurers because it could mean that insurers will have to deal with more claims than originally anticipated.

Moral hazard is accompanied by a variety of issues. First, the moral hazard factor means that insurers assume that the insured will demonstrate maximizing behavior—the notion of least amount of effort for the most reward. To be sure, individuals do weigh costs and benefits, but a multitude of factors come into play beyond the dollar values associated with various actions. If, for example, the market value of a house drops to $150,000 but is insured for $200,000, the insured will not necessarily torch his or her own house to collect the insurance, nor is that even likely to happen. Nevertheless, this is the reason why insurance coverage is usually for less than market value. Even though the possibility is relatively remote, the insurer must take this possibility into consideration. Second, moral hazard does not exclusively involve only intentional action, but may also involve carelessness, forgetfulness, or even ignorance. Taking fewer measures to protect property than the insured once did, represents a moral hazard to be considered by the insurer. A way for insurers to deal with moral hazards may be to either revoke the insurance contract (declare the party as uninsurable) or increase the premium payments to make the insurer's risk worth taking.

Terrorism and Insurance

Before September 11, 2001, terrorism was included as part of blanket commercial insurance coverage that guaranteed against more likely catastrophic events. After 9/11, which resulted in about $50 billion in insurance claims, new insurance policies were created to deal specifically with terrorist threat. In 2002, the United States passed the Terrorism Risk and Insurance Act (TRIA), ensuring that commercial property owners, including those who owned office buildings, factories, apartment buildings, and shopping malls, must be offered the opportunity to purchase terrorism coverage. Some corporations, however, found themselves in a position of being forced to buy terrorism insurance to satisfy their bankers who threatened to withdraw funding from clients who did not have this form of insurance. Terrorism insurance can be costly, however, and, as we know, the probability of terrorism varies from place to place and between states. Corporations in Iowa, for example, simply are not as likely to be targeted as those in New York. Furthermore, TRIA is a federally funded backstop, which suggests that taxpayers end up paying for the costs of added security even in low-risk areas that are unlikely to be targeted by terrorists.

Insurance policies for individuals also reflect the changing social nature of potential catastrophe. While standard home insurance policies typically include coverage for damage to property and personal possessions due to explosion, fire, and smoke, insurance coverage today varies with respect to exclusionary clauses and terrorist activity. In Canada, for example, most home insurance policies explicitly state that they will not cover damage due to explosion, fire, and smoke resulting from terrorist activity. Conversely, home insurance policies in the United States, thanks to TRIA, do not specifically exclude damages due to terrorism, nor do life insurance policies exclude terrorism as a cause of death.

The losses associated with 9/11 were the costliest ever endured by the U.S. insurance industry. While previous catastrophes such as Hurricane Andrew in 1992 also seriously disrupted the insurance market, the 2001 U.S. terrorist attacks are an example of an event with potential "open-ended liability losses, all of which are extremely difficult to estimate with any accuracy and which will probably take many years or even decades to be run off" (Doherty, Lamm-Tennant, & Starks, 2003, p. 182). Terrorist attacks have a much wider margin of error in terms of estimating both occurrence and losses than do most natural disasters that are characterized by more moderate error, especially due to the social factors involved in terrorist events.[2] The challenge for insurers and reinsurers (those who insure the insurers) is to make the incalculable calculable. As Bougen (2003) notes, "[the industry] in dealing with low probability events has a particularly fragile connection to statistical technologies" (p. 258). Furthermore, the liabilities associated with terrorist attacks are not simply monetary liabilities. Terrorist events, including other terrorist attacks in Northern Ireland, the UK mainland, and the Middle East, involve a sociopolitical dimension that is absent in other catastrophic situations. Terrorist events, like natural disasters, tend to be low-probability, high-damage events. Unlike natural events, however, the added dimension of moral uncertainty characterizes terrorism: What exactly are the intentions of those who perform such acts, and how does this relate to protecting against such events?

In terms of simple risk balance, the tendency has been to focus on events that have a moral character. The moral or immoral aspect of crime and terrorism fuels our concerns with these acts and our efforts to deal with them. Consider the funds that are spent in attempts made, essentially, to seek and destroy at least the signs of terrorism. The rationale behind putting millions of dollars into such efforts is often couched strictly in risk assessment terms, suggesting that the probability of this event is really quite large and therefore warrants our attention. The reality is that terrorism poses less threat than does the natural environment, such as earthquakes and storms, and less than man-made disasters such as chemical spills or manufacturing plant pollution. The difference between certain man-made disasters and terrorism, however, is that man-made disasters may be infused with issues of negligence, whereas terrorism and crime are intentional acts meant specifically to cause harm and instill fear. The immorality of such intentional acts grabs our collective attention and appears more worthy of our consideration than either the negligence associated with man-made disasters or natural disasters. Although man-made disasters are not absent a moral dimension, especially with respect to compensating the victims of such disasters, the causes of these disasters are not as clearly perceived, due to motivated individuals or groups of individuals intending to cause harm, although this view may be challenged by the claims made regarding the neglect of the poor who were stranded in New Orleans after Katrina.

Crisis Drills and Tabletop Exercises: Imagining Dire Consequences

The idea that both formal and informal sources contribute to preparing for danger leads us back to the idea of participation in information sessions. While there are many who advocate the significance of public contributions to information building (e.g., Mitchell, 2003), there are others who suggest that public participation is not effective. Sunstein (2001), for example, suggests that although public participation may increase power sharing in some cases, the involvement of the public may also undermine public trust in the experts who are sharing their specialized knowledge.

As we have seen, there are major difficulties in attempting to prepare for hazards that have not yet been experienced: it is difficult to prepare for the unimaginable. What is less difficult, however, is preparing for what is imaginable or seemingly possible. If an event or hazard can be imagined, responses to that event can also be imagined. One of the means of operationalizing an imaginable response is to conduct emergency or crisis simulations or drills. From lifeguards trained to identify and respond to blocked airways, to families developing escape routines from a burning house, to the evacuation of hospitals and geographic regions due to toxic spills, simulations are an attempt to reduce elements of these situations from unknown to knowable. Rehearsals, simulations, and drills are forms of practice responding so that when faced with actual hazardous, emergency, or crisis situations, responses will be simply that much more automatic and effective.

Imagined responses to hazards or threats differ in terms of complexity, as do the simulation methods that may be used to practice imagined responses. The varying complexity of the practice sessions depends on the goals of the organizations and individuals involved, as well as the knowledge of participants, the experience of the participants in dealing with particular hazards, and time and resource constraints. The literature on simulations and drills suggests that there are four primary types of drills: walk-throughs, tabletop exercises, event simulations, and full deployment drills (Kamer, n.d.; Friese, 2004). Prior to any simulation exercise, however, a number of items must fall into place.

According to Kamer (n.d.) there are a number of steps involved in developing crisis plans, which have been annotated for our purposes here.

1.   The first step is establishing the crisis team. Crisis teams should be cross-disciplinary and have representation from all stakeholders. At the same time, crisis teams function better with relatively few members.

2.   The next step is to articulate workable values in crisis. Crises are intense, often stressful periods that require clear articulation of what is important; the values that must define responses to hazardous situations must be evident. Furthermore, crises also consist of defining moments when true colors may be revealed. Kamer's (n.d.) advice to corporations is to ensure that crises are handled in a manner that puts the best spin on the company's standing. While spin is one issue, this advice can be applied to all forms of crisis plans: values will guide the prioritization of factors within specific scenarios. At this point, Kamer suggests that crises must be defined. For example, McMaster University in Hamilton, Canada, divides crises into public order crises and public welfare crises, which includes natural and man-made crises (McMaster, 2006).

3.   The next step is role definition. The

crisis team makes two important determinations. First, it divides up and assigns responsibility for the development of different aspects of the crisis plan. Next, it decides who will be on point for management roles in the event of certain kinds of crises. (Kamer, n.d.)

As we have identified throughout, jurisdiction is of primary importance. Following role assignment, interim measures are often put in place. As Kamer explains, this may involve reducing the likelihood of various crises by removing hazards of a variety of types from the area.

4. The fourth step calls for a thorough, precise plan to be written. As Kamer (n.d.) notes,

> The plan is necessary because it states the organization's approach to crisis management from values through execution. That needs to be memorialized in writing, because it needs to survive executive and employee turnover, and serve as a corporate policy and compliance document, a training manual, and a playbook. It's Showtime when the crisis hits, and the audience will have little tolerance for actors who still have to read their lines.

5. Following the written plan, feedback is achieved through training, which enables participants to see where potential problems might lie.

6. Finally, the simulation and drill step of crisis plans. (a) The first type of simulation is the *walk-through*, during which relevant parties are gathered together and the plan is discussed, especially with respect to roles and possible scenarios. (b) The next type of simulation is the *tabletop exercise*, whereby participants respond to a hypothetical situation as if it were real. The hypothetical situation involves details of a particular scenario, with participants stating what they would do if faced with that situation. Leadership skills are put to the test in this exercise. (c) *Event simulations* are the next level of practice response. In an event simulation, levels of intensity and authenticity are increased. This form of simulation is often carefully recorded by observers who later provide feedback; the media may report on this form of simulation. Evaluation is a critical component of this form of simulation. (d) The most intensive simulation is the *full deployment drill* (as played out in the Top Officials [TOPOFF] exercises that have been conducted in the United States since 2000). This form of drill lasts a long time, in order to get a sense of the fatigue factor that participants would face in real situations; employs the equipment and many of the same resources that are necessary in actual crises; and is made to seem as real as possible. The full deployment drill is used far less frequently than the other forms of rehearsals because it is resource intensive and costly.

Clearly, the creation and execution of full-fledged disaster plans is not the only means by which actors employ imagination in their anticipation of potential harm. Rehearsal on a smaller scale is also evident in the ways in which individuals consider or imagine current and future harms. Some individuals undertake specific activities to prepare themselves for possible victimization. For example, by their very nature, self-defense classes assume a certain level of crime and prepare individuals to defend themselves in the face of particular dangers. Self-defense classes do little to change the likelihood of crime, but they prepare individuals to minimize harm should, or when, they face such situations. A different example within the realm of health may be personal alarm systems worn by those with various health conditions. The individual may trigger these personal alarm systems when conditions warrant, but the alarm system does not prevent the occurrence of a heart attack, for example, and is rather a form of preparation for when it happens. Self-defense classes and personal alarm systems are a form of taking responsibility for one's own fate—of imagining a potential future and behaving in ways that reduce the harm associated with that future.

Here we observe some degree of slippage with respect to the notions of preparedness and prevention. On the one hand, we know that individuals lock their doors at night, arm their security systems, and stay away from crime-prone areas. On the other hand, at the same time that these individuals may prevent their own victimization, their activities do little to prevent the occurrence of crime more broadly, but may simply divert thieves and robbers to less well-protected homes and residents. What is prevented, it is hoped, is their own victimization, not the prevention of crime itself. Block Watch programs, for example, are simply a means of diverting crime to areas with less surveillance, but are not necessarily geared toward stopping the occurrence of crime more generally.

Cross-Agency Cooperation

Preparation with regard to hazards requires not only recognition that there are a number of potential stakeholders relative to any particular hazard, but also recognition of the significance of coordination among stakeholders. In particular, preparing for hazards is facilitated by coordinated efforts among a number of parties, each of whom has mutually agreed to prepare for or prevent the occurrence of particular hazards and their associated harms. Efforts must be made by stakeholders to ensure that they are not working at cross-purposes to each other. An example mentioned in Chapter 5, this volume, was the impact of Project Bioshield and the granting of the authority to agencies such as the Food and Drug Administration in crisis situations. This power circumvents the bureaucratic structures that often serve as barriers to hazardous, crisis, and emergency situations.

Another example is the case of food safety standards. The Food Standards Australia New Zealand emphasizes the notion of regulatory convergence, "the coming together of ideas, principles, legal requirements, enforcement mechanisms and organizational structures used by government to protect the population" (Peachey, 2005). Coordinated efforts to maintain standards are often forthcoming only in the context of a marketplace failure or with regard to a public health initiative. The idea behind regulatory convergence as a standardized method, however, is that it facilitates preparation for hazards by being able to pinpoint where breakdowns occur; as well as facilitates cooperation which may prevent threats from being actualized because of structures in place that are working toward a common goal.

Efforts to address identity theft provide a further example of cross-agency cooperation. The Canadian government has partnered with the U.S. government in an effort to address identity theft, and has come up with a number of suggestions that rely on the coordinated efforts of the two countries (Public Safety and Emergency Preparedness Canada [PSEPC], 2004). Similarly, the approach emphasizes converged interests between the private sector and government in dealing with this issue. First, because the public is not aware of the extent of identity theft, coordinated education and public awareness initiatives involving both government and the private sectors are advised. Second, since the public needs to be informed of the problem and how to report it and businesses need to consistently define identity theft as a crime, rather than as a cost of business, government needs to increase efforts to provide information to the public on reporting and must motivate business to report these incidents to authorities. Third, it is recommended that both countries review their laws and their effectiveness in addressing identify theft. Fourth, both countries need to work toward consistency in verification processes involving documents such as passports and birth certificates. Finally, the private sector must review their internal procedures, and take a close look at employees who work with sensitive data, to ensure that the privacy and security of their clients are respected.

A primary motivation behind coordinated efforts to address threats to security is the recognition that security interests among parties and perspectives are linked. While it is true that the definitions of security and hazards may vary, failure to recognize the definitions and needs of other actors increases the potential that security efforts will work at cross-purposes and will therefore be undermined. Independence, rather than reducing the likelihood of harm, may increase its likelihood. Rather than perceiving security interests as a zero-sum game, regulatory and other forms of convergence are based on the recognition that security interests may be best attained using multilateral versus unilateral strategies. Again, while our examples speak to the organizational and institutional level, examples also exist at the individual level. Multilateral strategies exist in the home: we ensure that cleaning products are kept away from infants, and initiate dietary changes at the family level, rather than only among particular family members. At work, colleagues who smoke do so only in designated areas, thus reducing the impact of that hazard for other parties.

Response

Once the time for preparation has passed and the threat has become a reality, individuals, institutions, and states must respond. In particular, we consider the response stage with respect to first responders and victims, the importance of leadership, and the significance of the media.

First Responders and Victims

Examining the reactions to threats is important not only from what we learn about the dangers posed by the physical and social worlds, but also for the insights provided from how people react to hazards, whether natural or man made. For example, we have learned from responses to calamities such as earthquakes and hurricanes that when these incidents occur, the first responders often are not emergency personnel but are instead members of the public. As Clarke (2006) points out, the first person at the site of a disaster is not usually the trained officer but the survivor who takes steps to help others. This pattern appears in many different types of disasters. It also emerged, not surprisingly, in the initial responses of people during the World Trade Center attacks, where nonprofessionals in the buildings acted to help evacuate people in the absence of police and fire department response teams.

Despite the public as the primary source of first responders, the responses of the public have been generally shrouded in myth (Quarantelli, 1989). Quarantelli explains that the first myth is the panic myth. While individuals feel fear and anxiety when faced with dangerous or hazardous situations, most individuals do not respond with irrational or inappropriate behavior. Rather, individuals tend to remain in place to facilitate efforts of others; converge on impact sites to offer their assistance; and, if possible, engage in deliberate and intentional activities to search for and help family, friends, and others. Quarantelli (p. 4) further notes the following with regard to individuals' responses to endangerment:

> In fact, instead (one could argue) they tend to show more rationality
> under stress than they do normally, if by rationality is meant conscious

weighing of alternative courses of action in a situation. None of us undertake much conscious weighing of optional courses of actions in performing the great majority of our daily routines. But those caught in the emergency time periods of disasters, when their very lives and those of others that are important to them may be at stake, become very conscious and aware of the behavioral choices they have and make.

A second myth is the passivity myth (Quarantelli, 1989). This myth presumes that individuals will be paralyzed, unable to help themselves or others. Associated with this myth is that victims passively wait for external help to arrive and wait helplessly for others to take action. In disaster situations, 90% of the missing are found by neighbors and others (Quarantelli, p. 4). A third myth is the antisocial myth, the idea that there is a violent, hidden "Mr. Hyde" nature that is revealed in the context of hazards. Quarantelli (p. 5) explains that this is largely untrue. While there are instances of looting and criminal activity associated with disasters, as was reported with Hurricane Katrina, this does not characterize the immediate or majority response to disasters.

A fourth myth is the traumatized myth, which suggests that serious mental illness characterizes those who have been exposed to various forms of trauma. New psychoses are rarely produced; while these events become etched into the minds of those who endure them, they have rarely been found to incapacitate those who experience such events (Quarantelli, 1989, p. 6). Finally, there is the self-centered myth, which suggests that low morale and low self-esteem is a response to these situations. As Quarantelli notes, the experience of disaster is not an isolating experience because often a large number of others have gone through recent similar experiences. Quarantelli sums up his analysis by suggesting that most of the problems experienced by individuals in the responsiveness phase of disasters have to do with the organizations helping them, as individuals themselves tend to cope reasonably well. He further suggests that "disasters are primarily disruptions in the routine behavior of groups rather than interruptions of the everyday actions of individuals" and that "disasters are public difficulties in collective social entities; they are not the personal problems some persons might have" (pp. 8–9).

It is important to note the situations to which these myths apply. Not all hazards that we have referred to in this text are collectively experienced. For example, crime victimization does not, technically, involve any collective familiarity. Although we have sometimes used the terms hazard and disaster interchangeably, it is important to keep in mind that disasters involve far greater numbers of individuals than hazards do. For many, the experience of crime is very personal. Drawing on the disaster literature, however, allows us to see incidents that are defined largely as individual are part of a range of behaviors that collectives also experience. For victims of sexual assault, for example, while the experience of the sexual assault itself is indeed personal, the behavior is recognizable as part of the collective understanding of similar others. A large part of the recovery phase for victims of crime is the recognition that they are not alone in their experiences, that similar incidents have occurred to others, and that there is some collective recognition of the pain that this has caused for a particular individual. The same can be said of health hazards: the individual who acquires breast cancer, although experienced individually, is part of a collective of individuals who have and will come to understand this illness. The personal understanding of hazard can be located within the experiences of collectives.

Whether those who first offer help are themselves victims or emergency response professionals, the types of support that victims require can vary substantially. While removing victims from harm's way and dealing with physical injury must first be dealt with, victims also require different forms of social support from various sources. Victims tend to rely first on family and friends and immediate social circles, and less on formal sources of support. The types of required support vary with the nature of the stressor under consideration (Norris, 2001, p. 471). Emotional support (comfort and acceptance) has been found to be most appropriate in uncontrollable situations, whereas informational support (advice and guidance) is best suited to conditions where the stressor can be controlled (Norris, p. 471). In situations where there is a loss of assets, tangible support to replace losses is hugely beneficial.

Recovery from disaster often requires more than one form of support. Norris (2001) investigates the variations in types of support required and offered in different disaster contexts and among victims of varying ethnicities and incomes. These authors find that support mobilization is complicated: "Whereas the rule of relative need means that the most help should go to those who need it the most, the rule of relative advantage acknowledges that one's position in the social structure also influences one's access to resources" (Norris, p. 472). The extent of harm and damage endured by victims explicitly depends on the social context in which victims find themselves. The parameters of natural versus man-made hazards may also influence the types of support that are forthcoming. Legal processes work to influence the acquisition of certain forms of support.[3]

How do these points relate to risk balance? We suggest that victims play a key role in the response phase of various hazardous events. The data that we have drawn on throughout this text suggests that actors most often draw on their own resources, but that the resources at their disposal vary widely. Support of efforts to help themselves or their family members and to help others in the face of hazards is crucial, as is acknowledging the efforts that actors make in this regard. While formal recognition of these efforts is likely impossible during the response phase, it is critical that the efforts of individual actors be formally acknowledged in the aftermath of these events. Recognition provides feedback and encourages similar behaviors in the case of subsequent and similar events.

Leadership in Response

In a study by Connell (2001) in the immediate aftermath of 9/11, an analysis of media reports containing first hand accounts from survivors focuses on the reported experiences of these victims and, in particular, the decision to evacuate and the evacuation process. Victims appeared to attribute their survival to three factors: social location, leadership, and level of perceived threat. Connell uses Turner and Killian's (1987) definition of *collective behavior* as existing when a "collective is oriented toward an object of attention and arrives at some shared objective, but these are not defined in advance and there are no formal procedures for reaching decisions" (Turner & Killian, p. 4, as quoted in Connell, p. 3). While formal evacuation procedures existed at the World Trade Center, the decision to evacuate was determined in a context fraught with extreme contingencies, including victims' injuries and destruction of the work area, including physical hazards such as fire, smoke, and broken glass, to name a few.

Leadership factors figured prominently in victims' decisions to evacuate the building. Interestingly, in some cases, the corporate culture of decision making even figured into this high stress situation. The study highlights one report of a group of coworkers who went into their conference room to discuss their options, eventually arriving at the conclusion that they needed to evacuate, after having weighed various options. Survivors mentioned the significant role played by officials such as police officers and firefighters; their role was highlighted due to their recognizable uniforms. Floor marshals played a significant role in the formal evacuation plans, but few were mentioned in the survivor accounts. Besides mentioning formal leadership roles played by uniformed authority figures, survivors focused on the informal leadership roles taken on by coworkers who worked to organize their colleagues' evacuation of the building.

While the above example focuses on a hazard of major proportions, effective leadership in response to less wide-ranging hazards, such as crime, is also particularly significant. Victims of crime are their own first responders, as it is most often crime victims who report their experiences to police. Similarly, individuals who experience illness or injury are also often their own first responders and report their symptoms to medical personnel. In their capacity as leaders, police officers and medical personnel play critical roles in responding to individual concerns. Differing trends can be observed, however. In the case of reports of criminal victimization, we see a trend toward a less hands-on approach by police: individuals often have to report their victimization in person, rather than to police arriving at their doorsteps. On the other hand, although people with suspected health problems typically do not receive house calls, more and more often batteries of tests are conducted to deduce or uncover health problems. Both of these examples speak, albeit differently, to the notion of validation, and the validation that effective leadership provides to those who find themselves victimized.

The Media and Response Coordination

Popular culture seems obsessed by the twin factors of crime and hardship. The preponderance of crime-related television shows, such as *Law and Order* (of which there are currently three versions), *Crime Scene Investigation* (or *CSI*, also three versions), among a host of others including *Medium*, *Cold Case*, *Crossing Jordan*, and *Without a Trace*, not to mention the numerous reality shows featuring cops and courts, suggests that the media is presenting people with a steady diet of the hazards of crime. Disaster films, on the other hand, are a genre that evolved during the 1970s, with movies such as *Airport* (1970), *The Poseidon Adventure* (1972), *Earthquake* (1974), and *Towering Inferno* (1974) topping the charts. More recently, the 1990s saw disaster-themed movies focusing on disease (*Outbreak*, 1995), natural events (*Twister*, 1996), Armageddon-style demise and extraterrestrials (*Independence Day*, 1996, and *Deep Impact*, 1998). The 21st century is keeping apace with films about experiments gone awry (*Stealth*, 2005, and *Black Hole*, 2006), avalanches and blizzards (*Avalanche*, 2004, and *Storm*, 2005) and even terrorism (*Black Friday*, 2005, *World Trade Center*, 2006, and *United 93*, 2006), it is quite likely that more of this genre will be seen during the last half of the current decade.

The mass media play a role in risk balance and, in particular, the response phase of hazards and disasters that goes well beyond the reputed entertainment value that crime-TV and disaster movies provide. In Chapter 5, this volume, we noted that the media facilitate the transmission of communications throughout the various stages of disasters and hazardous events. The media facilitate communications among those directly involved in hazardous events. As importantly, however, the media facilitate the communication of these types of events to the rest of the world. Spencer and Triche (1994) explain that the media use particular frames through which hazards are considered.

The focus of the media on hazardous occurrences is relatively rare considering the abundance of hazards that occur every day. As Spencer and Triche (1994) explain, few hazardous events are translated into "news events" (p. 200). The media use cultural frameworks to determine which occurrences are defined as newsworthy events. Not unlike the use of heuristics by individuals, hazards are newsworthy "when they question, or become the basis for questioning, the taken-for-granted safety of the every day world and our routine activities within that world" (Spencer & Triche, p. 200). At a very basic level, hazards are categorized according to whether they are natural or social, and whether they can be considered causes or consequences. The reporting of hazards is also influenced by the assumptions that are made with respect to the origins of the phenomenon, the newsworthiness of events, the sources of information, and ideologies and politics (Spencer & Triche, p. 201).

The varying frames that may be applied by the media suggest that the role of the media in risk balance will vary depending on the media itself. Local media, for example, have been found to spin news items differently depending on the relevance of particular stories to their audiences. In their study of local hazards in New Orleans (pre-Hurricane Katrina), Spencer and Triche (1994, p. 206) found that reporters tended to downplay the significance of the consequences of particular hazards and to minimize their seriousness. As well, local reporting tended to focus on expert opinions, rather than using quotes from locals, which tended to highlight local suffering. Experts and their respective quotes, conversely, diminished local impacts but highlighted possible consequences of various hazards. Spencer and Triche suggest that the focus on experts may have been a strategic choice to reduce public anxiety.

The ability of the media to render any sort of effect is limited, however, by the structure in which newscasts appear. In their study of news coverage following September 11, 2001, McDonald and Lawrence (2004) focus on the expanded news hole that was created due to the unprecedented nature of this particular event. The extraordinary circumstances following the attacks included the event requiring a few days to unfold—details in the hours following the attacks were sketchy. McDonald and Lawrence also note that in the immediate aftermath of 9/11, the media helped to provide a degree of emotional gratification for TV viewers by focusing on American values, American unity, and American strength. At the same time, these authors' examination of the news coverage immediately following this event suggested "emotional content outweighed informational in a way that did not necessarily serve the public's long-term interests" (McDonald & Lawrence, p. 329). Rather than employing any form of unconventional format for this out-of-the-ordinary event, McDonald and Lawrence find that a conventional crime script, breaking-news format prevailed. This script contains a description of a crime; accompanying visuals, including eyewitness testimony; a focus on witnesses, friends, and family members; and a focus on perpetrators and efforts to apprehend them (McDonald & Lawrence, p. 335).

In the immediate aftermath of 9/11, the media, despite the hours of time at their disposal, failed to provide the viewing audience with any more depth than what is normally offered on a daily basis. This suggests an effort to "routinize the unexpected" (Tuchman, 1980, quoted in McDonald & Lawrence, 2004, p. 336). Furthermore, by covering the terrorist attacks through a crime script, the details of the crime or terrorist event are the focus of reporting, and not any consideration of the social and political context in which the event has occurred. The crime script encourages consumers to expect some form of closure—focusing on the perpetrators (terrorists) deflects attention away from political issues at hand (terrorism), which are far less amenable to closure. McDonald and Lawrence argue that the media's focus on the sensational aspects of the story—body counts and perpetrators—was evidence of the media's "[un]willingness to depart from these ingrained habits of ordinary news delivery," (p. 339) to the detriment of the viewing audience, amounting to a lost opportunity to get Americans thinking about the hard problem of terrorism rather than its quick resolution.

The media can play a critical role in the delivery of information during hazardous or crisis times. However, the expectation that the media will actually deliver information that moves beyond a formulaic approach to news stories may be overly optimistic, especially as the event moves from the response stage to the aftermath.

Recovery and Prevention

A central question that guides the recovery and prevention process is the question of responsibility: "Who is responsible for the costs of harm incurred?" "How does this responsibility vary by hazard?" Below we high-light some of the methods of recovering costs, many of which imply that the costs of hazards are borne by specific actors—individuals, institutions, and the state.

Litigation

We have considered insurance as a form of compensation in the after-math of hazard and disaster, but there are other forms of compensation that may also apply: tort law and government compensation. While insur-ance speaks to identifying and dealing with the costs of life's potential misfortunes, tort law is another venue that allows for victims, whether plaintiffs or claimants, to recover some of their costs from offenders, or defendants. Specifically, tort law establishes the conditions that allow for costs to be shifted to those responsible for such costs—tort means wrong, and tort law establishes who is responsible for a particular wrong and who will pay the price of that wrong. Tort law differentiates between inten-tional and unintentional harm. Intentional harms may include battery and defamation, for example, while unintentional harms include accidents and other mishaps. As with insurance, the notion of liability figures promi-nently in tort law. In cases of tort that proceed to the courts, decisions must be made according to liability rules—rules that specify the conditions under which costs can be shifted from one to another party. Liability rules establish whether specific situations can best be described as involving fault liability or strict liability.

In the case of fault liability, it must be determined that the defendant breached some duty of care to the plaintiff. For example, a breach would occur when the defendant either does something that a reasonable person would not do or fails to do something that a reasonable person would do. The idea behind establishing fault is that there is a failure to take appro-priate precautions to avoid the harm that one could reasonably foresee. Examples of fault liability include defamation. Imagine a case where a book distributor distributes books that include defamatory statements about a particular person. Even though the distributor was not the author of the defamation (that is, did not commit the initial wrong), he or she would still be found to be liable, or at fault, because of not having taken appropriate care with respect to what he or she was distributing. Another example of fault liability is negligence—breaching a duty of care. Failing to provide a particular standard of care would be considered a form of negligence. Another example is trespass, causing direct interference. As noted earlier, strict liability falls under a set of rules that suggests that the liability clearly lies with one particular party. The authors of defamatory remarks are held strictly liable; the fault of defamation lies entirely with those who write defamatory comments.

With the possibility of recouping damages, tort potentially enables the costs of hardship to be redirected toward those who are responsible for causing the harm. This may work to enhance security: being able to establish blame and diminish costs may have the effect of reducing anxiety and subsequently enhancing security. As Menyawi (2003) explains, tort works on the basis of corrective justice: those who cause harm or damage are responsible for the costs they incur. The idea behind tort law is that of deterrence: if parties know that they will be held responsible for the damages they cause, more attention will be paid to reducing or eliminating harm or damage or the probability of it. The trend, however, is more toward no-fault compensation schemes than toward tort. In no-fault compensation schemes, such as third-party insurance, the focus is on distributive justice, with the underlying idea that all victims deserve to be compensated, in contrast to finding fault. Rather than establishing individual responsibility for damage, compensation schemes rely on the notion of collective support, and fault need not be established (Menyawi, p. 6). Collective support means that both defendants and victims pay for losses, however indirectly those payments are made. These types of compensation schemes may therefore provide security for defendants, but victims end up paying by participating in these compensation schemes in the first place.

The idea of perpetrators paying for the harms they commit via tort law is a common occurrence throughout the United States and elsewhere. Tort law has even been used to extract some degree of compensation for breaches of security from terrorist organizations. In perhaps one of the most well-known cases, *Klinghoffer v. the Palestine Liberation Organization* (*PLO*), a civil action was brought against a terrorist organization, the PLO (*Klinghoffer v. PLO*, 1990). A disabled American tourist was shot and killed, then thrown, with his wheelchair, over the side of a cruise ship during the ship's hijacking by the PLO. The family of the deceased victim initially sued the cruise line for negligent security. The cruise line, in turn, impleaded the PLO as a defendant. Once jurisdictional issues were sorted out, and questions that were raised as to whether state tort law or federal tort law would hear the case had been resolved, it took some 12 years before a verdict was eventually reached. The case culminated in the PLO paying the Klinghoffer family directly for damages, at the same time that the PLO denied responsibility for the event. While the amount of the damages paid was not made public, speculation was that the settlement was for tens of millions of dollars (Hume & Todd, 2003). As Hume and Todd note, "the Klinghoffers' determination to avenge the brutal murder committed on the Achille Lauro [cruise liner] stands as a path-breaking success to use the American legal system to hold terrorists and their allies to account." These authors suggest that although tort law may do little to inhibit terrorists, its use may be one of a toolbox of methods used against terrorists to extract some justice.

Government Compensation

Imagine this scenario: Individuals working in the Twin Towers of the World Trade Center on the morning of September 11, 2001. Until about 8:45 A.M., all accounts suggest that the workday was proceeding as one might expect it normally would. After 8:45 A.M., however, the day changed radically, and forever after, as the first of two planes hit the North Tower. A second plane hit the South Tower at approximately 9:03 A.M. In the aftermath of this event, a critical question has emerged: When, and to what extent, should the government compensate for unfortunate events?

Lascher and Powers (2004) suggest that this question has received much less attention in the aftermath of this event than other questions having to do with security, such as the focus on detection, interagency coordination, and so on. The question of compensation is not straightforward, and involves both moral and ethical issues. In terms of this particular terrorist event, what does the government owe victims, and how does the argument for compensation differ for victims of other terrorist events, as well as for other hazards and disasters? In the near immediate aftermath of 9/11, U.S. Congress enabled the establishment of the September 11th Victim Compensation Fund. This fund was geared to provide victims or their families with monetary compensation for the damages incurred as a result of the events of 9/11 (Lascher & Powers, p. 282). But what exactly is the rationale for providing compensation?

A paternalistic view of the state would maintain that the government should compensate for life's unfortunate events and uncertainties, "from cradle to grave" (Lascher & Powers, 2004, p. 286). Obviously, this is an untenable system and any government would quickly run out of funds. One issue that arises in this scenario is whether the availability of compensation would reduce motivation for individuals to privately purchase insurance. This may constitute a situation of moral hazard: if individuals know they will be compensated, individual efforts to obtain private insurance may be reduced. Beyond the notion that governments should take care of their citizens, another concept that emerges is that of liability or culpability (Lascher & Powers, p. 287). If government could have done more to protect citizens, does it not owe them some compensation in the event of harm or loss? This argument harkens back to tort law and reasonable levels of care. But how do we know if reasonable care has been taken? Lascher and Powers argue that the size of the group involved may serve as an indication of reasonable care to be taken: the larger the organization, the more culpable the government is. In other words, the greater the conspiracy, the more likely it is that the government should have been able to identify and prevent that group from acting. This would provide the rationale for compensating victims of 9/11, given the size of Al-Qaeda, and would provide a rationale for not providing compensation to the victims of the Alfred P. Murrah Building bombing in Oklahoma City, an event involving a conspiracy of far fewer individuals, with the implication that this event was less preventable.

Another issue that may determine whether compensation is to be awarded has to do with the concepts of brute bad luck versus option bad luck, both of which deal with the notion of contributory negligence, and the relative contributions of victims to their own demise. *Brute bad luck* is the situation that describes an outcome that could not be anticipated (Lascher and Powers [2004] provide the example of being hit by a meteor), whereas *option bad luck* is the outcome of a deliberate gamble, such as losing one's savings on the stock market. Brute bad luck would be worthy of government compensation, whereas option bad luck would not. Furthermore, as mentioned above, option bad luck would apply when individuals fail to personally address possible outcomes because of anticipating government compensation for these outcomes. This situation is known as *adverse selection*. These issues are addressed by Lascher and Powers's four principles of government compensation (Lascher & Powers, p. 287, p. 289):

   1. Government should compensate victims of unpredictable events whenever it has failed to take reasonable pre-event risk control and risk reduction measures (and especially in the extreme case in which government intentionally exposes certain individuals to risk).

   2. Government's responsibility to compensate victims under Principle 1 is lessened if the victims failed to take reasonable pre-event risk control or risk reduction measures (and especially if the compensation program itself were to create a significant problem of moral hazard).

3. Government's responsibility to compensate victims under Principle 1 is lessened if the victims failed to take reasonable pre-event risk financing measures (and especially if the compensation program itself were to create a significant commitment problem—e.g. adverse selection).

4. Government should compensate victims of unpredictable events when the failure to compensate is likely to cause additional and significant negative economic/social ramifications. (Lascher & Powers, 2004, pp. 287, 289).

These principles address basic considerations, but as Lascher and Powers (2004) note, secondary considerations also apply. First, these principles have not specified which level of government is to bear the financial burden of compensation. Is there a particular level of government that bears more responsibility than another level? A second issue has to do with who is compensated. What obligation does a government have to noncitizens and visitors? This question might best be answered by determining the level of involvement with citizens that noncitizens have. For example, if a U.S. embassy in an African country is bombed, it would make sense that the Africans employed at that embassy would also be compensated. In another instance, the issue of who is to receive compensation can be far more complicated. For example, the individuals killed on September 11, 2001, covered a range of the economic and social spectrum, from high-priced lawyers to cleaning crews. Given the respective differences in risk positions, should compensation be equally distributed? One might argue that, on the one hand, the government's failure to take reasonable actions was evenly distributed, therefore compensation should also be evenly distributed (Lascher & Powers, p. 293). On the other hand, some people experience greater losses than others and it could be argued that compensation should be in accordance with respective losses: Some may lose more than others (Lascher & Powers, p. 293).

Returning to Normal: Re-Establishing Routines

In the aftermath of hazards and disasters, there is often reference to the notion of returning to normal. In the early days after 9/11, President Bush encouraged Americans to return to and support the "American way of life." Essentially, the idea was to return to the everyday familiarity of the known, or routines. The ability and ease with which a return to prehazard ways of life is possible, however, is hazard dependent. In the aftermath of natural disasters, for example, cleaning up the immediate devastation as well as restoring basic features of survival—homes, water, and power—often takes precedence over other concerns. Infrastructures may have to be rebuilt, along with homes and workplaces. Restoring environments to their prehazard stage, however, will vary widely depending on the resources and time available for this task, as well as the political and social will to realize such changes.

Again, the devastation caused by Hurricane Katrina provides a living laboratory in terms of the multitude of factors and interests that converge, or fail to converge, in order to address the damages inflicted on New Orleans and the surrounding area. The stakeholders in this process are many: from individuals who lost their homes and families, to businesses who suffered economic losses or stand to gain from redevelopment, to politicians who may see the restoration of New Orleans as a means of saving face that was lost in the botched response to this disaster. Still others view the aftermath of Katrina as a time to re-evaluate the very idea of restoration: rather than restore particular neighborhoods (some of which were slums) to their former states, the idea is to transform these neighborhoods into different and better places. Returning to normal and establishing routines has a different outcome depending on whether a restorative or transformative vision is used. The difference between these two responses in the aftermath of hazards is paralleled in the criminological literature in terms of restorative and transformative justice. The concept of justice also figures into decisions and how they are made with regard to the allocation of resources to aftermath efforts. Who is deserving, and on the basis of what criteria, of the resources that may be available for restorative efforts?

The idea of returning to normal, and either establishing or re-establishing routines, is a feature of a wide range of hazardous events, including events that are experienced individually. Those who experience criminal victimization often must also re-establish themselves in the world that they inhabited prior to victimization. Again, the nature of the victimization will determine whether a return to routine is desirable. Victims who have been seriously injured in a criminal attack may look at their prior routines with a critical eye to determine if the routines that they had previously established are those to which they want to return, or should return. As we suggested at the beginning of this volume, routines can expose us to harm. Conversely, individuals whose cars have been stolen may consider their victimization as simply a case of bad luck and as having nothing to do with routine activities. Similarly, in the aftermath of heart bypass surgery, patients may vow explicitly not to return to their previously unhealthy lifestyles: the experience of this event may encourage the patient to replace old routines with those geared to promoting future healthiness.

The replacement of previous routines with new routines may not, however, necessarily instill feelings of security and well-being. In the aftermath of 9/11, the new routine of airport security has, in many ways, contributed to feelings of insecurity for those who experience these security measures, not to mention the many who simply feel inconvenienced by these new routines. Yet efforts to re-establish comfort with regard to past ways of life have been attempted at various times through what is known as reassurance policing. According to Bahn (1974), *reassurance policing* may be defined as "the feeling of security and safety that a citizen experiences when he sees a police officer or police patrol car nearby" (p. 340). Based on Wilson and Kelling's (1982) idea of broken windows and the signals that broken windows send (i.e., that no one cares and no one is available in particular neighborhoods), bringing the visibility of police officers to the foreground is meant to counteract this perception and suggest that, in fact, there is someone, or some agency, that cares. The more visible police officers are, the more comfort the public is provided: presumably, it is considered evident that the police indeed care by the very fact of their presence. While this method may be short term, police visibility signals to communities that the authorities are taking specific concerns seriously. After the bombings in England, British police officers undertook a campaign of reassurance policing that was meant to encourage a return to normal, although the omnipresence of officers indeed signaled a new definition of what it means to be "normal."

Conclusion

As we observed earlier in Chapter 2, this volume, certain factors prevail in balancing risk to achieve security, factors including knowledge, power, control, and vision. Many of these aspects are addressed by coming to terms with the significance and meaning of differences in resources, in the form of economic, cultural, and social capital, which are tightly bound to risk positions. Actions taken or not taken at various times and in particular places may work to alleviate potential harm, or to circumvent the occurrence of harm altogether. Conversely, opportunities for responding and planning may be missed, resulting in greater harm than had opportunities been taken advantage of, or had the landscape been viewed with an eye to various possibilities.

Not all means of addressing hazards are equally successful. The efficacy of personal or institutional responses to hazards is dependent on an ability to mobilize resources to respond, and to correctly judge the risk of injury or loss. There are variations both across and between levels in terms of their assessments of what is needed to minimize harm. Not all individuals and institutions will be able to mobilize resources equally successfully: risk positions determine how and to what extent this can be accomplished. Between levels, we know that efficacy can also vary, as will judgments as to what constitutes effective mobilization of resources.

Notes to Chapter 6

1. As noted in Chapter 4, this volume, false positives occur when predictions are made that certain behaviors will occur but they do not; false negatives occur when predictions are made that certain behaviors will not occur but they do.

2. This depends, of course, on both the type, as well as the location of the natural disaster. The estimated damage and loss of life associated with the 2004 tsunami in Southeast Asia is expected to take some time yet to finalize.

3. These forms of support are usually tangible. We consider victim compensation and litigation in our discussion of recovery, later in the present chapter.

7

Concluding Thoughts

Becoming Secure: What Have We Learned?

References to security are extensive and are often preceded by adjectives that add some insight into what is at stake: discussions of social security, financial security, national security, private security, homeland security, border security, and Internet security tend to prevail. A recent Google search (in May 2007) came up with nearly 6 billion hits associated with the term, compared with 1.9 billion hits less than 2 years before, in September 2005. No longer a concept limited to the realm of politics and state relations (as in national security), security has become a marketable commodity—at all levels, from the individual and institutional levels, to the state level. Spending on items that supposedly enhance personal security and corporate security has soared over the past 20 years, as consumers attempt to secure self, home, and business against harm.

As we have noted, knowledge and power are central features of security, and those who have the power to do so are able to define hazards and threats. Both power and knowledge are central components of the resources that actors bring to bear in defining hazards. In most cases, institutional and state definitions prevail over individual definitions of threats. Yet, as Béland (2007, p. 83) notes, "terrorism has taken a global form that both challenges and legitimizes the protective mission of the state." In terms of the relationship of individual and state interests in security, the state obviously has greater resources at its disposal to facilitate prioritizing state interests over security interests at other levels. At the same time, security at any particular level cannot be understood apart from security at other levels.

We have seen the importance at the individual level of heuristic devices, or mental shortcuts, that enhance or undermine security. These are often put into play when an individual is attempting to decipher or categorize various elements as benign or harmful. Heuristics depend on the store of knowledge on which actors rely, which is built through experience and the formal acquisition of knowledge. These heuristic devices also influence the identification of hazards at the institutional and state levels. The use of heuristic devices depends on their availability: the accessibility of these devices and their use relates to respective risk positions and locations relative to the hazards that are identified. Furthermore, the identification of hazards and threats is often influenced by cultural idiosyncrasies. The cultural determination of what is at risk and therefore what is threatening varies substantially around the globe, depending on the nature of the harms and the contexts in which these identifications are made.

We have documented the importance of trust in the reliability of both human and nonhuman objects in our collective sense of security. Trust contributes to social order by providing expectational maps: interacting parties learn to have compatible expectations of each other or others. An *expectational map* is like a map of short-term prospects; it is a map of what we can expect will happen in the short term, at least, if not farther into the future. We are able to develop such maps because of trust; we place our confidence in someone, something or some system. Coleman (1993) further suggests that trust involves rationality with parties determining whether or not to trust on the basis of calculations regarding probable loss or gain, yet some of these calculations are far less mathematical than we tend to think. These maps contribute to ontological security, that is, the confidence that life will continue as we know it. If trust is not developed or is ambivalent, the outcome is anxiety, a defining characteristic of modern society.

Giddens (1990) suggests that trust is particularly critical when we are faced with a lack of information. If access to information were entirely open, or transparent, then trust would be a nonissue. But since we are often faced with less knowledge than we might prefer, experts' knowledge, or disciplinary expertise, enables experts to capture a front and center position in our navigation of hazards and threats.

Of central importance in formulating our argument is Beck's notion of risk society. As we demonstrated, this perspective builds on the recognition that the value accorded expertise and trust in experts has declined over the past few decades. As Douglas (1992) notes, there is an emphasis in contemporary society on charging to someone's account responsibility or blame for negative outcomes. Part of establishing responsibility is establishing jurisdiction. As Timmermans (2002) points out jurisdiction is the "tie between an organizational group and its work" (p. 551), with some degree of struggle often characterizing efforts to claim and maintain jurisdiction. When viewed this way, jurisdiction is a form of control, with both abstract and specific knowledge often characterizing jurisdictional claims. Having said this, an actor can only claim jurisdiction in the face of agreement from others with whom it interacts. Jurisdiction, therefore, has implications for accountability and responsibility.

We have discussed the importance of accountability across agencies; this is demonstrated in the local role of police in U.S. homeland security efforts. Thacher (2005) notes that the politics of policing emphasize attention paid to certain areas over others: "police take responsibility for law and order mainly within their assigned beats, ignoring or even contributing to illegality and disorder elsewhere" (p. 639). With a rather narrow view of jurisdiction, Thacher notes that geography is often the key determinant of police responsibility. In our analyses of the case of Jane Doe and the case of Karla Homolka and Paul Bernardo, in Chapter 3, this volume, we find support for this observation: the quest to capture these offenders was impeded by the perceived barriers imposed by police jurisdictions and the failure to share information between jurisdictions.

How does the concept of jurisdiction relate to risk balance? We have emphasized that the determination of what constitutes a hazard often varies by perspective (individual, institution, or state); the means to address various hazards, in terms of available resources, also varies by perspective. We have learned that establishing jurisdiction has an impact on responsibilities and rights, and further implies accountability and control over particular situations prior to, during, and after hazards. Admittedly there are many hazards and disasters that pose problems for jurisdictions: Under whose jurisdiction is the restoration of basic amenities for the victims of the 2004 tsunami? For the victims of Hurricane Katrina? Is this the jurisdiction of individuals, local government, or the national or even world communities?

Establishing jurisdiction is not an easy task, and is one that requires more than simply geographic or incident-based determinations.[1] It is not difficult to establish that fires are the jurisdiction of the fire department, or that burglaries are the jurisdiction of the police department, or that heart attacks are the jurisdiction of emergency medical personnel. Each of these events, however, assumes that an event has already transpired. What is less clear is establishing jurisdiction in the pre-event stage or establishing jurisdiction over chronic harms. Furthermore, establishing jurisdiction for events that reside outside the domain of any one particular disciplinary boundary is also plagued by difficulties and challenges.

This leads us to some practical problems that are informed by our perspective. Consider the pre-event stage. Who has jurisdiction for establishing that appropriate dietary requirements are met among school-aged children? Is it the jurisdiction of parents or guardians to feed children adequately, or is it the responsibility of schools to identify children who might be inadequately fed? Into which jurisdiction does this task fall if parents are unable to provide for children, due to limited resources? What if parents are able to provide for children but do not: does this mean that schools have no responsibility for these students? In the years prior to Hurricane Katrina, was replacing and repairing inadequate levees the jurisdiction of local government or federal government? What duty do the various levels of governments owe to citizens? Who was responsible for the levees?

There are also difficulties in establishing security for hazards that reside in more than one disciplinary domain. What about the case of starving children? Is it the jurisdiction of health authorities, school authorities, or the police to intervene? Whose responsibility is the prevention of hazard in this case? In the example of terrorism, who is responsible for the identification of members of terrorist plots? Is this a community issue? Does the membership of various religious organizations, for example, need to bring particular individuals to the attention of the authorities, or is it an issue specific to policing and security specialists? Is terrorism the jurisdiction of the host country alone, in the case of international terrorists, or does the export country also bear some responsibility for the activities of terrorists? Again we see that values come into play in establishing jurisdiction for hazards, taking us well beyond geography and incident-specific approaches to hazards.

Establishing Security

Security is not as simple as locking one's doors or avoiding certain types of people: it is also about regular health check ups, buying insurance, and recycling. As we have maintained, contexts are critical to determining how people evaluate their security. From an institutional perspective, security may be just as diverse: from corporations offering compensation packages to employees; to the police conducting criminal background checks; to the school board placing schools in particular geographical locations. Similarly, the activities in which states participate may work to undermine security both domestically and internationally, especially if behaviors undermine international reputations. Values are central to determining what it is that people and institutions are willing to do in the name of security—both their own security and that of others.

It is therefore important to ask, "Who or what is endangered?" Or, "Whose security interests are being taken into account?" National security, for example, suggests that the referent subject is the nation—the nation requires securing with respect to some form of endangerment. Although national security might at first appear, to be the purview of nation states, national security is clearly bound to other levels in particular ways. Yet, as Buzan (1983) notes, "since the security of any one referent object or level cannot be achieved in isolation from the others, the security of each becomes, in part, a condition for the security of all" (p. 13).

An interesting example of the referent subjects and objects of security can be found in a recent article titled "Come One, Come All, Join the Terror Target List," in the *New York Times* (Lipton, 2006), focusing on the National Asset Database:

> It reads like a tally of terrorist targets that a child might have written: Old MacDonald's Petting Zoo, the Amish Country Popcorn factory, the Mule Day Parade, the Sweetwater Flea Market and an unspecified "Beach at the End of a Street."

A recent report issued by the inspector general of the Department of Homeland Security questioned the inclusion of a number of sites on the National Asset Database, which is a database that has been used by the DHS to allocate resources to various parts of the country to address the threat of terrorism. The report calls into question the inclusion of various "unusual or out-of-place" locations "whose criticality is not readily apparent" (quoted in Lipton, 2006). Indeed, it is difficult to make sense of the fact that a state such as Indiana lists 50% more potential terrorist targets than does the state of New York. Given the differences in populations (New York far exceeds Indiana), the subsequent differences in population densities and critical infrastructure, not to mention the record of terrorist activity associated with each of these states, the criteria by which targets are determined is not self-evident. As the inspector general points out, the credibility of the data is at issue with the inclusion of such seemingly innocuous sites (Lipton).

Interestingly, the insecurity associated with the identified targets appears not to be a product of the targets themselves. In Illinois, an organizer of

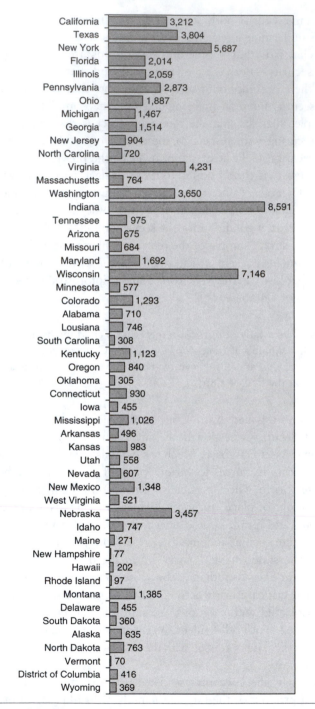

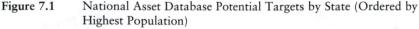

Figure 7.1   National Asset Database Potential Targets by State (Ordered by Highest Population)

the Apple and Pork Festival, listed in the database, remarks, "Seems like someone has gone overboard" (Lipton, 2006). Similarly, the owner of Amish Country Popcorn company states, "I am out in the middle of nowhere. . . . We are nothing but a bunch of Amish buggies and tractors out here" (Lipton). It seems that if the targets are wondering how it is that they have been included in the database, the determination of security is being left in the hands of the experts who determine threat independent of any assessment by the targets themselves. As was noted in Chapter 2, this volume, Ripley and Frank (2004) suggest that the arguments for the inclusion of these targets may draw on the notion of relative worth, rather than relative vulnerability. Reminiscent of the compensation argument that we considered in Chapter 6, this volume, this argument is based on the idea that the state owes an equal duty to protect, despite unequal vulnerability.

Regardless of whether the threat is terrorism or avian flu, policy decisions across a variety of domains must come to terms with the allocation of limited dollars to address variations in vulnerability. The idea that relative worth could be a rationale for the allocation of funding points in the direction of political suasion playing a key role in how resources are allocated: political figures with more power, or at least more power behind them, will likely be more successful in obtaining resources. The legitimacy of actions to acquire funding will depend, to a certain degree, on the ability of those in power to construct convincing arguments. Clearly, the comments included in the *New York Times* article suggest that legitimacy with respect to these claims is some way off: "Their time could be better spent doing other things, like providing the security for the country" (Lipton, 2006). Figure 7.1 provides an overview of the ranking of states, on the basis of population, in the National Asset Database.

Being safe—that is, providing adequate protection in the face of varying probabilities—is clearly a challenge, but this should not dissuade us from addressing this challenge in a systematic way in order to achieve some measure of security. In an approach that includes consideration of the risk assessment issues raised in this book, the RAND Corporation recently issued a report, *Estimating Terrorism Risk*, which offers a model whereby we can determine an appropriate allocation of resources in response to risk (Willis, Morral, Kelly, & Medby, 2005). These authors note, "There are two important sources of uncertainty in estimating terrorism risk. The first includes variability and error in estimates of threats, vulnerabilities, and consequences. The second involves how we should value different types of consequences" (p. xvii).

In their calculations, Willis and colleagues demonstrate that we can, through a series of estimates, make sense of relative vulnerabilities that contribute to risk. We can then calculate the resources that need to be differentially applied in response to these risks. While we may make some mistakes in this calculation, we cannot include all relevant factors in these equations. Our degree of regret from miscalculating low risk if something does happen could be offset by knowledge that we did everything we could to respond to where the greatest danger exists.

Practical Steps to Security

Not all members of society define security similarly. Individual biographies, including past experience and social location, have much to do with how security appears to particular actors. Understandings of and orientations to security also vary at the institutional level. The institutional machinery, however, often does not speak with one voice any more than any one voice can speak for all individuals. In addition, any consideration of security must begin by recognizing that each point in history is characterized by factors that are unique to that particular historical period, at the same time recognizing that many factors have emerged out of the momentum of the past.

When considering the three stages of events, we observe that the first and last phases are open ended, at least until it is recognized that a particular threat is likely to be actualized. While many of our examples of hazards suggest discrete events, there may be other threats that are seemingly continuous and do not as obviously pass through the pre-event to post-event stages. We earlier mentioned how it is that smoking may be considered a chronic event at the societal level; a certain proportion of individuals continue to smoke despite the harm that this brings on themselves and others. Similarly, crime may also be seen as a chronic problem at the societal level, with perhaps a certain amount of crime posing a threat to the general population. At the individual level, however, these hazards can be seen as event based. Individual smokers begin to smoke, then hopefully quit, while individual crime events follow an event pattern: individuals move from a state of nonvictim, to victim, to recovering victim. Similarly, preparedness may occur for some time in advance of a particular incident. At the same time, recognizing that a particular occurrence is possible does not necessarily mean that it can be adequately prepared for. Critical to our understanding of risk balance is the observation that there are resource limitations: hazards vie for attention and are often prioritized among other threats and demands for resources. Although individuals may live in areas known for crime, limited resources may mean prioritizing groceries over adequate locks.

The term *all hazards* has been increasingly used in the security literature, as well as by those charged with maintaining security. The Department of Homeland Security (Government Accountability Office [GAO], 2005), for example, defines an all-hazards approach as follows:

> All-hazards emergency preparedness efforts seek to prepare all sectors of American society—business, industry and nonprofit, state, territorial, local and tribal governments, and the general public—for all hazards the nation may face, i.e., any large scale emergency event including terrorist attacks and natural or accidental disasters. (footnote 2)

The basis of this initiative was 9/11. While commonalities among terrorist and national disasters are clear, the all-hazards approach appears to prioritize certain types of events over others; in the case of the Department of Homeland Security, that event is terrorism. The reality, clearly, is that all hazards are not equal and are perceived in different ways depending on the perspective taken. While it is increasingly popular to talk about risk assessment in an all-hazards environment, we propose here a set of principles that may help to guide how risk balance is negotiated.

Principle 1. Choice

We cannot apply infinite resources to address all of the threats that we face in modern life. We are confronted by a number of hazards, which demand that we make difficult choices and attempt to balance risk by fully considering identified hazards against the resources we have at our disposal. Priorities are then selected for action. Choices, however, are not made in a social vacuum. The ability to direct resources to respective hazards does not always mean that resources will in fact be applied. Social and political factors—as well as risk positions—play a role in decision making, and the willingness to prioritize preparedness, response, and prevention measures to identified hazards. Importantly, for many of the hazards faced—with the exception of certain natural hazards—choices can be made in advance to minimize harm.

Principle 2. Decision Making

A central theme running throughout our discussion is the need to make decisions regarding risk balance based on information, trust, and other resources. The first element of decision making—information—is central to risk balance: resources are typically allocated on the basis of what is known. Information is one distinct type of resource. While what is unknown, either due to a lack of imagination or lack of resources, also figures into decision-making, information is typically a required element influencing how seriously harms are perceived. It must also be noted, however, that having correct information does not necessarily imply particular action. Information alone will not ensure that smart decisions are made, but the probability of having appropriate information greatly enhances the probability of harm reduction. A second element in decision making is trust in the source of information. If the information source is not trusted, it is unlikely that this information will figure into assessments of risk—information is really only as good as its source. The third element of decision making is resources. Resources have surfaced continually in our discussion of risk balance and security. With regard to decision making, decisions are based not only on information and trust, but also on the availability of resources. If individuals recognize that they live in a floodplain—if they both have the information and trust the source of that information—the decisions they make with respect to that threat must be weighed against other available resources. Those who have less economic resources, for example, may determine that while they recognize the threat, they do not have the financial means to remove themselves from harm's way.

Principle 3. Cooperation

Effective decision making requires cooperation across groups that have not dealt with one another in an easy fashion or that suspect one another in the ongoing battle over jurisdictional turf. Developing a common language with respect to security may be difficult, but the contributions of risk balance suggests that problem solving, which manages tough decisions and forces resource choices, should become a central part of the security lexicon. Furthermore, it is critical that security not be seen as a zero-sum game: the bolstering of security in one realm or by one actor does not necessarily diminish or enhance security in other realms or for other actors.

Principle 4. Planning

Planning for disasters needs to extend beyond treating one type of hazard as completely different from another. The agencies involved in emergency planning, for example, also emphasize two aspects of response: (1) practice prepares for a quick and decisive response, which is a lesson learned in England during the transit bombings; and (2) quick response relies on fail-proof communication. This is not the end of the story, however. Success extends to preparation for the next incident based on lessons quickly learned from the recent incident. It also depends on the level of preparation that was put in place prior to the incident that may have mitigated the damage or quickened the response: closed-circuit television did not deter the first set of bombs in London but it helped quickly unravel the source of the bombs, leading to the suspects. As importantly, it became a vital tool in the dragnet that was set out in pursuit of the second set of unsuccessful bombers who were tracked down quickly after their failed attack. While planning is important and comes from practice, in order to be effective plans must be well formed, pertinent, and involve all stakeholders affected by potential hazards. Planning is central to all stages of hazards, from the preparation, to the response, to the recovery.

We need to move past the recognition of hazards and the application of resources to risk balance in order to demonstrate that security is not a given but is negotiated through tough decisions. We are not going to be free of all hazards, but it may be impossible to respond to any hazard if we spread ourselves too thin and refuse to make strategic choices. Again, the negotiation aspect of risk balance points in the direction of jurisdiction; clearly, we cannot know everything nor can we prepare for everything, but we can encourage a dialogue that facilitates the recognition and acceptance of responsibilities, as well as the recognition and acceptance of limitations.

Principle 5. Institutional Learning

While we remember Hurricane Katrina vividly for the carnage that it left and the ineptitude of the government's response, we have much less of a memory of Hurricane Rita that struck soon after but was managed far more effectively. Similarly, many more people survived the devastation of 9/11 than perished. The institutional learning of government agencies can facilitate a more competent response, contain the damage, and assist in a quicker response.

Threats to our security are tied to one another, and our responses are based on innovating around routines that we have learned in managing risk in our daily lives. Some of the daily prevention activities that we engage in provide model behavior for reducing potential harm. Much can be borrowed in our discussion from the examples we have drawn from across the disciplines: an example is the insurance model as a device that encourages prevention and mitigates the costs of hazards.

Principle 6. Communication

The mobilization of resources to prepare for, respond to, and recover from hazards is dependent on communication both within and between jurisdictions. By communication, we mean the process of both informing stakeholders of the hazards that affect them and, in turn, listening to stakeholders regarding their perceptions of and experiences with hazards. The Environmental Protection Agency (EPA; 2002) provides advice for risk communication, starting with basic first steps: Determine what the message is that needs to be communicated. Deliver the message in a way that goals will be met. The EPA then suggests answering the following questions as a means of maximizing the effectiveness of hazards communication. As can be seen, these questions can apply to a range of hazardous situations:

> Why are we communicating? Who are our target audiences? What do our audiences want to know? What do we want to get across? How will we communicate? How will we listen? How will we respond? Who will carry out the plans? When? What problems or barriers have we planned for? Have we succeeded? (EPA, p. 4)

These questions assume that communication about hazards is at least a two-way street: stakeholders are encouraged to ask questions and provide feedback, while those providing information are encouraged to listen. Table 7.1 provides further information with respect to hazards communication.

Concluding Thoughts

Early on in this book, we mentioned the significance of getting back to normal and returning to routines in the aftermath of hazards. Prior to the occurrence of harm, however, we build routines and often structure

Table 7.1 Cardinal Rules of Risk Communication

1. Accept and involve the public as a legitimate partner. The goal is to produce an informed public, not to defuse public concerns.

2. Plan carefully and evaluate your efforts. Different goals, audiences, and media require different actions. Analyze the audience; learn what works for each situation.

3. Listen to the public's specific concerns. People often care as much about credibility, competence, and empathy as they do about risk levels, statistics, and details.

4. Be honest, frank, and open. Trust and credibility are difficult to obtain; once lost, they are almost impossible to regain.

5. Coordinate and collaborate with other credible sources. Conflicts among organizations make communication with the public more difficult.

6. Meet the needs of the media. The media are usually more interested in simplicity than complexity, danger than safety. Make sure they have what they need to portray the situation fairly.

7. Speak clearly and with compassion. Never let your efforts prevent acknowledgment of the tragedy of an illness, injury, or death.

SOURCE: Environmental Protection Agency, 2002.

our lives around them because of the way in which routines reassure. Knowing flows and ebbs of daily and yearly life is often a form of comfort. However, returning to normal may well involve establishing a new normal, taking into account and being aware of harms and making adjustments that are required to address these. The point of this volume has been to consider the commonalities among the ways in which we register and deal with both the possibility and the reality of negative contingencies. While it would be difficult to suggest that a tsunami is a contingency in the same way that a heart attack may be a contingency, what we have illustrated is that these events, as disparate as they are, involve common threads.

The study of security has been belated and the disciplinary fit of this research has been an uncomfortable one (Kennedy & Sherley, 2005). There is general acknowledgment that conventional disciplinary approaches are not likely to satisfy the accounting of the large-scale changes that have taken place in our conceptualization and response to these threats. A more comprehensive approach, based on a way of integrating the different perspectives is needed. Our consideration of risk balance provides a beginning step.

Note to Chapter 7

1. One approach that has been taken is the establishment of a National Incident Management System (NIMS), which relies entirely on an incident-based approach. In March 2004, President Bush directed the secretary of the Department Homeland Security, Tom Ridge, to establish "a comprehensive national approach to incident management, applicable to all jurisdictional levels across functional disciplines" (Federal Emergency Management Agency [FEMA], 2004b, p. 1). An assumption embedded in this system is that the majority of incidents can be handled by one jurisdiction, but NIMS allows for the smooth operation and inclusion of more than one jurisdiction should the nature of the incident dictate the involvement of other jurisdictions. What is important from our point of view, however, is the inclusion and importance of values that help guide how jurisdiction is established.

References

Agnew, Robert. 2006. Storylines as a neglected cause of crime. *Journal of Research in Crime and Delinquency* 43 (2): 119–47.

Alberts, Sheldon. 2005 (August 31). Hurricane victims blame Bush: Approval rating sinking in wake of Katrina. *The Calgary Herald*, p. A5.

Alexander, Don. 1997. The backlash caused by the past. *Social Alternatives* 16: 30–31.

Ali, S. Harris. 1997. Trust, risk and the public: The case of the Guelph Landfill Site. *Canadian Journal of Sociology* 22: 481–504.

Allstate Insurance. 2006. Allstate official site. http://www.allstate.com/.

Alphonso, Caroline. 2006 (November 11). Universities move to hide work from U.S. eyes. *The Globe & Mail*.

Anarumo, Mark C. 2005. What are we really afraid of? The practitioner view of the terrorist threat in the United States. PhD diss., Rutgers University, p. 66.

Ang, Ien. 2002. After "911": Defending the global city. *Ethnicities* 2: 160–62.

Appell, David. 2001. Precautionary principle: The new uncertainty principle. *Scientific American*: 18–19. http://www.biotech-info.net/uncertainty.html.

Appleborne, Peter, Christopher Drew, Jere Longman, and Andrew Revkin. 2005 (September 4). A delicate balance is undone in a flash, and a battered city waits. *The New York Times*, pp. A19, A22–A23.

Arendt, Hannah. 1951. *The Origins of the New Totalitarianism*. New York: Harcourt, Brace, Jovanovich.

Armstrong, David. 1995. The rise of surveillance medicine. *Sociology of Health & Illness* 17: 393–404.

Bahn, C. 1974. The reassurance factor in police patrol. *Criminology* 12 (3): 338–45.

Barbalace, Roberta C. 2004. Asbestos: A manufacturing health hazard dating to prehistoric times. October. http://EnvironmentalChemistry.com/yogi/environmental/asbestoshealthhazards2004.htm.

Bauman, Zygmunt. 2002. Violence in the age of uncertainty. *Crime and Insecurity: The governance of safety in Europe,* ed. Adam Crawford. Portland, OR: Willan Publishing, pp. 52–74.

Bayley, David. 2005. Keynote address. Presented at the annual meeting of the Australia and New Zealand Society of Criminology, Wellington, New Zealand, February 10.

BBC. 2007. ID cards: An action network briefing. http://www.bbc.co.uk/dna/actionnetwork/A2319176.

Beck, Diana L. 2004. Health, wealth and the Chinese Oedipus. *Society* 41 (2): 64–68.

Beck, Ulrich. 1989. On the way to the industrial risk society? Outline of an argument. *Thesis Eleven* 23 (1): 86–103.

Beck, Ulrich. 1992. *Risk Society: Towards a New Modernity.* Newbury Park, CA: Sage.

Beck, Ulrich. 2003. The silence of words: On terror and war. *Security Dialogue* 34: 255–67.

Béland, Daniel. 2007. *States of Global Insecurity: Policy, Politics, and Society.* New York: Worth Publishers.

Bélanger, Claude. 2000. Chronology of the October crisis, 1970, and its aftermath. Department of History, Marianopolis College, Montréal, Quebec, Canada. http://www2.marianopolis.edu/quebechistory/chronos/october.htm.

Bernardo investigation flawed. 1996. http://www.thecanadianencyclopedia.com/index.cfm?PgNm=TCE&Params=M1ARTM0010959.

Blair, Tony. 2005. News conference. http://www.number-10.gov.uk/output/Page8041.asp.

Blaser, Martin J. 2006. Statement of Infectious Diseases Society of America (IDSA) concerning Project BioShield reauthorization issues. April 6. http://www.idsociety.org/Template.cfm?Section=Home&Template=/ContentManagement/ContentDisplay.cfm&ContentID=15896.

Blatchford, Christie. 2005 (September 10). The haunted of New Orleans. *The Globe & Mail,* p. A21.

Bobbitt, Philip. 2004 (August 11). Being clear about present dangers. *The New York Times,* p. A19.

Bougen, Philip D. 2003. Catastrophe risk. *Economy and Society* 32: 253–74.

Bourdieu, Pierre. 1983. The forms of capital. [Okonomisches Kapital, kulturelles Kapital, soziales Kapital.] Trans. Richard Nice. *Soziale Welt Supplement* 2: 183–98.

Bracing for Katrina. 2005 (August 25). *The Globe & Mail,* p. A1.

Bradley, Ben S., and John R. Morss. 2002. Social construction in a world at risk: Toward a psychology of experience. *Theory & Psychology* 12: 509–32.

Brainard, Lael. 2002. A turning point for globalisation? The implications for the global economy of America's campaign against terrorism. *Cambridge Review of International Affairs* 15: 233–44.

Brandt, Allan M. 1987. *No Magic Bullet: A Social History of Venereal Disease in the United States Since 1880.* New York: Oxford University Press.

Brodeur, Jean-Paul. 1983. High policing and low policing: Remarks about the policing of political activities. *Social Problems* 30: 507–20.

Buzan, Barry. 1983. *People, States and Fear: The National Security Problem in International Relations.* Chapel Hill: The University of North Carolina Press.

Calhoun, Laurie. 2002. The terrorist's tacit message. *Peace Review* 14: 85–91.

Center for American Progress. 2005. Who are Katrina's victims? http://www.americanprogress.org/kf/katrinavictims.pdf.

Chan, Kit Yee, and Daniel D. Reidpath 2003. "Typhoid Mary" and "HIV Jane": Responsibility, agency and disease prevention. *Reproductive Health Matters* 11: 40–50.

Clarke, Lee. 2006. *Mission Improbable: Using Fantasy Documents to Tame Disaster*. Chicago: University of Chicago Press.

Clarke, Lee, and James F. Short. 1993. Social organization and risk: Some current controversies. *Annual Review of Sociology* 19: 375–99.

Clarke, Ronald, and Graeme Newman. 2006. *Outsmarting the Terrorist*. Westport, CT: Praeger.

Cohen, Lawrence E., and Marcus Felson. 1979. Social change and crime rate trends: A routine activity approach. *American Sociological Review* 44: 588–608.

Coleman, James S. 1993. The rational reconstruction of society: 1992 presidential address. *American Sociological Review* 58: 1–15.

Connell, Rory. 2001. Collective behavior in the September 11, 2001 evacuation of the World Trade Center. Preliminary Paper #313, University of Delaware Disaster Research Center, Newark, DE, pp. 1–21.

Cornish, Derek B., and Ronald V. Clarke. 1987. Understanding crime displacement: An application of rational choice theory. *Criminology* 25: 933–48.

C-TPAT. *See* Customs-Trade Partnership Against Terrorism.ctv.ca. 2005. http://www.ctv.ca/servlet/ArticleNews/story/CTVNews/1117799451154_113208651?s_name=&no_ads=.

Cummins, J. David, and Christopher M. Lewis. 2003. Catastrophic events, parameter uncertainty and the breakdown of implicit long-term contracting: The case of terrorism insurance. *Journal of Risk and Uncertainty* 26: 153–78.

Customs-Trade Partnership Against Terrorism (C-TPAT). 2004. Securing the Global Supply Chain Customs-Trade Partnership Against Terrorism: Strategic Plan. U.S. Customs and Border Protection, Washington, DC.

Dawson, Jane I. 2000. The two faces of environmental justice: Lessons from the eco-nationalist phenomenon. *Environmental Politics* 9: 22–60.

Deflem, Mathieu. 2004. *Terrorism and Counter-Terrorism: Criminological Perspectives*. Amsterdam: Elsevier.

Department of Homeland Security. n.d. Ready. http://www.ready.gov/america/_downloads/ready_trifold_brochure.txt.

Department of State. 2007. U.S. electronic passport: Frequently asked questions. http://travel.state.gov/passport/eppt/eppt_2788.html#Two.

Dimitrov, Radoslav S. 2002. Water, conflict, and security: A conceptual minefield. *Society & Natural Resources* 15: 677–91.

Doe v. Metropolitan Toronto (Municipality) Commissioners of Police. 1998. Ontario Court of Justice (General Division). Jane Doe and Board of Commissioners of Police for the Municipality of Metropolitan Toronto, Jack Marks, Kim Derry and William Cameron. Court File No. 87-CQ-21670, Judgment July 3.

Doherty, Neil A., Joan Lamm-Tennant, and Laura T. Starks. 2003. Insuring September 11th: Market recovery and transparency. *Journal of Risk and Uncertainty* 26: 179–99.

Douglas, Mary. 1992. *Risk and Blame: Essays in Cultural Theory*. London: Routledge.

Douglas, Mary, and Marcel Calvez. 1990. The self as risk taker: A cultural theory of contagion in relation to AIDS. *Sociological Review* 38: 445–64.

Dudley, Gail, and Robin B. McFee. 2005. Preparedness for biological terrorism in the United States: Project Bioshield and beyond. *Journal of the American Osteopathic Association* 105: 417–24.

Economist. 2002. Leaders: Preparing for terror. 365 (8301): 11–12 (November 30).

Eddy, Elizabeth. 2004. Environmental security: Securing what for whom? *Social Alternatives* 23: 23–28.

Environmental Protection Agency. 2002. *Risk Communication* (www.epa.gov/superfund/tools/pdfs/37riskcom.pdf)

Ericson, Richard. 1994. The division of expert knowledge in policing and security. *British Journal of Sociology* 43: 149–75.

Ex-FEMA chief tells of frustration and chaos. 2005 (September 15). *The New York Times*, p. A1.

Faist, Thomas. 2002. Extension du domaine de la lutte: International migration and security before and after September 11, 2001. *International Migration Review* 36: 7–28.

Farrell, Graham, Coreta Phillips, and Ken Pease. 1995. Like taking candy. *British Journal of Criminology* 35: 384–99.

FDA. See Food and Drug Administration.

Federal Emergency Management Agency (FEMA). 2004a. Are you ready? An in-depth guide to citizen preparedness. Department of Homeland Security, Washington, DC. http://www.fema.gov/pdf/areyouready/areyouready_full.pdf.

Federal Emergency Management Agency (FEMA). 2004b. http://www.fema.gov/pdf/nims/nims_training_development.pdf.

Federal Trade Commission (FTC). 2006. Consumer fraud and identity theft victim complaint data: January 1 through December 31, 2005. Federal Trade Commission, Washington, DC. http://www.consumer.gov/idtheft/pdf/clearing-house_2005.pdf.

FEMA. *See* Federal Emergency Management Agency.

Fischetti, Mark. 2001. Drowning New Orleans. *Scientific American* (October), pp. 76–85.

Food and Drug Administration (FDA). 2004a. Project BioShield: Protecting Americans from terrorism. http://www.fda.gov/fdac/features/2004/604_terror.html.

Food and Drug Administration (FDA). 2004b. Fact sheet. http://www.cfsan.fda.gov/~comm/bsefact2.html.

Freedman, L. 1992. The concept of security. *Encyclopedia of Government and Politics* (Vol. 2), ed. M. Hawkesworth and M. Kogan. London: Routledge, pp. 730–41.

Friese, Greg. 2004. Emergency response drills for camping. *Camping Magazine* 77 (3). http://findarticles.com/p/articles/mi_m1249/is_2004_May-June/ai_n6134202.

Frohlich, Katherine L., Ellen Corin, and Louise Potvin. 2001. A theoretical proposal for the relationship between context and disease. *Sociology of Health and Illness* 23: 776–97.

From Muslims in America. 2005 (July 28). *The New York Times*, p. A14.

FTC. *See* Federal Trade Commission.

GAO. *See* Government Accountability Office.

Gibbs, Lois Marie. 1998. Learning from Love Canal: A 20th anniversary retrospective. http://arts.envirolink.org/arts_and_activism/LoisGibbs.html.

Giddens, Anthony. 1990. *The Consequences of Modernity*. Stanford, CA: Stanford University Press.

Gillis, Justin. 2006 (May 10). Production of anthrax vaccine delayed again. *The Washington Post*, p. D01.

Glass, Thomas A., and Monica Schoch-Spana. 2002. Bioterrorism and the people: How to vaccinate a city against panic. *Clinical Infectious Diseases* 34: 217–23.

Glassner, Barry. 1999. *The Culture of Fear: Why Americans Are Afraid of the Wrong Things*. New York: Basic.

Goodnough, Abby. 2006 (May 31). As hurricane season looms, states aim to scare. http://www.nytimes.com/2006/05/31/us/31prepare.html?ex=1306728000&en=467e0e3692fdbce3&ei=5088&partner=rssnyt&emc=rss.

Gosselin, Peter. 2006 (November 28). Insurers learn to pinpoint risks—and avoid them. *The Los Angeles Times*.

Government Accountability Office (GAO). 2005. *DHS's efforts to enhance first responders' all-hazards capabilities continue to evolve*. Government Accountability Office, Washington, DC.

Greaves, David. 2000. The creation of partial patients. *Cambridge Quarterly of Health Ethics* 9: 23–37.

Greider, William. 2004. Orange Alert at Sebago. *Nation* 278: 16.

Grief in Russia now mixes with harsh words for government. 2004 (September 7). *The New York Times*, p. 3.

Hamm, Mark. 2007. *Terrorism as Crime*. New York: NYU Press.

Hamre, John J. 2002. Science and security at risk. *Issues in Science and Technology* XVIII: 51–57.

Harpham, Geoffrey Galt. 2002. Symbolic terror. *Critical Inquiry* 28: 573–79.

HarrisInteractive. 2005. Fewer Americans than Europeans have trust in the media—press, radio and TV. http://www.harrisinteractive.com/harris_poll/index.asp?PID=534.

Heymann, David L. 2002. The microbial threat in fragile times: Balancing known and unknown risks. Bulletin of the World Health Organization 80: 179.

Hills, Alice. 2002. Responding to catastrophic terrorism. *Studies in Conflict and Terrorism* 25: 245–61.

Hoffman, Bruce. 2006. *Inside Terrorism*. New York: Columbia University Press.

Hollway, Wendy, and Tony Jefferson. 1997. The risk society in an age of anxiety: Situating fear of crime. *British Journal of Sociology* 48 (2): 255–66.

How green was our warning? 2003 (March 30). *The Washington Post*, p. F01. http://www.washingtonpost.com/ac2/wp-dyn/A42116-2003Mar28?language=printer.

Hubbard, Phil. 2003. Fear and loathing at the multiplex: Everyday anxiety in the post-industrial city. *Capital & Class* 80: 51–75.

Hume, Hamish, and Gordon Dwyer Todd. 2003. Ambulance chasing for justice: How private lawsuits for civil damages can help combat international terror. *Federalist Society* online. http://www.fed-soc.org/Publications/Terrorism/ambulancechasing.htm.

Hunt, Alan. 1999. Anxiety and social explanation: Some anxieties about anxiety. *Journal of Social History* 33 (1): 509–28.

Innes, Martin, Nigel Fielding, and Nina Cope. 2005. The appliance of science? *British Journal of Criminology* 45 (1): 39–57.

Insurance plans you can avoid. 2005 (September 4). *Business Week*. http://www.businessweek.com/investor/content/jan2006/pi20060113_9383.htm?chan=search, p. xx.

Jenish, D'Arcy. 1996. Bernardo investigation flawed. *Macleans* online. http://www.thecanadianencyclopedia.com/index.cfm?PgNm=TCE&Params=M1ARTM0010959.

Johnson, Richard. 2002. Defending ways of life: The (anti-) terrorist rhetorics of Bush and Blair. *Theory, Culture and Society* 19: 211–31.

Johnston, David, Eric Schmitt, David E. Sanger, Richard W. Stevenson, and Steven R. Weisman. 2004 (April 4). Uneven response seen to terror risk in summer '01. *The New York Times*, p. A1.

Kahn, Laura H. 2003/2004. Viral trade and global public health. *Issues in Science and Technology* 20: 57–63.

Kamer, Larry. n.d. Preparing and fine-tuning your crisis plan: A workable methodology. The Business Forum, Beverly Hills, CA. http://www.bizforum.org/whitepapers/kamer.htm.

Karp, David R., Gordon Bazemore, & J. D. Chesire. 2004. The role and attitudes of restorative board members: A case study of volunteers in community justice. *Crime and Delinquency* 50 (4): 487–515.

Kelly, Peter. 2001. Youth at risk: Processes of individualization and responsibilisation in risk society. *Discourse* 22: 23–33.

Kennedy, Leslie W., and Alison Sherley. 2005. Making a case for the study of public security in criminal justice. *Criminologist* 30: 1, 3–4.

Keohane, Nathaniel O., and Richard J. Zeckhauser. 2003. The ecology of terror defense. *Journal of Risk and Uncertainty* 26: 201–29.

Klinghoffer v. PLO, 739 F. Supp. 854 (S.D.N.Y. 1990), 937 F.2d 44 (2d Cir. 1991).

Kushner, Harvey W. 2002. *Encyclopedia of Terrorism*. Thousand Oaks, CA: Sage.

Lascher, Edward L., and Michael R. Powers. 2004. September 11 victims, random events, and the ethics of compensation. *American Behavioral Scientist* 48: 281–94.

Lash, Scott, and Brian Wynne. 1992. Introduction. *Risk Society: Towards a New Modernity*, by Ulrich Beck. London: Sage, pp. 1–8.

Laxness, Halldor. 2002. *World Light*. New York: Random House.

Levidow, Les. 1994. De-reifying risk. *Science as Culture* 3: 440–56.

Lianos, Michalis, and Mary Douglas. 2000. Dangerization and the end of deviance. *British Journal of Criminology* 40: 261–79.

Lilly, J. Robert, Francis T. Cullen, and Richard A. Ball. 2002. *Criminological Theory: Context and Consequences*. Thousand Oaks, CA: Sage.

Lipton, Eric. 2006 (July 12). Come one, come all, join the terror target list. *The New York Times* online. http://www.nytimes.com/2006/07/12/washington/12assets .html?ex=1310356800&en=cc3091801be419b5&ei=5088&partner=rssnyt & emc=rss.

Luers, Jeffrey. 2007. Who is Jeffrey Luers? http://www.freefreenow.org/whois.html.

Luhmann, Niklas. 1988. Tautology and paradox in the self-descriptions of modern society. *Sociological Theory* 6: 21–25.

Lum, Cynthia, Leslie W. Kennedy, and Alison Sherley. 2006. Are counter-terrorism strategies effective: The results of the Campbell systematic review on counter-terrorism evaluation research. *Journal of Experimental Criminology* 2 (4): 489–516.

Lupton, Deborah, ed. 1999. *Risk and Sociocultural Theory: New Directions and Perspectives*. New York: Cambridge University Press.

Manning, Peter K. 1977. *Police Work: The Social Organization of Policing*. Cambridge: MIT Press.

Margolis, Howard. 1996. *Dealing with Risk*. Chicago: University of Chicago Press.

Marshall, Brent K., J. Steven Picou, and Duane A Gill. 2003. Terrorism as disaster: Selected commonalities and long-term recovery for 9/11 survivors. *Research in Social Problems and Public Policy* 11: 73–96.

May, Thomas, Mark P. Aulisio, and Ross D. Silverman. 2003. The smallpox vaccination of health care workers: Professional obligations and defense against bioterrorism. *Hastings Center Report* 33: 26–33.

McCullagh, Declan. 2005. FAQ: How real ID will affect you. http://news.com. com/FAQ+How+Real+ID+will+affect+you/2100-1028_3-5697111.html.

McDonald, Ian R., and Regina G. Lawrence. 2004. Filling the 24 X 7 news hole. *American Behavioral Scientist* 48: 327–40.

McMaster University. 2006. The McMaster University crisis response plan. http:// www.mcmaster.ca/newsevents/crisismanagement/.

Memorial Institute for the Prevention of Terrorism (MIPT). n.d. Terrorism Knowledge Database. http://www.tkb.org/Home.jsp.

Menyawi, Hassan El. 2003. Public tort liability: Recommending an alternative to tort liability and no-fault compensation. *Global Jurist Advances* 3 (1, Article 1). http://www.bepress.com/gj/advances/vol3/iss1/art1.

Merriam-Webster Online Dictionary. 2007 Jurisdiction. http://209.161.33.50/dictionary/jurisdiction.

Miethe, Terance D., and Robert F. Meier. 1994. *Crime and Its Social Context: Toward an Integrated Theory of Offenders, Victims, and Situations.* Albany: State University of New York Press.

MIPT. *See* Memorial Institute for the Prevention of Terrorism.

Mitchell, James K. 2003. The fox and the hedgehog: Myopia about homeland security in U.S. policies on terrorism. *Research in Social Problems and Public Policy* 11: 53–72.

Moore, Dawn, and Mariana Valverde. 2000. Maidens at risk: "Date rape drugs" and the formation of hybrid risk knowledge. *Economy & Society* 29: 514–31.

MSNBC. 2005. New Orleans mayor orders looting crackdown: Thousands feared dead from Katrina's wrath; stadium evacuation begins. September 1. http://www.msnbc.msn.com/id/9063708/.

Mueller, John. 2006. *Overblown: How Politicians and the Terrorism Industry Inflate National Security Threats, and Why We Believe Them.* New York: Free Press.

Murphy, Christopher. 1998. Policing post-modern Canada. *Canadian Journal of Law and Society* 13: 1–25.

National Commission on Terrorist Attacks Upon the United States. 2004. *Final Report. The 9/11 Commission Report.* New York: Norton. http://www.9-11commission.gov/report/911Report.pdf.

Nelson, Stephen A. 2004. Earthquake hazards and risk. Tulane University, New Orleans, LA. http://www.tulane.edu/~sanelson/ge01204/eqhazards&risks.pdf.

New Republic. 2003. Ready or not. February 27. https://ssl.tnr.com/p/docsub.mhtml?i=20030310&s=editorial031003.

Norris, Fran. 2001. 50,000 disaster victims speak: An empirical review of the empirical literature, 1981–2001. Report prepared for The National Center for PTSD, U.S. Department of Veterans Affairs, Washington, DC; and the Centre for Mental Health Services, Washington, DC, pp. 1–12.

O'Malley, Pat. 1992. Risk, power and crime prevention. *Economy and Society* 21: 252–75.

O'Malley, Pat. 2000. Uncertain subjects: Risks, liberalism and contract. *Economy & Society* 29: 460–84.

O'Malley, Pat. 2004. The uncertain promise of risk. *Australian and New Zealand Journal of Criminology* 37: 323–43.

OnLine NewsHour. 2003. Newsmaker: Tom Ridge. September. http://www.pbs.org/newshour/bb/terrorism/july-dec03/ridge_9-02.html.

Partnership for Public Warning (PPW). 2004. Testimony before the House of Representatives Subcommittee on National Security, Emerging Threats and International Relations Committee on Government Reform: The Homeland Security Advisory System: Threat Codes and Public Responses. http://www.ppw.us/ppw/docs/hsas_testimony.pdf.

Peachey, Graham. 2005. Regulatory convergence in a global marketplace. Food Standards Australia New Zealand, Sydney. http://www.foodstandards.gov

.au/mediareleasespublications/speeches/speeches2005/grahampeacheyregulat 2998.cfm.

Perez-Lugo, Maria. 2004. Media uses in disaster situations: A new focus on the impact phase. *Sociological Inquiry* 74: 210–25.

Petersen, A.R. 1996. Risk and the regulated self: The discourse of health promotion as politics of uncertainty. *Australian and New Zealand Journal of Sociology* 32: 44–57.

Picou, J. Steven, Brent K. Marshall and Duane A Gill. 2004. Disaster, litigation, and the corrosive community. *Social Forces* 82: 1493–1522.

Plummer, Ken. 2003. Queers, bodies and postmodern sexualities: A note on revisiting the sexual in symbolic interactionism. *Qualitative Sociology* 26: 515–30.

Police chief wants appeal of Doe case. 1998 (July 23). *Toronto Star*, p. C3.

Posner, Richard A. 2004. *Catastrophe, Risk and Response.* New York: Oxford University Press.

PPW. *See* Partnership for Public Warning.

PSEPC. *See* Public Safety and Emergency Preparedness Canada.

Public Safety and Emergency Preparedness Canada (PSEPC). 2004. Report on identity theft: A report to the Minister of Public Safety and Emergency Preparedness Canada and the Attorney General of the United States. Bi-national Working Group on Cross-Border Mass Marketing Fraud. October. http://www .psepc-sppcc.gc.ca/prg/le/bs/report-en.asp.

Quarantelli, E. L. 2003. A half century of social science disaster research: Selected major findings and their applicability. Disaster Research Center, University of Delaware, Newark, Delaware.

Quarantelli, E.L. 1989. Conceptualizing disasters from a sociological perspective. *International Journal of Mass Emergencies and Disasters* 7: 243–51.

Record, Jeffrey. 2003. Bounding the global war on terrorism. Record for the Strategic Studies Institute. http://www.strategicstudiesinstitute.army.mil/pubs/ display.cfm?pubID=207.

Reichman, Nancy J. 1986. Managing crime risks: Towards an insurance based model of social control. *Research in Law, Deviance and Social Control* 8: 151–72.

Reiner, Robert, Sonia Livingstone, and Jessica Allen. 2001. Casino culture: Media and crime in a risk society. *Crime, Risk and Injustice: The Politics of Crime Control in Liberal Democracies*, ed. Kevin Stenson & Robert R. Sullivan. Devon, UK: Willan, pp. 175–93.

Rigakos, George. 2002. *The New Parapolice: Risk Markets and Commodified Social Control.* Toronto: University of Toronto Press.

Riley, K. Jack, Gregory F. Treverton, Jeremy M. Wilson and Lois M. Davis. 2005. *State and Local Intelligence in the War on Terrorism.* Washington, DC: RAND Corporation.

Ripley, Amanda, and Mitch Frank. 2004. How we got homeland security WRONG. *Time* 163: 32–38.

Russia's grief turns to anger. 2004 (September 6). *The Globe & Mail*, p. AO1.

Sacco, Vincent, and Leslie W. Kennedy. 2002. *The Criminal Event: An Introduction to Criminology in Canada*. Toronto: Nelson Thomson Learning.

Schwartz, John. 1995 (May 11). An outbreak of medical myths. *The Washington Post*, p. 38.

Scott, S., S. Jackson, and K. Backett-Milburn. 1998. Swings and roundabouts: Risk anxiety in the everyday worlds of children. *Sociology* 32: 689–705.

Seligman, Adam B. 1998. Between public and private. *Society*: 28–36.

Shannon, Lyle W. 1985. Risk assessment versus real prediction: The prediction problem and public trust. *Journal of Quantitative Criminology* 1: 159–89.

Shields, Chris, Kelly R. Damphousse, and Brent L. Smith. 2006. Their day in court: Assessing plea bargaining among terrorists. *Journal of Contemporary Criminal Justice* 22: 261–276.

Short, James F. 1984. The social fabric at risk: Toward the social transformation of risk analysis. *American Sociological Review* 49: 711–25.

Silver, Eric, and Lisa L. Miller. 2002. A cautionary note on the use of actuarial risk assessment tools for social control. *Crime and Delinquency* 48: 138–61.

Simon, Jonathan. 1988. The ideological effects of actuarial practices. *Law and Society Review* 22: 772–800.

Slovic, Paul. 1993. Perceived risk, trust, and democracy. *Risk Analysis* 13: 675–82.

Slovic, Paul, Melissa Finucane, Ellen Peters, and Donald G. MacGregor. 2002. Rational actors or rational fools: Implications of the affect heuristic for behavioral economics. *Journal of Socio-Economics* 31: 239–342.

Soroos, Marvin S. 1995. Environmental security: Choices for the twenty-first century. *National Forum* 75: 20–25.

Spector, Malcolm, and John I. Kitsuse. 2001. *Constructing Social Problems*. New Brunswick, NJ: Transaction Publishers.

Spencer, William, and Elizabeth Triche. 1994. Media constructions of risk and safety: Differential framings of hazard events. *Sociological Inquiry* 64: 199–213.

Starr, Chauncey. 1969. Social benefit versus technological risk. *Science* 165: 1232–38.

Stone, Deborah A. 1993. The struggle for the soul of health insurance. *Journal of Health Politics Policy and Law* 18: 287–317.

Sunstein, Cass R. 2001. Laws of fear. Olin Working Paper #128 (2D Series), University of Chicago Law & Economics, Chicago, pp. 1–42.

Sunstein, Cass R. 2005. *Laws of Fear: Beyond the Precautionary Principle*. Cambridge, UK: Cambridge University Press.

Tanner, Robert. 2005. New Orleans, Pakistan united in misery. Charleston, SC. http://www.wciv.com/news/stories/1005/270983.html.

Taylor-Butts, Andrea. 2004. Private security and public policing in Canada. Statistics Canada, Catalogue no. 85-002-XIE, 24 (7). Ottawa: Statistics Canada.

Thacher, David. 2005. The local role in Homeland Security. *Law and Society Review* 39: 635–76.

The Brookings Institution. 2002. The CNN effect: How 24-hour news coverage affects government decisions and public opinion. http://www.brookings.edu/comm/transcripts/20020123.htm, p. 1.

The rise of the rent-a-cop. 2004 (September 11). *The Globe & Mail*, p. F1.

Timmermans, Stefan. 2002. The cause of death vs. the gift of life: Boundary maintenance and the politics of expertise in death investigation. *Sociology of Health and Illness* 24: 550–74.

Tseloni, Andromachi, and Ken Pease. 2003. Repeat personal victimization: 'Boosts' or 'flags'? *British Journal of Criminology* 43: 196–212.

Tuchman, G. 1980. *Making News*. New York: Free Press.

Turner, Ralph H., and Lewis M. Killian. 1987. *Collective Behavior*, 3rd ed. Englewood Cliffs, NJ: Prentice-Hall.

Tversky, Amos, and Daniel Kahneman. 1974. Judgment under uncertainty: Heuristics and biases. *Science* 185: 1124–31.

Tversky, Amos, and Daniel Kahneman. 1986. Judgment under uncertainty: Heuristics and biases. *Judgment and Decision Making: An Interdisciplinary Reader*, ed. H. R. Hammond & K. R. Arkes. Cambridge, UK: Cambridge University Press, pp. 38–55.

UN. *See* United Nations.

United Nations. 1999. Report of the Secretary General. Recommendations on institutional arrangements for disaster reduction activities of the United Nations system after the conclusion of the International Decade for Natural Disaster Reduction. General Assembly, fifty-fourth session. Economic and Social Council, Geneva. http://www.un.org/documents/ecosoc/docs/1999/e1999-89.htm.

View from abroad (The). 2005 (September 4). *The New York Times*, pp. 4, 5.

Viscusi, W. Kip, and Richard J. Zeckhauser. 2003. Sacrificing civil liberties to reduce terrorism risks. *Journal of Risk and Uncertainty* 26: 99–120.

Wallington, T., L. Berger, B. Henry, R. Shahin, B. Yaffe, B. Mederski, et al. 2003. Update: Severe acute respiratory syndrome—Toronto, Canada. *Morbidity and Mortality Weekly Report* http://www.cdc.gov/mmwr/preview/mmwrhtml/mm5223a4.htm.

Wells, Celia. 1999. Inquiring into disasters: Law, politics and blame. *Risk Management: An International Journal* 1: 7–19.

White House. 2002. Gov. Ridge announces Homeland Security Advisory System Press release. http://www.whitehouse.gov/news/releases/2002/03/20020312-1.html.

White House. 2003. President details Project BioShield. http://www.whitehouse.gov/news/releases/2003/02/20030203.html.

White House. 2005. President arrives in Alabama, briefed on Hurricane Katrina. http://www.whitehouse.gov/news/releases/2005/09/20050902-2.html.

Wildavsky, Aaron B. 1995. *But Is it True?: A Citizen's Guide to Environmental Health and Safety Issues*. Cambridge, MA: Harvard University Press.

Williams, Simon. 2001. From smart bombs to bugs: Thinking the unthinkable in medical sociology and beyond. *Sociological Research Online* 6 (3). http://www.socresonline.org.uk/6/3/contents.html.

Willis, James J., Stephen D. Mastrofski, and David Weisburd. 2004. CompStat and bureaucracy: A case study of challenges and opportunities for change. *Justice Quarterly* 21: 463–96.

Wilson, James Q., and George Kelling. 1982. Broken windows: The police and neighborhood safety. *Atlantic Monthly* 249 (3): 29–38.

Wynne, Brian. 1996. May the sheep safely graze? A reflexive view of the expert-lay knowledge divide. *Risk, Environment and Modernity: Towards a New Ecology*, ed. Scott Lash, Bronislaw Szerszynski, and Brian Wynne. London: Sage, pp. 44–83.

Young, Alison. 1996. *Imagining Crime*. London: Sage.

Young-Bruehl, Elisabeth. 2002. On the origins of a new totalitarianism. *Social Research* 69: 567–78.

Suggested Readings

Abbott Chapman, Joan, and Carey Denholm. 1997. Adolescent risk taking and the romantic ethic: HIV/AIDS awareness among year 11 and 12 students. *Australian and New Zealand Journal of Sociology* 33: 306–21.

Ballard, Karen, and Mary Ann Elston. 2005. Medicalisation: A multi-dimensional concept. *Social Theory & Health* 3: 228–41.

Baron, Stephen W., and Leslie W. Kennedy. 1998. Deterrence and homeless male street youths. *Canadian Journal of Criminology* 40: 27–60.

Beck, Ulrich. 1992a. How modern is modern society? *Theory, Culture and Society* 9: 163–69.

Beck, Ulrich. 1992b. From industrial society to the risk society: Questions of survival, social structure and ecological enlightenment. *Theory, Culture and Society* 9: 97–123.

Birkland, Thomas A. 2004. Introduction: Risk, disaster, and policy in the 21st century. *American Behavioral Scientist* 48: 275–80.

Blau, Judith R. 1996. Organizations as overlapping jurisdictions: Restoring reason in organizational accounts. *Administrative Science Quarterly* 41: 172–79.

Blomley, Nicholas. 2004. Un-real estate: Proprietary space and public gardening. *Antipode* 36: 614–41.

Brown, Barry. *Geographies of Technology: Some Comments on Place, Space and Technology*. Glasgow, UK: University of Glasgow Press.

Campbell, Murray. 2005 (September 3). How the crisis caught the southern U.S. off guard: Katrina: 'You can do everything for other countries but you can't do nothing for your own people.' *The Globe & Mail*, pp. A1, A10–11.

Clarke, Lee. 1988. Explaining choices among technological risks. *Social Problems* 35: 22–35.

Clarke, Lee. 1997. Dealing with risk: Why the public and the experts disagree on environmental issues. *Contemporary Sociology* 26: 462–63.

Comfort, Louise K. 2002. Governance under fire: Organizational fragility in complex systems. *Governance and Public Security*. Syracuse, NY: Syracuse University, pp. 113–27. http://www.businessofgovernment.org/pdfs/RobertsReport.pdf.

Department of Homeland Security. Citizen guidance on the homeland security advisory system. http://www.dhs.gov/xlibrary/assets/CitizenGuidanceHSAS2.pdf.

Douglas, Mary, and Aaron Wildavsky. 1983. *Risk and Culture: An Essay on the Selection of Technological and Environmental Dangers.* Berkeley: University of California Press.

Douglas, Mary. 1966. *Purity and Danger: An Analysis of Concepts of Pollution and Taboo.* New York: Frederick A. Praeger.

Environmental Protection Agency (EPA). 2002. Risk communication. http://www.epa.gov/superfund/tools/pdfs/37riskcom.pdf.

EPA. *See* Environmental Protection Agency.

Ericson, Richard, and Kevin Haggerty. 1997. *Policing the Risk Society.* Toronto: University of Toronto Press.

Freudenberg, William R. 1993. Risk and recreancy: Weber, the division of labor, and the rationality of risk perceptions. *Social Forces* 71: 909–32.

Gans, Herbert J. 1962. *The Urban Villagers: Group and Class in the Life of Italian-Americans.* New York: Free Press.

Goldstein, Bernard. 2001. The precautionary principle also applies to public health actions. *American Journal of Public Health* 91: 1358–61.

Hunt, William K., Hector F. Myers, and Monica Dyche. 1999. Living with risk: Male partners of HIV-positive women. *Cultural Diversity and Ethnic Minority Psychology* 5: 276–86.

Kennedy, Leslie W., and Stephen W. Baron. 1993. Routine activities and a subculture of violence: A study of violence on the street. *Journal of Research in Crime & Delinquency* 30: 88–112.

Liebow, Elliot. 1967. *Tally's Corner.* Boston: Little Brown.

Lipton, Eric. 2006 (June 27). "Breathtaking" waste and fraud in hurricane aid. *The New York Times,* p. A1.

Livingstone, Sonia, Jessica Allen, and Robert Reiner. 2001. Audiences for crime media 1946–91: A historical approach to reception studies. *Communication Review* 4: 165.

Margolis, Eric, and Lisa Catanzarite. 1998. Sexual behavior and condom use among injection drug users. *Research in Social Policy* 6: 59–82.

Morris, Julian. 2000. Defining the precautionary principle. *Rethinking Risk and the Precautionary Principle,* ed. Julian Morris. Boston: Butterworth Heinemann, pp. 1–21.

Norris, Fran H., and Krzysztof Kaniasty. 1992. A longitudinal study of the effects of various crime prevention strategies on criminal victimization, fear of crime, and psychological distress. *American Journal of Community Psychology* 20: 625–48.

O'Malley, Pat. 1999. Governmentality and the risk society. *Economy and Society* 28: 138–48.

Park, Robert E., Earnest W. Burgess, and R. D. McKenzie. (1925) 1967. *The City: Suggestions for Investigation of Human Behavior in the Urban Environment.* Chicago: University of Chicago Press.

Privacy Rights Clearinghouse. Fact Sheet #26: Clue insurance databases. http://www.privacyrights.org/fs/fs26-CLUE.htm.

Purcell, Kristen, Lee Clarke, and Linda Renzulli. 2000. Menus of choice: The social embeddedness of decisions. *Risk in the Modern Age*, ed. Maurice J. Cohen. Houndmills, UK: Macmillan, pp. 62–79

Reed, Brian J., and David R. Segal. 2000. The impact of multiple deployments on soldiers' peacekeeping attitudes, morale, and retention. *Armed Forces & Society* 27: 57–78.

Reiner, Robert, Sonia Livingston, and Jessica Allen. 2000. No more happy endings? The media and popular concern about crime since the Second World War. *Crime, Risk and Insecurity*, ed. Tim Hope and Richard Sparks. London: Routledge, pp. 107–26.

Rose, Peter R. 1999. Exploration Economics, Risk-Analysis, and Prospect Evaluation. Austin, TX: P. R. Rose.

Rountree, Pamela Wilcox, and Kenneth C. Land. 2000. The generalization of multilevel models of burglary victimization: A cross-city comparison. *Social Science Research* 29: 284–305.

Sedelmaier, Christopher, and Mark Anarumo. 2005. Terrorist incident reporting: How much don't we know? Presented at conference of American Society of Criminology (unpublished).

Singer, Lawrence. 2004. Reassurance policing: An evaluation of the local management of community safety. Home Office Research, London.

Slovic, Paul. 1997. Trust, emotion, sex, politics, and science: Surveying the risk-assessment battlefield. *Environment, Ethics, and Behavior: The Psychology of Environmental Valuation and Degradation*, ed. Max H. Bazerman and David M. Messick. San Francisco: The New Lexington Press/Jossey-Bass, pp. 277–313.

Sokolsky, Joel J. 2004. Realism Canadian style: National security policy and the Chrétien legacy. *Policy Matters* 5: 3–44.

Sunstein, Cass R. 2002. Hazardous heuristics. Olin Working Paper #165, University of Chicago Law & Economics, Chicago, pp. 1–32, and University of Chicago Public Law Research Paper #33, Chicago.

Trudeau, Pierre Elliot. 1970. Notes for a national broadcast, October 16. Library and Archives Canada.

White House. 2005. National Incident Management System: National Standard Curriculum Training Development Guidance.

Whyte, William Foote. 1943. *Street Corner Society*. Chicago: University of Chicago Press.

Wilkinson, I. 2001. Social theories of risk perception: At once indispensable and insufficient. *Current Sociology* 49: 1–22.

Willis, Henry H., Andrew R. Morral, Terrance K. Kelly, and Jamison Jo Medby. 2005. *Estimating Terrorism Risk*, ed. RAND Corporation. Arlington, Center for Terrorism Risk Management Policy, RAND, Virginia, pp. 1–94.

Zaretsky, Eli. 2002. Trauma and dereification: September 11 and the problem of ontological security. *Constellations* 9: 98–105.

Index

About the Authors

Erin Gibbs Van Brunschot has been at the University of Calgary for the past eight years, the last two years as Associate Dean (Academic Programs) in the Faculty of Social Sciences. Dr. Van Brunschot received her PhD from the University of Alberta, and her BA and MA degrees from the University of Calgary.

Dr. Van Brunschot's research interests have included prostitution, violence, and risk taking, with publications in each of these areas. More recently, Dr. Van Brunschot's research interests have evolved into the areas of risk and security as these relate to both individuals and institutions.

Leslie W. Kennedy, Professor of Criminal Justice, served as Dean of the Rutgers School of Criminal Justice from 1998 to 2007. He received his BA from McGill University, his MA from the University of Western Ontario, and his PhD from the University of Toronto. Dr. Kennedy has published extensively in the areas of fear of crime, victimology, and violence. Among his published works, he is the coauthor with Vince Sacco of *The Criminal Event*, appearing in its fourth edition this year, in which they advocate a holistic approach to the study of crime in social context. In addition, he has published extensively on spatial and temporal analysis of crime patterns.

Dr. Kennedy's current research in public security builds on his previous research in event analysis and understanding the social contexts in which hazards to society are identified and deterred. He has recently published (with Cynthia Lum and Alison Sherley) an extensive review of counterterrorism studies in the *Journal of Experimental Criminology*.

Dr. Kennedy is currently the Director of the Rutgers Center for the Study of Public Security. The Center's primary focuses are to conduct original analytical and objective research on how risk assessment can be applied to the study of security, and to inform public policy discussions in this area.